Delaware
Prehistoric Archaeology

Delaware
Prehistoric Archaeology

An Ecological Approach

Jay F. Custer

1984

Newark: University of Delaware Press
London and Toronto: Associated University Presses

Associated University Presses
440 Forsgate Drive
Cranbury, N. J. 08512

Associated University Presses
25 Sicilian Avenue
London WC1A 2QH, England

Associated University Presses
2133 Royal Windsor Drive
Unit 1
Mississauga, Ontario
Canada L5J 1K5

Library of Congress Cataloging in Publication Data

Custer, Jay F., 1955–
  Delaware prehistoric archaeology.

  Bibliography: p.
  Includes index.
  1. Indians of North America—Delaware—Antiquities.
2. Delaware—Antiquities. I. Title.
E78.D3C97 1983   975.1′01   83-40130
ISBN 0-87413-233-9

Printed in the United States of America

For Sharon

Contents

Tables

Plates

Figures

Preface

Almost forty years have passed since the 1944 publication of C. A. Weslager's *Delaware's Buried Past,* which discussed both the history of archaeological research in Delaware and the findings of that research. Although an updated version was published in 1968, the pace of archaeological research in Delaware, and the Middle Atlantic in general, has accelerated to the point where a new overview is necessary. My goal in this book is to provide such an overview with a regional perspective for the interested layperson, as well as for students and professional researchers. For the interested layperson, the book may stand alone as a summary of the prehistoric archaeology of Delaware as of 1982. For the serious student and professional researcher I have included numerous citations to the original literature so that additional information may be gathered if needed. Additional references to Delaware archaeology may also be obtained from critical bibliographies written by Weslager (1978) and Porter (1979). The reader interested in a narrative of recent developments in Delaware archaeology strictly as a discipline is referred to Weslager's more recent overview (Weslager 1976), as well as Willey and Sabloff's (1980) review of the history of American archaeology.

Not only has the quantity of archaeological data increased, but new theoretical viewpoints regarding the goals and aims of archaeology have emerged. Probably the most important aspect of the new ideas emerging in archaeology over the past fifteen years was the recognition that prehistoric archaeology could be more than the source of a chronicle of people and events from the preliterate past. Since the publication of Lewis R. Binford's (1962) article "Archaeology as Anthropology," many archaeologists have come to believe that prehistoric archaeological data can shed light on the processes by which people adapt to their biosocial environment. According to this newer view, it is no longer sufficient to develop a chronicle of events in the past, or even to reconstruct past lifeways. It is necessary to seek to understand the ways by which a population of individuals in the remote past adapted themselves to their natural and social environments. Although not all archaeologists believe that such an understanding is possible, many researchers are trying to understand human adaptive response. This book seeks to develop such an understanding for the various human societies in Delaware's prehistoric past.

The archaeological data that will be used to study these ancient biosocial adaptations come from a variety of sources. Because the newer theoretical viewpoints have developed only recently, past studies of Delaware archaeology may be examined in a new light. In this book I attempt to do this. I also extensively review recent archaeological data, which come from a variety of sources. Traditional academically oriented research by state-sponsored agencies, such as the Bureau of Archaeology and Historic Preservation, and institutions, such as the University of Delaware, provides a large portion of the data. However, an increasingly larger portion of the archaeological research in Delaware is being funded and carried out by agencies such as the Delaware Department of Transportation and the United States Department of Agriculture Soil Conservation Service. Recent federal legislation (King et al. 1977) places prehistoric archaeological sites in the category of "cultural resources" and excavation and salvage of these sites is required when they will be destroyed by construction projects. Equally important are archaeological surveys that seek to identify locations of archaeological sites within the limits of proposed projects. These kinds of research have generated large amounts of data, much of which is unpublished except for technical reports circulated among the agencies involved. Where possible, I have drawn on this rapidly expanding data base. A final source of data includes the mass of information reported by the interested and dedicated individuals who enjoy the collecting of Indian artifacts in their spare time. Although a dwindling number of irresponsible individuals destroy sites and data and do not share information, many people join organizations like the Archaeological Society of Delaware and participate in an important way in the progress of Delaware archaeology. Much of the data, old and new, reviewed here are derived from the work of these private individuals and I greatly appreciate their efforts.

Acknowledgments

I could not have written this book without the help of many people. Their cooperation and assistance are gratefully acknowledged; however, any errors of fact or interpretation are solely my responsibility. Included among the people who helped with this book are William M. Gardner, who graciously gave his time for discussion and shared portions of his own unpublished manuscript on the archaeology of the Middle Atlantic; R. Michael Stewart, who read the manuscript and provided useful comments; W. Fred Kinsey, who shared his experience in Middle Atlantic culture history; Daniel Griffith, who introduced me to Delaware archaeology and shared his experience with Delaware's prehistoric archaeological record; Cliff Lefferts and Fay Stocum, who helped me find the necessary manuscripts, site data photos, and artifacts for analysis; Alice Guerrant and Cara Wise, who shared their knowledge of Delaware historic archaeology; C. A. Weslager, who provided advice and a historical perspective on many of the earlier studies; Ron Thomas and Kevin Cunningham, who provided data from the research funded by the Delaware Department of Transportation; Joseph McNamara and Karen Zukerman, who helped me compile many of the more recent radiocarbon dates; members of the Society for Pennsylvania Archaeology who shared their site data; Elwood Wilkins and the Archaeological Society of Delaware, who shared their collections and knowledge; Neill Wenger, who did the artwork; the Delaware Division of Historical and Cultural Affairs, who gave permission for the use of the plates; the University of Delaware College of Arts and Sciences and the Department of Anthropology, who provided funding and support for the preparation of the final manuscript; and especially my wife, Sharon, and my son, Jason, who provided support through the project.

Delaware
Prehistoric Archaeology

[1]

Introduction

There are many ways to approach the study of Delaware's prehistoric archaeology. In this chapter I describe the approach used here, along with its basic assumptions and organizational principles.

Theoretical Perspective

In many ways the types of materials found in the archaeological record influence the ways archaeologists study human behavior. Stone tools, house remains, living debris, and pottery fragments comprise the bulk of the archaeological record for Delaware, and as a result, archaeologists are usually able to best understand the technology and subsistence patterns of past groups. Similarly, plant remains and other data can be found to reconstruct ancient environments. Consequently, many archaeologists are drawn to anthropological theories that focus on how human cultures adapt to their natural environments.

Anthropologists who primarily study the effects of technology and environment on human behavior are labeled as cultural materialists (Harris 1968, 240–41), cultural ecologists (Steward 1955), or ecological anthropologists (Vayda and McKay 1975). Although they view culture as a form of adaptation, these anthropologists recognize that people must not only adapt to the biological world—equally important is the social environment created by the other humans of their own group and other neighboring societies. As a result, the *biosocial* environment's effects are seen as the key variable in understanding how culture works. Indeed, for these anthropologists culture is defined as human extrasomatic adaptation, emphasizing the nonbiological ways by which people adapt to all aspects of their environment (White 1949). In this book I try to examine the extrasomatic adaptation to biosocial environments of prehistoric groups in Delaware. Consequently, my approach is from a cultural ecological perspective and is derived from similar work by William M. Gardner (1978, 1982) throughout the Middle Atlantic region.

Adoption of a cultural ecological perspective creates a number of problems for archaeologists. It has been stated that the interaction of humans with the biosocial environment is of particular interest. Also, it has been noted that archaeologists are especially good at dealing with the components of culture that most closely connect with the biological portion of the environment. However, given that the social portion of the environment is equally important, how are prehistoric archaeologists to study its effects on past societies? As some researchers have noted, archaeologists do not excavate social organizations and kinship systems. Nevertheless, the patterned behavior that results from participation in shared social and religious systems creates patterned distributions of archaeological remains that can be excavated and understood (Binford 1965). Also, even though there are an infinite number of possible combinations of technologies, social organizations, and ideologies that can arise as human response to varied biosocial environments, a relatively limited number of combinations have occurred throughout human history (Murdock 1949; Steward 1955). These cross-cultural regularities suggest a pattern to the selective effects of the biosocial environment (Steward 1955, 27; Harris 1968, 241). In reviewing the prehistory of Delaware I examine socially derived patterns in the archaeological record as well as cross-cultural regularities and controlled comparisons (Eggan 1954) to reconstruct the social and ideological components of past cultures in Delaware and to study the process of their adaptive changes.

Although I have stressed the relatively limited number of combinations of cultural features seen in human adaptations, the variability that does exist can take on bewildering complexity. Even within a small state like Delaware, the 15,000 years of human occupation create a great deal of cultural variability to be studied. In fact, there is sufficient variability to necessitate the development of smaller units of study. The work of Albert C. Spaulding provides insights on how to develop such units. Spaulding (1960) has noted that the study of archaeology is focused upon three dimensions: form, time, and space, The formal dimension includes the cultural variability noted above, while the temporal and spatial dimensions provide sources of variability within the formal dimension. Different places and different times are likely to produce different biosocial environments and adaptations; therefore, time and space are two ways to divide up Delaware's prehistory into smaller units of study. Given an interest in studying human adaptations to varied biosocial environments, the smaller units of study are defined as units of time and space that represent similar biosocial environments.

Spatial Units

The definitions of spatial units used to organize the study of Delaware's prehistory must define areas that would have supported similar plant and animal communities in the past. Odum (1971) has noted that the composition of any biotic community is dependent upon two types of factors: climatic and edaphic. Climatic factors include available atmospheric moisture, solar radiation, and temperature, while edaphic factors include soils, topography, exposure, and slope. In dealing with past environments, climatic factors are best considered from a temporal perspective and are discussed later. Division of the state into smaller units of similar past environments explicitly considers edaphic factors.

Numerous studies have mapped out regions within Delaware that have some applicability to studies of prehistoric archaeology. Included are studies of soils (Matthews and Lavoie 1970; Matthews and Ireland 1971; Ireland and Matthews 1974), drainage systems (Delaware Division of Historical and Cultural Affairs n.d.), physiographic zones (Fenneman 1938; Thornbury 1965), geological formations (Delaware Geological Survey 1976), and coastal sedimentary environments (Kraft et al. 1976). Of all these studies, the descriptions of physiographic zones that represent areas of similar geography, geology, and topography, provide the most useful initial division of Delaware for the study of prehistoric cultures. A brief description of each zone is provided below.

Piedmont Uplands/Fall Line Zone

The Piedmont portion of Delaware is characterized by a diversified relief dissected by narrow and deep stream valleys with isolated knolls rising above the general upland level (Spoljaric 1967, 3). Thornbury (1965, 88) notes that within the Piedmont Uplands there are no large tributaries of the older incised river systems, the Susquehanna and the Delaware. Instead, there are a number of smaller drainage systems. Some large floodplains can be found along the Brandywine; however, these areas are uncommon in the Delaware Piedmont. Elevation differences of up to 82 meters (270 feet) can be found between small floodplains of the numerous drainages and the tops of the adjacent knolls; these elevation differences are sufficient to cause changes in tree community distribution (Braun 1967, 192–94). Soils of the Piedmont Uplands can generally be characterized as well drained with some poorly drained areas in floodplains and upland flats.

Resembling a gigantic alluvial fan, the Fall Line zone represents a transition from the Piedmont Uplands to the flatter Coastal Plain areas in the southern part of the state. Streams flowing from the Piedmont with steep

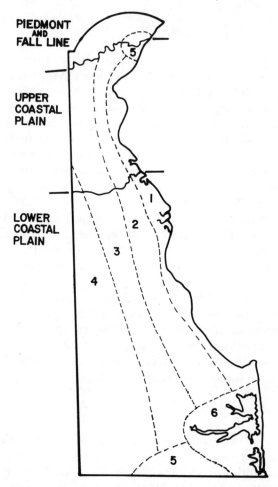

Fig. 1. Physiographic zones of Delaware. Coastal Plain zones: 1 = Delaware Shore; 2 = Mid-drainage; 3 = Drainage Divide; 4 = Chesapeake Headwater drainage; 5 = interior swamps; 6 = coastal bay.

gradients reach the Fall Line zone, which is less steep, and drop their bed loads. At present, the bed loads of the Piedmont streams are quite small; however, at various times in the past these streams carried tremendous sediment loads and dropped gravels, cobbles, boulders, and various sorted sands that make up the Columbia Formation described by Jordan (1964). This deposition created a series of well-drained soils and interspersed cobble beds in the vicinity of the Fall Line zone. Elevation differences range up to 52 meters (170 feet) from the floodplains of the White Clay Creek to the edge of the Fall Line scarp. Water resources are abundant and are comprised primarily of the White Clay Creek, which flows parallel to the Fall Line itself.

High Coastal Plain

Located between the Fall Line and the Smyrna River, the High Coastal Plain represents the southeastern extension of the very coarse gravel deposits of the Columbia sediments (Jordan 1964, 40). In many areas these coarse deposits resisted erosion, creating a rolling topography with up to 16 meters (50 feet) of elevation difference between the headlands bordering the larger streams and the adjacent floodplain marshes. Even though these elevation differences are considerably less than those noted for the Piedmont and Fall Line, they are great enough to significantly influence seasonal differences in plant communities (Braun 1967, 246–47). Water courses tend to be deeply incised and are lined by a veneer of relatively recent sediments that is thin along the upper reaches of drainages and thickens moving toward their mouths (Kraft et al. 1976, 13). Most streams are tidal and the saltwater/freshwater mix allows for a wide range of resources. Soils include a variety of well-drained and swampy settings that are distributed in a mosaic pattern across the region.

Low Coastal Plain

Underlain by the sands of the Columbia Formation (Jordan 1964; Delaware Geological Survey 1976), the Low Coastal Plain includes most of Kent and Sussex counties. These sands have been extensively reworked by various geological processes and the result is a very flat and relatively featureless landscape. Elevation differences range up to 10 meters (30 feet) and these small differences are further moderated by long gradual slopes. Surface water settings have been severely affected by rising sea level; most river systems are tidal in their middle and lower reaches, with extensive salt marshes found along the Delaware Bay and barrier island/salt marshes found along the Atlantic Coast (Kraft et al. 1976). These riverine systems would combine a wide range of environments and represent especially attractive human habitation areas. Much of the area is well drained; however, some extensive poorly drained areas are found.

Although the physiographic zones provide a useful organizing device for the study of prehistory, in the Coastal Plain areas they obscure some additional significant environmental differences. These additional sources of environmental variability, generally distributed in broad belts parallel to the Delaware River and Bay shore, are described below.

Midpeninsular Drainage Divide

Thomas (1966a, 3) has described the Midpeninsular Drainage Divide as the "backbone" of the Delmarva Peninsula. This area is defined by the stretch of low rolling topography that separates the headwaters of streams that drain into the Delaware River from streams that drain into the Chesapeake Bay. Elevation differences are slight and flowing surface water is restricted to the low order headwaters of larger streams and rivers. Additional water sources of the Midpeninsular Drainage Divide include a number of swamps that have formed in areas of poorly drained soils surrounded by sand ridges. Bay/basin features, known locally as whale wallows, represent another water source in this area. Geomorphological evidence seems to indicate that they were formed during the end of the Ice Ages, or Pleistocene, and many seem to have held water ever since (Rasmussen 1958, 82). The combination of headwater drainages, swampy areas, and bay/basin features with interspersed well-drained areas creates a mosaic of edaphic settings. This mosaic pattern is reflected in the varied poorly drained soils and well-drained soils in the area.

Interior Swamps

Churchman's Marsh on the White Clay Creek in northern new Castle County and Cedar Swamp on the headwaters of the Pocomoke in extreme southern Sussex County are included in this zone. The main difference between these two swamps and other swamps and marshes in Delaware is their large size and the fact that at least initially in their development both Churchman's Marsh and Cedar Swamp were probably fresh water and not tidal. Very little geomorphological research has been carried out at these two locations; however, their formation histories are similar to Dismal Swamp on the Virginia-North Carolina border and Mattawoman and Zekiah swamps in the lower Potomack River Valley of Maryland. Using research from Dismal Swamp (Whitehead 1972; Rappleye and Gardner 1979) as a model, Churchman's Marsh and Cedar Swamp can be viewed as special resource settings throughout much of their history. Although the soils in this zone are mostly poorly drained, there are some pockets of well-drained soils on headlands adjacent to the marshes.

Delaware Shore Zone

Included in the Delaware Shore zone are the remnant terraces of the Delaware River as well as the various tidal marshes that fringe the Delaware River and the Delaware Bay. These marshes are found throughout the area and include broad marshes with sandy barriers, more narrow marshes with continuous sandy barriers, and the Cape Henlopen spit complex (Kraft et al. 1976). Soils in the Delaware Shore edaphic zone are generally poorly drained; however, pockets of well-drained soils in areas of higher elevation may be found.

Mid-drainage Zone

The Mid-drainage zone is a strip of land located between the Delaware Shore and the Midpeninsular Drainage Divide and includes the central sections of all the Coastal Plain tributaries of the Delaware River. The modern tidal limit along the drainages marks the center of this zone and the major drainages and their tributaries are fresh throughout the inland half of the zone. Some tidal marshes and poorly drained areas are found in the floodplains of the major drainages. Well-drained soils are found on upper terraces of the drainages and on isolated headlands between the major drainages and their tributaries. The combination of brackish and freshwater resources makes this zone one of the richest in Delaware.

Coastal Bay Zone

Rehoboth Bay, Indian River, and Little Assawoman Bay are the major water courses of the Coastal Bay zone. Large embayed areas with fringing barrier islands of the Baymouth Barrier complex (Kraft et al. 1976) and tidal marshes are found within the area. Some minor water courses in the area are fresh. Much of the area is poorly drained; however, some well-drained areas are found on higher elevations and upper terraces of the major drainages. Elevation differences are quite low.

Chesapeake Headwater Drainages

The upper reaches of the Choptank and Nanticoke are included in this zone. In terms of available surface water, soils, and tidal resources, the Chesapeake headwater drainages resemble the Mid-drainage zone. The major difference between the two zones is that the extent of tidal brackish water settings in the Chesapeake headwater drainages is smaller than in the Mid-drainage zone.

The locations of these zones have not remained constant since the end of the Pleistocene because some zones have been subject to extensive land-

scape modification. The most important factor in this landscape
modification is post-Pleistocene sea level rise. Numerous studies by Kraft
(1971; 1977; Kraft et al. 1976) have shown that sea level has been rising
along the Atlantic Coast of Delaware and the Delaware Bay and River for
the past 12,000 years. This sea level rise has transformed the Delaware
River of 10,000 B.C. into the current drowned estuary. Many old land
surfaces have become submerged and the configuration of the Delaware
Bay and River has changed dramatically. The effect of the sea level rise can
be most easily seen in the Delaware Shore, Mid-drainage, and Coastal Bay
zones. In the past these zones would have been located further to the east;
with time they have migrated to the west and their present positions.

By combining the physiographic zones and the environmental zones of
the Coastal Plain, one can divide Delaware into regions that would have
had similar environments in the past. These zones provide spatial reference points throughout this review of Delaware prehistory; however, at
times it is necessary to use additional reference points such as drainages,
modern political boundaries, and town locations.

Temporal Units

The 15,000-year-long time span of Delaware prehistory is divided into
units, called "periods," defined by similar biosocial environments and similar adaptations or lifeways. Use of the term *period* avoids many of the
outdated connotations of the term *stage,* as noted by Snow (1980, 14),
although the sequence of adaptations revealed by the study of these periods represents a unique cultural evolutionary sequence of cultures re-
sponding to various biosocial environmental changes (Harris 1968, 656).
However, the existence of this sequence does not imply that the prehistoric
cultures of Delaware marched through a series of universal evolutionary
stages. The time periods used to organize this book are listed in Table 1,
along with their approximate dates.

Although for the Paleo-Indian and Archaic periods information is
sparse, the period is useful for discussion. However, during the Woodland I and Woodland II periods, where much more data are available, it is
possible to recognize finer temporal and spatial distinctions in adaptations
and lifeways. These smaller temporal/spatial units are called *complexes* and
are composed of a set of archaeological sites showing similar adaptations to
the biosocial environments with limited spatial and/or temporal distributions. The primary consideration of similar adaptations in addition to spatial and temporal integrity makes the term *complex* preferable to the more
restricted term *phase* used in the traditional literature (Willey and Phillips
1958). The complexes and their spatial and temporal distributions are
noted in Table 2.

Fig. 2. Drainage Locations. 1 = Brandywine; 2 = White Clay; 3 = Christina; 4 = Chesapeake and Delaware Canal; 5 = Appoquinnimink; 6 = Smyrna; 7 = Leipsic; 8 = St. Jones; 9 = Murderkill; 10 = Mispillion; 11 = Cedar Creek; 12 = Slaughter Creek; 13 = Broadkill; 14 = Indian River; 15 = Upper Pocomoke; 16 = Nanticoke; 17 = Marshyhope; 18 = Choptank.

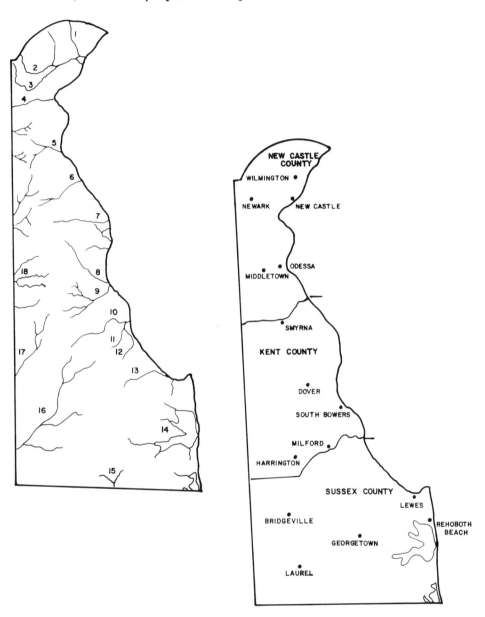

Fig. 3. Modern political boundaries and town locations.

Table 1: Delaware Cultural Periods and Dates

Period	Date*
Paleo-Indian	12,000 BC–6500 BC
Archaic	6500 BC–3000 BC
Woodland I	3000 BC–AD 1000
Woodland II	AD 1000–AD 1600

*These dates and all others noted herein are based on radiocarbon age determinations (See Michels 1973 for a complete description). Traditional methods of converting radiocarbon dates to calendar dates have recently been questioned (Ralph et al 1974) and numerous correction methods recommended. However, there is no single agreed-upon method and Stuckenrath (1977) suggests that until agreement is reached no corrections should be made. I have followed Stuckenrath's suggestion and no radiocarbon dates in this book have been corrected or recalibrated. Appendix I lists all of the available radiocarbon dates for Delaware.

Paleoenvironments

Because I have emphasized the study of adaptation to biosocial environments, some introductory remarks are necessary on the reconstruction of ancient environments, paleoenvironments, and climates. Some general information about past climate can be derived from a knowledge of how weather patterns may have worked in the past. The climatic changes noted during almost all of the prehistoric human occupation of Delaware were related to the major climatic shift that marked the end of the Ice Age

Table 2: Culture Complexes of Delaware

Dates	Period	Low Coastal Plain	High Coastal Plain	Piedmont/Fall Line
AD 1600				
	Woodland II	Slaughter Creek Complex		Minguannon Complex
AD 1000				
AD 500		Late Carey Complex	Webb Complex	Delaware Park Complex
AD 0	Woodland I	Carey Complex		
500 BC		Wolfe Neck Complex	Delmarva Adena Complex	Wolfe Neck Complex
		Clyde Farm Complex	Barker's Landing Complex	Clyde Farm Complex
3000 BC				
6500 BC	Archaic	(No Special Complexes)		
12,000 BC	Paleo-Indian	(No Special Complexes)		

environments of the Pleistocene and the development of the modern environments of the Holocene. During the Pleistocene the climate of Delaware was determined by the Laurentide ice sheet, which covered most of the northeastern portion of the continent. The cold air mass associated with this ice sheet combined with warm southern air to produce extensive frontal activity in the Middle Atlantic region (Carbone 1976, 19). Cloudy and wet conditions would have dominated the Delmarva Peninsula area and the average temperature would have been markedly colder, in the range of 5 degrees Farenheit (Carbone 1976, 91). After 8500 B.C., a rapid shift in air mass patterns was caused by the fairly rapid melting of the Laurentide ice sheet. Throughout the retreat of the glaciers the Laurentide air mass still had an important role and increased moisture in the atmosphere caused levels of precipitation significantly higher than those noted today (Carbone 1976, 93). However, the degree to which the Delmarva Peninsula was affected by this air mass lessened as the ice sheets retreated to the north. Following the dramatic shift in climate that marked the end of the Pleistocene and the beginning of the Holocene, the climatic patterns are somewhat more difficult to categorize. Westerly winds became increasingly prevalent (Carbone 1976, 20) and brought increased warmth and dryness to the Middle Atlantic region. In general, the degree of seasonal variation became greater throughout the Holocene, eventually approximating modern conditions.

More detailed information can be derived from palynology, the study of pollen. The work of Wendland and Bryson (1974) provides the theoretical basis for interpreting the pollen data. Wendland and Bryson analyzed discontinuities in the global geologic-botanic record and developed an "episodic model" of environmental change based on a series of significant environmental change dates. The episodic model notes that climatic change was not a set of incremental changes, but rather was a series of time periods, or episodes, of fairly stable climatic patterns disrupted at various times by marked, abrupt changes. The significant dates, their correlation with Delaware prehistoric culture periods, and the episodes are noted in Table 3. Although this model was developed with worldwide applicability in mind, Wright (1976) has noted that local paleoenvironmental data must be evaluated in order to insure that the model is indeed applicable.

Table 3: Environmental Episodes

Episode	Dates	Culture Period
Late Glacial	15,000 BC–8080 BC	Paleo-Indian
pre-Boreal	8080 BC–7350 BC	Paleo-Indian
Boreal	7350 BC–6540 BC	Paleo-Indian
Atlantic	6540 BC–3110 BC	Archaic
sub-Boreal	3110 BC–810 BC	Woodland I
sub-Atlantic	810 BC–AD 1000	Woodland I
Recent	AD 1000–AD 1600	Woodland II

Table 4:   Transitional Area Pollen Sequences

Episode	Date	Crystal Lake(1)	Buckles Bog(2)	Cranberry Bog (3)	High Point State Park(4)	Saddle Bo (5)
Sub-Atlantic	Recent 800 BC	Pine		Pine(?)	Oak,pine,hemlock, chestnut	Birch,spr oak
Sub-Boreal	800 BC 3100 BC	Oak,hickory	Oak,chestnut		Oak,pine,hickory	Oak,hicko
Atlantic	3100 BC 6500 BC	Hemlock,oak, beech		Hemlock,oak	Oak,pine,hemlock	Oak,hemlo
Pre-Boreal/Boreal	6500 BC 8000 BC	Pine,oak	Pine Spruce,pine	Pine	Spruce,pine, fir	Pine
Late Glacial	8000 BC 10,000 BC	Spruce,fir, oak,pine	Sedge,grasses	Spruce,fir, pine	Grasses,sedges, composites	park tund

Sources: 1 - Walker and Hartman 1960
           2 - Maxwell and Davis 1972
           3 - Gehris 1964
           4 - Niering 1953
           5 - Sirkin and Minard 1972

The most useful approach to the study of pollen data from Delaware is to look at these data in a regional context. The work of Carbone (1976) is used as a framework for this regional context. Carbone (1976, 20) notes that the Middle Atlantic can be divided into subareas on the basis of dominant fossil pollen characteristics. Delaware is located on the southern margin of what Carbone describes as the transitional area of the Middle Atlantic, which is composed of the states of Pennsylvania, New Jersey, Maryland, and Delaware (Carbone 1976, 21). The term *transitional* refers to the fact that the geomorphological, floral, and faunal characteristics of this area were typical of both glaciated and unglaciated regions (Carbone 1976, 23). Because the pollen samples are so few it is necessary to examine pollen data from throughout the transitional area.

The first pollen data to be considered are located in the Allegheny Plateau and the Ridge and Valley sections of the transitional area and are summarized in Table 4. The Crystal Lake—Hartstown Bog profile from northwest Pennsylvania (Walker and Hartman 1960) is one of the most important for the Middle Atlantic area. The sequence of vegetation revealed by the pollen data corresponds nicely to the episodic model and can be seen as representative of the glaciated sections of the transitional area (Carbone 1976, 27). Similar sequences from a variety of locations in the Ridge and Valley and Allegheny Plateau areas, including Buckles Bog (Maxwell and Davis 1972), Cranberry Bog (Gehris 1964), High Point State Park Bog (Niering 1953), and Saddle Bog (Sirkin and Minard 1972) confirm the general episodic model. (See Table 4 for tabular summaries.) As a group these sequences represent the higher elevation settings within

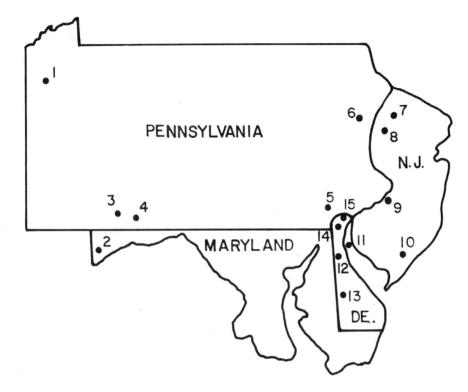

Fig. 4. Pollen sampling locations. 1 = Hartstown Bog, Crystal Lake, Mercer County, Penn.; 2 = Buckles Bog, Garrett County, Md.; 3 = Glades Bog, Somerset County, Penn.; 4 = New Paris No. 4 Sinkhole, Bedford County, Penn.; 5 = Marsh Creek, Chester County, Penn.; 6 = Cranberry Bog, Monroe County, Penn.; 7 = High Point, Sussex County, N.J.; 8 = Saddle Bog, Sussex County, N.J.; 9 = Delaware Terraces, Trenton to Camden, N.J.; 10 = Oswego Bog, Pine, N.J.; 11 = Reedy Island, New Castle County, Del.; 12 = Borthwick Basin, New Castle County, Del.; 13 = Dill Farm (7K-E-12), Kent County, Del.; 14 = Delaware Park (7NC-E-41), New Castle County, Del.; 15 = Mitchell Farm site (7NC-A-2), New Castle County, Del.

Table 5: Delmarva Peninsula Pollen Data

Episode	Date	Marsh Creek(1)	Borthwick Basin(2)	Reedy Island(3)	Delaware River(4)	Chesapeake Bay(5)	Dill Farm(6)	7NC-E-41 (7)	7NC (
	Recent								
Sub-Atlantic		Oak,chestnut					Oak,alder, aspen, aquatics		
	800 BC								
Sub-Boreal	800 BC		Hickory, graminae	Hickory	Pine,oak, hickory	Oak,pine, hickory		Grasses, oak,pine	
	3100 BC								
Atlantic	3100 BC	Hemlock, oak	Oak	Hemlock	Oak,hemlock	Oak,hemlock			Oa: he:
	6500 BC								
Pre-Boreal/ Boreal	6500 BC	Pine	Pine, spruce		Pine,spruce	Pine			Pi oa
	8000 BC								
Late Glacial	8000 BC	Grasses, sedges, pine	Spruce, pine	Pine	Pine,birch, spruce, grasses	Spruce, grasses	Pine, grasses		Sp pi bu
									Pi sp
	10,000 BC								bu

Sources: 1 – Martin 1958   5 – Harrison, Malloy, Rusnak, and Teresmae 19
         2 – Rasmussen 1958   6 – Unpublished manuscript, Island Field Muse
         3 – Owens, Steffanson, and Sirkin 1974   7 – Thomas 1981
         4 – Sirkin, Owens, Minard, and Rubin 1970   8 – Custer 1981

the transitional area and correspond to areas that were associated with tundra conditions at the end of the Pleistocene. Therefore, their applicability to events on the Delmarva Peninsula is limited to the fact that they do correspond to the episodic model and provide some clues to the nature of the interaction between climate and edaphic factors.

Pollen data that pertains directly to the Delmarva Peninsula can be divided into three groups corresponding to the physiographic divisions of Delaware. Within the Piedmont and Fall Line zones there are three pollen samples available for analysis. One of these sites is Marsh Creek in Chester County, Pennsylvania (Martin 1958). The results from the analysis of the pollen from this location are summarized in Table 5. The pollen record from Marsh Creek tends to be somewhat compressed; however, a good picture of Late Pleistocene fluctuations is presented. Low zones dated to approximately 11,500 B.C. show a series of oscillations between grasses and sedges and boreal species, indicating that taiga/tundralike communities were interspersed among one another, with their distributions shifting slightly in response to climatic and edaphic conditions. The postglacial record from the site begins with a pine dominance and follows a standard sequence of northern hardwoods to temperate hardwood forests (Carbone 1976; 28–31).

The Mitchell site (7NC-A-2) is located in the Hockessin area of northern New Castle County. A sequence of pollen samples was recovered from within an inactive sinkhole and is summarized in Table 5. The lowest levels, dominated by pine and nonarboreal pollen, including burnet, has an associated radiocarbon date of 9530 B.C. (UGa-4323). Overlying layers also contain burnet, nonarboreal pollen, and spruce. An oak-hemlock zone is associated with a radiocarbon date of 5840 B.C. (UGa-4322). Levels just below the plowzone area show increases in hickory and nonarboreal pollen. In general, the sequence of plant communities revealed in the Hockessin sinkhole corresponds nicely to the episodic model described by Carbone.

The final data for the Piedmont and Fall Line zone come from the Delaware Park Site (7NC-E-41) in northern New Castle County (Thomas 1981). Ten pollen samples were taken from dated archaeological refuse features. The pollen data from these features and the radiocarbon dates are listed in Table 6. Note that the species composition of the samples remains remarkably constant from 1850 B.C. to A.D. 640. Nonaboreal pollen comprises the majority of the species in the samples in all cases, with arboreal pollen indicating an oak-pine-elm or oak-elm-pine forest setting. These pollen assemblages and their dates correspond nicely to other pollen data from this time period that show a warm-dry maximum during the late Atlantic and early Sub-Boreal episodes.

Three sets of pollen data are available for the High Coastal Plain section of Delaware and are summarized in Table 5. The only published data come from a series of single samples taken along the terraces of the Delaware River (Sirkin, Owens, Minard, and Rubin 1970). This set of pollen data does not represent a continuous column, but only a series of single samples with associated radiocarbon dates. In general the New Jersey Coastal Plain data is contrasted to the rest of the transitional area by the preponderance of pine pollen in most of the samples. Carbone (1976, 38) stresses the

Table 6: Pollen Percentages from Dated Features at 7NC-E-41

Feature	Date	Lab #*	Grasses	Herbaceous	Wetland	Total NAP**	Pine	Oak	Elm	Hickory
Fea. 63	AD 640	UGa-3439	18 .3	23.3	18.3	59.9	5.8	8.7	7.2	2.6
Fea. 51	AD 455	UGa-3438	24 .6	14.9	19.8	59.3	7.7	11.1	8.2	0.0
Fea. 39	AD 275	UGa-3501	24.4	22.9	16.6	63.9	7.8	10.2	7.3	0.4
Fea. 56	AD 100	UGa-3467	20.8	20.3	21.3	62.4	7.8	10.9	7.2	0.5
Fea. 45	AD 85	UGa-3503	22.3	17.1	19.7	59.1	9.8	14.0	12.5	2.6
Fea. 43	AD 80	UGa-3465	18.2	26.1	19.1	63.4	6.3	9.2	7.3	1.2
Fea. 12	AD 65	UGa-3504	17.8	21.3	20.8	59.9	8.4	9.9	7.9	0.9
Fea. 149	10 BC	UGa-3500	18 .9	21.0	12.6	52.5	8.0	12.2	7.6	2.6
Fea. 138	740 BC	UGa-3469	17.6	22.3	19.2	59.1	6.0	9.1	9.3	2.5
Fea. 94	1850 BC	UGa-3440	15.9	24.2	17.6	57.7	7.9	11.0	7.9	1.3

Source: Thomas (1981:IX-135)

*Wherever radiocarbon dates from Delaware are used in the text, the laboratory number is noted in parentheses following the date or in footnotes. Appendix I lists all radiocarbon dates from Delaware with the laboratory number, radiocarbon years, standard deviation, site location, and significant associated artifacts

**Non-arboreal pollen

effects of edaphic factors at the expense of climatic factors in the area. However, in spite of the importance of the edaphic effects and the preponderance of pine pollen, there are still changes in other species that seem to correspond to the episodic model. An additional pollen sequence was obtained from the area of Reedy Island, Delaware (Owens, Stefansson, and Sirkin 1974). The sample came from the area of the Reedy Island dike and is somewhat anomalous in that the species composition is relatively constant throughout. The only available date is an estimation at 8820 B.C. Owens et al. (1974) note a correlation with the Oswego Bog profile (Florer 1972; Potzger 1945, 1952); however, the data from these samples are somewhat compressed and the estimated age makes the correlations suspect. The most that can be said concerning the Reedy Island sequence would be that the importance of the edaphic effects of the Coastal Plain is emphasized by the constant species composition. The final pollen data for the High Coastal Plain come from the Borthwick Basin in southern New Castle County, Delaware (Rasmussen 1958). The pollen is derived from a bay-basin feature and no radiocarbon dates are available. The bottom portion of the sequence (Rasmussen 1958, 88, fig. 4) is characterized by a spruce-pine dominance with a shift to pine-spruce moving up through the sequence. The top third of the sequence is characterized by an oak dominance. Especially interesting is a section with a pronounced increase in nonarboreal pollen associated with a slight increase in hickory located in the middle of the oak-dominated pollen zone. Correlation of this sequence with others is difficult due to the absence of dates; however, Table 5 offers a rough correlation based on comparable vegetation communities.

Three sets of pollen data are pertinent for the Low Coastal Plain section of Delaware. The Oswego Bog in the Pine Barrens of New Jersey (Florer 1972; Potzger 1945, 1952) has been discussed previously and indicates the importance of the edaphic effects of the Coastal Plain settings. It is questionable, however, whether or not the effects of edaphic factors in an area like the Pine Barrens can be generalized to the Coastal Plain as a whole. At best it can be stated that the edaphic effects are important and should be carefully considered before attempting to reconstruct environments in Coastal Plain settings. A series of borings carried out near the mouth of the Chesapeake Bay (Harrison, Malloy, Rusnak, and Teresmae 1965) are also applicable to the Low Coastal Plain areas of the Delmarva Peninsula. A strong coniferous assemblage is noted prior to 13,330 B.C. with a nonarboreal pollen component comprising almost 20 percent of the assemblage. The remaining sequence consists of a pine-dominant assemblage about 8390 B.C. followed by an oak-hemlock zone and an oak-pine-hickory zone. In general, the Chesapeake samples fit with the episodic model and represent a good picture of vegetation communities that were not heavily influenced by special seral successions or edaphic factors (Carbone 1976, 53). The final sequence from the Low Coastal Plain comes from the Dill Farm site (7K-E-12) in Kent County, Delaware. Two pollen samples with associated radiocarbon dates were taken from a buried swamp in the interior Drainage Divide zone. The older of the samples was dated to approximately 7940 B.C. (I-6045) and showed a pine dominance with some associated hemlock, birch, and oak. A strong nonarboreal component is also noted for this sample. Thus, the Dill Farm data from the Late Glacial/Pre-Boreal transition closely parallels the data from the Chesapeake Bay samples. The second sample from Dill Farm dates to approximately 500 B.C. (I-6891) and is characterized by an oak dominance with associated beech, maple, alder, aspen, and some associated aquatics. The oak dominance fits the pattern for the rest of the Coastal Plain and the hydrophytic association mirrors local edaphic effects.

A series of applicable pollen samples are available for Coastal Plain areas to the south in southeast Virginia, North Carolina, and Georgia. These pollen samples are discussed by Carbone and have some bearing on the Delmarva Peninsula. In general, the pollen data from the Coastal Plain areas of the south Atlantic Coast fit with the general episodic model (Science Applications Incorporated 1979). To a large degree the effects of the Holocene warming trends were felt somewhat earlier in the South Atlantic Coastal Plain; however, the general pattern of vegetation communities corresponds to some of the Low Coastal Plain settings of the Delmarva Peninsula. Especially important are some of the swamp-forest succession patterns seen at Dismal Swamp, Virginia (Whitehead 1972; Rappleye and Gardner 1979) and Rockyhock Bay, North Carolina (Whitehead 1973), which can be used as models for the interpretation of similar edaphic settings such as those at Cedar Swamp and Churchman's Marsh in Delaware.

In sum, the pollen data from Delaware and surrounding regions fit with the episodic model and support the correlations of environmental episodes and cultural periods noted in Table 3.

Archaeological Site Data

As was noted in the Preface, the basic archaeological data upon which this book is based come from a variety of sources. Published site reports and technical reports prepared for various state agencies comprise a large bulk of the data and where these reports have been used they are cited. Additional sources of information are the unpublished site survey records maintained by the Bureau of Archaeology and Historic Preservation in Dover. These records include all known prehistoric archaeological sites in Delaware and note the locations of sites as well as information on the artifacts found there. Sites are given a registration number, which uses a system developed in 1954 (Thomas 1966a, 2). Each county is divided into blocks bounded by lines of latitude and longitude or state and county boundaries; each block is given a letter designation beginning with the northernmost or westernmost division, continuing in alphabetical order to the east and south. The individual sites are then given a designation, including the state, the county, the block, and the site's numerical order within the block. A New Castle County site might be designated 7NC-A-3, with 7 referring to Delaware's numerical order in the alphabet among the states.

As part of a research project to assess the archaeological resources of Delaware, I systematically examined these site files and the artifacts collections maintained at the Island Field Museum in South Bowers, Delaware. The results of the analysis were reported to the Delaware Bureau of Archaeology and Historic Preservation (Custer 1980b, 1981) and are included as part of the data reported here. In order to ensure that my interpretations of settlement patterns (i.e., the distribution of sites across the landscape—Willey 1953) are correct and can be duplicated, references to the individual sites by their state numbers are included. These sites are referenced by their registration number assigned by the state and, where available, by their common name. Appendix 2 gives a list of all Delaware prehistoric archaeological sites noted in the text and includes their state number and the periods and complexes present at each.

[2]

Paleo-Indian Period:
The Earliest Inhabitants of Delaware

The Paleo-Indian period begins with the arrival of the earliest inhabitants of Delaware and ends with the emergence of the relatively modern environments of the Holocene. An adaptation to the distinctive Pleistocene environments of the Delmarva Peninsula characterizes the Paleo-Indian period and the emergence of Holocene environments brings these adaptations to an end. In general, the first arrival of people on the Delmarva Peninsula took place sometime at the end of the Pleistocene. These early inhabitants of Delaware were portions of populations of hunters and gatherers who had crossed from Asia into northwestern North America several thousand years earlier. The question of when this crossing took place is open to some debate and is a major focus of research in current North American archaeology. At present two schools of thought concerning this question can be identified. Although both agree that people could have entered North America from Asia up to 30,000 years ago, they differ over the presently available evidence for human entry into North America. One theory advocates that, for the time being, the earliest well-documented dates for human habitation of North America are less than 14,000 years old (Haynes 1977). The second school of thought believes that evidence is presently available to support the contention that people could have entered North America up to 30,000 years ago (Humphrey and Stanford 1979). Although most of the debate focuses on available evidence rather than on possibilities, it can become quite acidulous.

Over the years the Delaware River Valley has provided archaeological data relevant to the question of early human entry into North America. Although most of the work was done in the middle and late nineteenth century, debate over some of the finds still goes on today. Some of the earliest work was by C. C. Abbott in the middle Delaware River Valley near

Trenton, New Jersey. Abbott (1872, 1876) reported finding very crude stone tools made from argillite, which he claimed dated from within the Middle Pleistocene. Willey and Sabloff (1980, 47) and Griffin (1977, 3) note that Abbott's work is typical of a period when various researchers were trying to push the antiquity of humans in the New World back to time levels comparable to those recognized in the Old World, particularly Western Europe. Unfortunately, the data used by Abbott and other early researchers were not good. For example, Abbott's "early" tools were thought to be quite old because they were very crude. However, the tools looked crude because they were unfinished and had been discarded very early in the process of biface manufacture. Later research showed that similar tools can be found in assemblages dating from times as recent as European Contact (about A.D. 1600). Also, geological research showed that the strata which produced the tools dated from well within the Holocene (Richards 1939).

About the same time that Abbott's finds were being reported, Hilbourne T. Cresson (1888, 1892) carried out archaeological investigations in Delaware near Naaman's Creek. While examining dredge spoil piles, Cresson allegedly found an assemblage of artifacts that resembled the argillite tools found by Abbott. Also included in the assemblage was a whelk shell incised with the drawing of a mammoth. Over the years the engraved shell, known as the Holly Oak pendant, and the associated artifact assemblage have been the center of controversy. Recent examination of the Holly Oak assemblage (Galasso 1981), now housed at the Smithsonian Institution, shows that based on diagnostic tool types, none of the stone tools are more than 5,000 years old. Also, Weslager's (1968, 30–44) summary of early responses to Cresson's work notes that the circumstances of the find are curious and that the shell's authenticity has always been questioned. Kraft (1977; Kraft and Thomas 1976) has recently published reevaluations of the geological setting of the find, along with a reexamination of the shell itself that raises the possibility that the pendant may be quite old and authentic. Analysis of the geology of the area of the reported find reveals the existence of a Sangamon age landscape (ca. 40,000 years old) overlain by a much younger Holocene marsh (Kraft 1977, 43, Fig. 7). Presumably the shell pendant could have been dredged from either landscape. However, because the shell supposedly was found in dredge spoils, its location in relation to the surrounding sediments will never be known and the geological analysis does not provide any clear answers to the question of the shell's age. Additional microscopic analysis of the shell showed similar weathering of the shell on both the unaltered surface and within the incised lines. This similar weathering indicates that the engraving was not done in recent times on an old shell; however, it is still possible that a recent shell could have been engraved and both the shell surface and the incising altered to resemble an older, weathered shell. Therefore, the question of the shell's age and authenticity remains open. Probably the only way to resolve the problem would be to date the shell, using some form of chronometric dating techniques. Amino acid racemization tests have been proposed to the Smithsonian Institution; however, the Smithsonian has declined to allow the shell to be sampled because it has been treated with a variety of preservatives that might skew the date. Presumably, other methods could be used, although it is likely that the preservatives would still cause inaccurate dates. Until the shell can be dated it must remain a tantalizing enigma in the search for very early inhabitants of Delaware and North America.

In light of the fact that the Holly Oak pendant provides little help in the determination of the maximum age for man's presence on the Delmarva Peninsula, one must look at comparable sites elsewhere in the Middle Atlantic area. Traditionally, the oldest sites in the Middle Atlantic area are associated with fluted projectile points (Griffin 1977, 8). These distinctive bifacially flaked stone tools are characterized by a groove or flute removed from the base of the point on both sides. Shapes and sizes vary greatly among fluted points in eastern North America; however, the oldest fluted points seem to be fairly uniform in morphology and are very similar to the Clovis fluted points found in the western United States (Haynes 1964). Because of the similarity in form, eastern fluted points from the earliest portion of the Paleo-Indian period are also known as Clovis points and are believed to be associated with a similar point in time. In the West, fluted points have been associated with a variety of extinct Pleistocene megafauna at a number of sites (Haury et al. 1953, 1959; Hester 1972; Wendorf and Hester 1975; Haynes 1964). Organic material from these western sites has yielded radiocarbon dates that range between 10,000 and 9500 B.C. (Haynes 1964). Because of the similarity of form, the earliest Clovis points found in eastern North America and the Delmarva Peninsula appear to date to a similar period (Griffin 1977, 4). Only a few dates for Clovis points are known from the Middle Atlantic and Northeast. At the Debert site in Nova Scotia, Clovislike points were dated about 9000 B.C. (MacDonald 1968). At the Shawnee-Minisink site in the Upper Delaware Valley of Pennsylvania a date of about 8700 B.C. has been reported (Kauffman and Dent 1978, 1; McNett et al. 1975). These dates tend to be quite late compared to the western dates; however, the key point for this discussion is the fact that they are not any earlier.

There are, however, older dates obtained for stone tools, not including fluted points, from the Middle Atlantic area. At the Meadowcroft Rockshelter in western Pennsylvania, Adovasio et al. (1977) have obtained dates of approximately 13,000 B.C. for an assemblage of nondiagnostic flake tools and bifaces. However, even though the Meadowcroft Rockshelter probably represents the finest example of controlled excavation techniques in the Middle Atlantic area, there are a number of questions about the early dates. These questions have been summarized by Mead (1980) and Haynes

Plate 1. Clovis points from central Delaware. (Courtesy Delaware Division of Historical and Cultural Affairs.)

(1977, 1980) and note the following anomalies in the Meadowcraft data: an absence of megafauna, an absence of diagnostic Paleo-Indian and Early Archaic materials from the chronological series that is otherwise complete, the presence of pollen from nut-bearing trees close to the glacial front, and the absence of a buried soil to correspond to discontinuities in the radiocarbon dates near the bottom of the soil profile. In addition, the presence of a large roof fall could have produced pronounced disturbance of the cultural deposits and would have been masked by later soil profile development. Adovasio et al. (1980) replied to these objections; however, the early dates for the Meadowcroft Rockshelter remain somewhat suspect, as noted by Dincauze (1981). In light of the above data it would seem that the earliest dates for man on the Delmarva Peninsula that are not subject to criticism are in the vicinity of 10,000 B.C. or later.

Given a beginning date of approximately 10,000 B.C. for the Paleo-Indian period, chronological divisions within and ending dates of the period can be explored. Time divisions within the Paleo-Indian period have been derived from the work of William M. Gardner at the Flint Run Paleo-Indian complex in the northern Shenandoah Valley of Virginia (Gardner 1974, 1977). Excavation at the Thunderbird site, a stratified Paleo-Indian base camp included within the Flint Run complex, indicates that three separate divisions are observable within the time period during which fluted points are manufactured. These three time periods are defined on the basis of different diagnostic artifacts, stratigraphic separation of living floors, and different methods of stone tool production (Gardner 1974). The three periods, or phases, recognized by Gardner (1974, 38) are Clovis, Mid-Paleo, and Dalton-Hardaway. Unfortunately, no radiocarbon dates are available for the phases. Further analysis of fluted points by Gardner and Verrey (1979) in western Virginia and Brown (1979) in Maryland indicates that Gardner's time divisions can probably be generalized for the Middle Atlantic area, although further stratigraphic data from other areas would be useful. Therefore, these time divisions will be applied to the Delmarva Peninsula Paleo-Indian data with the understanding that stratigraphic data from future sites may necessitate some revision.

Gardner's work also includes an additional phase in the Paleo-Indian period of the Middle Atlantic area. Gardner (1974, 1977) includes early side- and corner-notched projectile points such as Palmer, Amos, and Kirk types (Coe 1964, Broyles 1971) and the cultures that produced them within the Paleo-Indian period. Traditionally, the transition from fluted points to notched points was seen as a break in the chronological continuum that indicated basic lifeway changes (Coe 1964; Broyles 1971). Little information on anything other than projectile point morphology was ever included in the analyses presented by Coe and Broyles. Nevertheless, on the basis of these morphological changes the traditional researchers projected a new chronological period, the Early Archaic. Gardner (1974, 1977, 1978) has questioned the validity of this scheme based on data from the Flint Run complex sites. At both the Fifty and the Thunderbird sites there is evidence of a continuous use of the sites through the Paleo-Indian and Early Archaic periods. Use of jasper as a basis for nonprojectile point portions of the stone tool kit and settlement pattern continuity seem to indicate that the changes in projectile point forms from fluted to notched forms do not indicate any substantial changes in the lifestyle of these prehistoric peoples. Therefore, Gardner would include those cultures, traditionally referred to as Early Archaic, within the Paleo-Indian period. Lifeway shifts are not apparent until approximately 6500 B.C., when the dominant projectile point form is a small point with a notched base called a bifurcate. A variety of type names are ascribed to these bifurcate points in the traditional literature and are usually included in the Early Archaic continuum with the early notched points. However, because the notched points have been shown to be part of the Paleo-Indian continuum, and because the break in lifestyles occurs at the same time as the appearance of the bifurcate points,

Gardner (1978) would use the bifurcate points to mark the beginning of a different time period. Similarly, the bifurcate point would not be a part of the Early Archaic continuum of projectile point technology. For want of a better term, Gardner labels the bifurcate points *Middle Archaic* and sees them as indicative of the adaptation of people to the fully emerged Holocene.

Environmental Setting

The Paleo-Indian Period corresponds to the Late Glacial, Pre-Boreal, and Boreal environmental episodes (Table 3), and knowledge of these environments is crucial to an understanding of Paleo-Indian adaptations. In general, the environments from 15,000 B.C. to 6500 B.C. represent a transition from Late Pleistocene environments to those characteristic of the Holocene.

Late Glacial (15,000 B.C.–8080 B.C.)

The Late Glacial episode is associated with the very end of the Pleistocene and with the last effects of the glaciers upon climate in the Middle Atlantic area. By about 12,000 B.C. the Laurentide ice sheet had retreated just north of the headwaters of the Delaware River (Ogden 1977, 24, Fig. 4) and was still an important determinant of climatic patterns for the Delmarva Peninsula. By the end of the Late Glacial episode the ice sheet would have retreated to an area north of the Great Lakes and the Saint Lawrence River, and its effects upon the climate of the Middle Atlantic would have been severely reduced. Examination of the sections of Tables 4 and 5 pertaining to the Late Glacial episode reveals that a variety of plant communities are indicated by the pollen record. During the early parts of the Late Glacial some of the areas in the northern portion of the transitional area might have been characterized by tundra conditions (Carbone 1976, 68; Bernabo and Webb 1977, 72). In areas further south the Late Glacial episode was characterized by a hodge-podge, or mosaic, of different vegetation communities (Whitehead 1965; Brown and Cleland 1968). The wide variation of pollen found in Late Glacial assemblages, such as those noted in Tables 4 and 5, lend support to this view. Therefore, the nonarboreal elements of the pollen assemblages from the Delmarva Peninsula would have represented grassland settings within a broader coniferous matrix. Deciduous elements would also have been present in mixed hydrophytic seres and other communities.

Faunal evidence also supports the mosaic interpretation of Late Glacial environments (Carbone 1976, 68). Small mammals such as voles, lemmings, mice, and ground squirrels, all of which are extremely sensitive to environmental conditions and which are found today in markedly different environmental zones, are often found together in a single "disharmonious assemblage" in Late Glacial deposits (Brown and Cleland 1968, 114). Assemblages of this sort have been found in the Middle Atlantic at New Paris No. 4 Sinkhole in Pennsylvania (Guilday et al. 1964), Natural Chimneys (Guilday 1962), and Saltville, Virginia (Ray et al. 1967). Similarly, large mammals, or megafauna, from the end of the Pleistocene show certain anomalous associations. Carbone (1976, 67) notes that single locations often will contain a mix of woodland musk ox, grazing mammoth, browsing mastodon, giant moose of swampy forests, woodland peccaries, as well as white-tailed deer, caribou, elk, and giant beaver. Therefore, the mosaic interpretation seems to be upheld by a variety of sources of information and can be applied to the Delmarva Peninsula as well as to upper reaches of the Delaware River Valley (Eisenberg 1978) and is more accurate than the reconstructions offered by Sirkin (1977) and Edwards and Merrill (1977).

Although the general pattern of environmental distributions can be described, it is very difficult to specify the exact environmental setting for a given area during the Late Glacial episode. There are probably no modern analogues for the faunal and floral communities of this episode (Brown and Cleland 1968, 114) and, therefore, it is difficult to hypothesize interactions of species and the effects of this interaction upon their distributions. Post-Pleistocene sea level rise has also greatly altered the Delaware River Valley topography, making it difficult to predict even broad-scale faunal and floral community distributions in those areas. Consequently, the description of Late Glacial settings in the Delmarva Peninsula presented below is at best very generalized.

The pollen data from Table 5 indicates that the mosaic pattern for the Delmarva Peninsula was dominated by boreal components, most likely spruce. Spruce dominance from areas as far south as Rockyhock Bay, North Carolina (Whitehead 1973) suggests that the entire peninsula was dominated by spruce settings. Interspersed with the spruce would be various grassland settings, which produced the nonarboreal pollen noted in the samples. Within the Piedmont and Fall Line edaphic zones the grassland settings were probably restricted to swampy floodplains, scattered upland bogs and meadows (Martin 1958), and areas with special edaphic effects such as the serpentine barrens (Braun 1967, 248). Grassland settings within the Delaware Shore, Middrainage, Coastal Bay, and Chesapeake Headwater zones would probably be found in the low-relief floodplains of the Delaware River, which are now inundated and buried by post-Pleistocene sea level rise and in poorly drained areas. Rasmussen's (1958) data seem to indicate that bay and basin features were open and active during the Late Glacial episode, as does the work of Bonfiglio and Cresson (1978) in the New Jersey Coastal Plain. These areas would have supported some aquatics and surrounding swampy grasslands. Similarly, the data from Dill Farm indicates that the Midpeninsula Drainage Divide zone of the Delmarva

Peninsula also would have supported some grassland settings. The work of Foss et al. (1978) on the Maryland Eastern Shore indirectly indicates the existence of a certain amount of open settings in that windblown loess deposits are found across the peninsula. The ultimate source of the sediment is probably across the ancestral Susquehanna River Valley (Foss et al. 1978, 331) and the deposition seems to be scattered pockets. The implication would be that high wind velocities would be generated across the open grassland areas and the deposition would occur at the interface of the grasslands and the broad coniferous forest stands.

Although no megafaunal and other faunal remains from Late Glacial times are known for the Delmarva Peninsula, a few statements about faunal distributions can be made. The mosaic vegetation patterns noted for northern Delaware have been hypothesized for similar areas in Pennsylvania (Kinsey and Custer 1979, 40, Table 3), so based on similar vegetation settings, similar faunal distributions can be projected. Kinsey (1977a, 22) notes both grazing mammoth and browsing mastodon finds for the Piedmont areas of Lancaster County, Pennsylvania. Similarly, a variety of Pleistocene fauna were recovered from Bootlegger Sinkhole in the York County Piedmont (Reich 1974, 89–90). Included in the Bootlegger assemblage is a variety of small mammals such as moles, shrews, squirrels, lemmings, soles, and mice; various species of bat such as the Pleistocene big brown bat; carnivores such as wolf, skunk, otter, weasel, and fox; and caribou and white-tailed deer (John Guilday, personal communication). The variety of the small mammals and the inclusion of caribou at the Bootlegger Sinkhole seem to correspond nicely to the mosaic interpretation, and a similar assemblage can be extrapolated to the Delaware Piedmont during the Late Glacial times.

Also relevant to a discussion of Delaware faunal assemblages is a series of dated megafaunal finds from the Upper Delaware River Valley. Included in these megafaunal finds are the Highland Lake mastodon from Vernon, New Jersey, dated at 8940 B.C. ± 200 (Jepson 1964, 16), the Bojak Mastodon from Liberty Township, New Jersey, dated at 9045 B.C. ± 750 (Kraft 1974, 5), the Marshalls Creek Mastodon from Delaware Water Gap, Pennsylvania, dated at 10,210 B.C. ± 180 and 10,070 B.C. ± 180 (Huff 1969, 2–7), and Orange County, New York, caribou dated at 7910 B.C. ± 225 and 8050 B.C. ± 160 (Funk, Fisher, and Reilly 1970). Based on the dates of these finds and the similarity of environmental settings, it is likely that megafauna, including mastodons and mammoth, would be found in the Delaware Piedmont. Similarly, a number of mastodon and mammoth finds for the New Jersey Coastal Plain noted by Kraft (1977, 270, Fig. 5) can be used as the basis for an extrapolation of the distribution of these animals into the Delaware Coastal Plain.

In general, the faunal distributions for the Late Glacial times in the Delmarva Peninsula and in the Piedmont can be described as a mosaic setting with a high variety of species observable over small areas. The greatest variety of animals would be found in the grassland/woodland interface. Perennial and seasonal water sources would also act as focal points attractive to game. Included in these water settings would be lower order streams, bays and basins, and poorly drained areas in the drainage divide zones. Another focal point associated with the water sources would be salt and mineral licks in swampy areas such as the floodchutes of major drainages and poorly drained interior settings.

At this point it is necessary to consider the possible resources associated with the Delaware River both in terrestrial settings and estuarine settings. Extrapolating from published sea level rise curves for the Delaware Bay (Belknap and Kraft 1977, 620, Fig. 8), one can see that sea level was 30–24 meters lower than the present level during the Late Glacial episode. Geomorphological and paleotopographic studies of the ancestral Delaware River (Kraft 1971, 2137, Fig. 6) show a deeply incised river channel extending almost 50 kilometers beyond the present mouth of the Delaware Bay. Increased precipitation during the end of the Pleistocene as well as the presence of glacial melt water would have produced a very high volume of water within the Delaware River, as well as a high rate of flow and very low water temperature. Given the rapidly flowing cold river system, it is highly unlikely that there would be any significant estuarine resources (Gardner and Stewart 1977, 4; Ogden 1977, 26). Also extrapolating from Belknap and Kraft's (1977, 620, Fig. 8) sea level curve, a rate of sea level rise of 3 centimeters per decade can be generalized for the Late Glacial episode. Because most estuarine species require a certain stability in salinity and temperature conditions (Daiber et al. 1976), it is unlikely that this rapid sea level rise would have allowed sufficient stability for these species to exist.

Pre-Boreal/Boreal (8080 B.C.–6540 B.C.)

The Pre-Boreal/Boreal episode is a transition between the end of the Pleistocene and the beginning of the Holocene. Marked changes in floral environmental settings occurred, with the major effect being a reduction of open grassland environments and a spread of woodland settings dominated by boreal elements. For the Middle Atlantic area these changes in the environments are best viewed as the climax and culmination of changes that had begun as early as 10,700 B.C. (Carbone 1976, 74). The replacement forest was dominated by boreal elements; however, some oak pollen is evident in the Delaware Bay region by 8000 B.C. (Sirkin 1977, 213). Carbone (1976, 75) notes the development of a northern hardwood character for the Coastal Plain forests by 8500 B.C. Tables 4 and 5 reveal that a general replacement of the dominant, spruce, by pine can be seen in all pollen profiles from the Middle Atlantic where there are data available for the Pre-Boreal/Boreal episode.

The environmental changes of the Pre-Boreal/Boreal episode undoubtedly had a significant effect on faunal distributions, especially for those animals adapted to grassland and forest-edge settings. Reduction of openland habitats played an important role in the extinction of many of the Pleistocene megafauna, and habitats for many animals were significantly reduced in most areas. However, Gardner has noted that some areas in the South Atlantic Coastal Plain may havè retained their openland settings longer than other areas, creating a refugium setting (Science Applications Incorporated 1979, chap. 2:63). This pattern probably can be extrapolated to the Delmarva Peninsula. Low Coastal Plain areas in the southern part of the peninsula might have retained their open space and associated megafauna later than did the Piedmont, Fall Line, and High Coastal Plain zones. However, the dominant vegetation throughout Delaware regardless of soils and other edaphic effects would have been closed boreal forests. The overall effect was a significant reduction of carrying capacity as coniferous elements spread and brought about a reduction in food sources for browsing and grazing species. With the disappearance of the forest/grassland interfaces, or at least a sharp reduction in their number and extent of distribution, poorly drained swampy areas and other perennial and seasonal water sources would have been the focal points for animal populations that would include game species such as deer, elk, and moose.

Estuarine resources were still fairly impoverished. Again extrapolating from Belknap and Kraft's (1977, 620, Fig. 8) sea level curve, one can see that sea level was 24 to 19 meters lower than at present and that sea level was at a rate of approximately 3.33 centimeters per decade. This rate of rise is a little more rapid than the rate for the Late Glacial and it is unlikely that there would be sufficient stability of salinity and temperature for the establishment of rich and predictable estuarine settings. It should be noted, however, that by the Pre-Boreal/Boreal episode the effects of meltwater in the Delaware River itself were significantly reduced and temperatures within the river and its embayed mouth were rising slightly. The effect of this temperature rise would be felt in later climatic episodes as the estuarine conditions stabilized.

Archaeological Data and Paleo-Indian Adaptations

Archaeological sites from all four Paleo-Indian phases are found on the Delmarva Peninsula according to fluted-point surveys in the Maryland and Delaware portions of the peninsula by Thomas (1966b, 1974a), Brown (1979), Reynolds and Dilks (1965), Mason (1959), and Kinsey (1958, 1959a). Early notched-point find locations have not been surveyed because they were not originally considered part of the Paleo-Indian period when

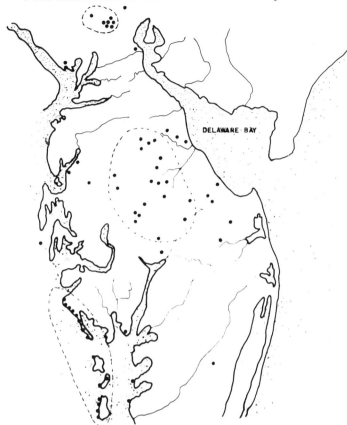

Fig. 5. Fluted Point Sites—Delaware and Maryland Upper Eastern Shore. Dots represent single and multiple fluted point finds.

most of the above studies were carried out. All sites are surface finds and information on associated artifacts is scanty. Consequently, in order to reconstruct the lifeways and settlement patterns of Paleo-Indian peoples in Delaware, one must look to other excavated Paleo-Indian sites in the Middle Atlantic area.

Numerous studies of Paleo-Indian sites in the Middle Atlantic area can be found in the archaeological literature. Several studies present listings of fluted point finds on a state or regional basis (Kinsey 1958, 1959a; Mason 1959; Kraft 1974; Brown 1979); however, these studies provide little, if any, analysis concerning the locations of Paleo-Indian sites. The literature also includes site-specific reports (McNett and McMillan 1974; McNett et al. 1975; Kraft 1973), but these site reports usually do not include any analysis that places the sites in a regional perspective.

Eisenberg (1978) has combined elements of both regional studies and site-specific reports in an analysis of Paleo-Indian sites in the Hudson and Upper Delaware drainage; however, Eisenberg's artifact analysis is somewhat flawed (Stewart 1979) and his data are not from well-excavated contexts. Gardner's (1974, 1977) study of the Flint Run complex of Paleo-Indian sites in western Virginia combines aspects of both regional studies and site-specific reports and can be used to develop an understanding of Paleo-Indian man-land relationships, or settlement patterns. The analysis of the Flint Run sites is especially useful in that a number of sites, each used for different functions, were studied, enabling Gardner (1977, 258–59) to develop a set of types of Paleo-Indian sites. This typology led to the development of a model of man-land relationships during the Paleo-Indian period.

The relationships between human beings and Late Glacial, pre-Boreal, and Boreal environments are especially important to Gardner's model. Within the mosaic parkland settings of the Late Glacial episode and boreal forest settings of the Pre-Boreal/Boreal episodes, the Paleo-Indian lifestyle is assumed to have been one of hunting and gathering, with an emphasis on the hunting (Griffin 1977, 12). Among most Paleo-Indian tool assemblages specialized tools for the processing of plant foods are generally rare. In general, most tools found from the Paleo-Indian time period are associated with the processing of products of the hunt. Included in this tool kit would be projectile points for the killing and butchering of the animals, biface knives for butchering and the manufacture of other tools, as well as a variety of flake tools for various purposes such as working bone or hide.

Although specialized plant food processing tools are not found in Paleo-Indian assemblages, plant foods probably played some role in Paleo-Indian diets (Griffin 1977, 12). Recent excavations by American University at the Shawnee-Minisink site in the Upper Delaware Valley (McNett and McMillan 1974; McNett et al. 1975; Kauffman and Dent 1978) have provided some carbonized plant remains from a hearth in a Paleo-Indian context. *Chenopodium, Acalypha*-like, *Phytolacca,* grape, *Amaranth, Silene,* Blackberry, *Lactula,* smartweed, *Physalis,* ragweed, sedge, hackberry, and hawthorne plum remains were included, as well as fish bones (Kauffman and Dent 1978, 5). These plant remains show that at least some portion of Paleo-Indian diets was made up of gathered wild plants. Nethertheless, given the overwhelming portion of the tool kit that is oriented toward procurement of hunted animal foods, gathering of wild plants seems to have played a relatively minor role in Paleo-Indian diets.

Because the Paleo-Indian hunters and gatherers lacked efficient and extensive technologies for the long-term storage of foods, they were unable to stay at a single location year round. Similarly, local group size had to be adjusted so as not to exhaust the available resources of the local area. As resources in an area became exhausted, social units had to change locations and readjust their size to fit new conditions. A flexible band-level social organization similar to those reported for living hunters and gatherers (Steward 1955, 101–50; Lee and DeVare 1968) is the most likely organization. However, not much more can be noted about Paleo-Indian social organization except to note that movement of groups had to be timed so as to coincide with the availability of certain critical resources that may have varied on a seasonal basis. Thus, the location of sites and the timing of their occupation were primary components of Paleo-Indian adaptations (Judge 1973).

For hunters and gatherers of the Paleo-Indian period, critical resources included food, shelter, and water. However, Gardner (1974, 1977, 1979) has suggested that the most critical resource was stone for the manufacture of tools, since mobile hunters and gatherers needed to have a set of tools to kill and process game and other resources when the time arose. Goodyear (1979) has noted that in the case of mobile hunters and gatherers it was more efficient to have tools and go looking for game than to have found game and then go looking for suitable tools. Similarly, high-quality lithic materials such as cryptocrystalline cherts and jaspers that are easily fashioned into tools, that have durable working edges, and that can be refurbished into tools with a variety of functions would have been the most efficient for mobile hunters and gatherers (Goodyear 1979). Callahan (1979) has shown that a biface technology produces the most useful tools for a mobile hunting and gathering lifestyle because the biface itself is a multipurpose tool: it can serve as a core and a source for the manufacture of special purpose flake tools, and the end product of its reduction-through-flake production is a projectile point with high length-width and width-thickness ratios especially suiting it for penetrating and cutting uses. Considering these data, then, the most basic component of Paleo-Indian adaptation was a biface technology that utilized high-quality lithic materials.

Given that the lithic use patterns described above form the basis of the Paleo-Indian adaptation, a logical assumption is that the use of space by Paleo-Indian groups was conditioned primarily by the status of their tool kits. It would be disastrous for a Paleo-Indian group to have its tool kit depleted without a source of lithic material nearby. Consequently, it would be reasonable to assume that lithic resources would form the focal point of Paleo-Indian settlement systems. The nature of the Late Glacial and early Holocene climate also contributes to the fact that the lithic resource would be most crucial. Carbone (1976) notes that seasonal variation was minimal. Therefore, movement from place to place was most likely related to depletion of the local resources in an area, rather than the appearance of newly (seasonally) available resources in another area. Movement was conditioned by local resource availability; however, ultimately the status of the tool kit and the proximity to suitable lithic raw materials influenced settlement and wandering decisions. Therefore, lithic resources would provide fixed points in Paleo-Indian settlement systems (Gardner 1977, 258). As such, lithic resources, along with game-attractive settings and loci of other resources would provide the most useful predictive factors for Paleo-Indian sites.

Elaborating on the general basis detailed above, Gardner has defined a typology of functionally distinct Paleo-Indian sites. The initial version of the typology was generated from the Flint Run Paleo-Indian complex data (Gardner 1974), and later versions (Gardner 1977, 1979) were generated based on data from a variety of other studies. In the most current model (Gardner 1979, 8–9), the following types of sites are noted:

Quarry Sites

Located at either primary or secondary (cobble) outcrops of high-quality lithic material, quarry sites were the location of initial procurement of materials for the manufacture of stone tools. Common artifacts are large numbers of waste flakes and bifaces that show signs of having been rejected early in the manufacturing process due to flaws in the raw materials. Finished, diagnostic artifacts are commonly absent, and quite often quarry sites are somewhat removed from water sources.

Quarry Reduction Stations

These sites are usually located at level ground and at water sources closest to the quarries. A limited range of artifacts have been found, including many waste flakes and bifaces that were apparently rejected early in the manufacturing process due to errors in flint knapping or flaws in the raw materials that were not detected at the quarry. Debris is less extensive than at quarry sites and usually represents later tool manufacturing stages. Quarry reduction stations seem to be places where large flakes, cores, and very early stage bifaces obtained at the quarry site were taken for further reduction into smaller primary-thinned bifaces (Callahan 1979) for transport.

Base Camps

Representing the main habitation sites of Paleo-Indian groups, base camps are characterized by houses and a wide variety of tools related to domestic activities. Chipping debris may be limited in number and reflective of tool maintenance, or it may occur in very large amounts if the base camp is close to quarry areas. Base camps are usually located close to water in areas of southern exposure and in areas of maximum habitat overlap. The largest base camps are quarry-related and show extensive tool manufacturing activities, mainly late-stage biface reduction and finishing of tools.

Base Camp Maintenance Stations

Maintenance stations were resource procurement sites located near especially rich gathering locations or game-attractive hunting locations within 10 to 15 kilometers of base camps. Tools associated with the processing of products of the hunt and blocky cores that served as sources of unmodified flake tools are the most common artifacts. Presumably, base camp maintenance stations would be periodically revisited and their resources exploited by groups staying at a nearby base camp.

Outlying Hunting Sites

These resource procurement sites are generally located within 40 kilometers of base camps and are found at junctions of large and small stream terraces and near game-attractive areas such as bogs, swamps, and other poorly drained areas. Artifacts are similar to those found at base camp maintenance stations, although they are not as numerous.

Isolated Point Finds

Isolated point finds comprise the majority of Paleo-Indian sites and it is difficult to discuss their role in Paleo-Indian settlement patterns. They may be either ephemeral occupations or hunting sites, remnants of disturbed and destroyed sites, or portions of larger unknown Paleo-Indian sites.

Gardner (1979) perceives all of the above described sites combined in various patterns to form settlement systems that vary in size and exact location given the particular environmental setting. For example, he (1979, 11) sees the Flint Run settlement system extending over an area 40 kilometers in diameter. However, in the Fall Line zone of southeastern Virginia, he (1979, 15) sees the settlement system ranging over 150 kilometers between outlying hunting sites and quarry-related sites. Just as the size of Paleo-Indian settlement systems can vary, so can the relationships among the sites. In the model of relationships described by Gardner (1977), a group began a cycle of movements at the quarry complex of sites. When their tool kits were completely refurbished and a suitable number of bifaces had been manufactured, the group would leave the quarry area and move to a new base camp location. While at the base camps, a series of hunting sites and base camp maintenance stations would have been utilized for resource procurement. When the local resources were depleted, the group would move to a new base camp. While moving from base camp to base camp, the tool kit would be continually utilized; attrition of artifacts would occur as tools were lost, broken, and continually resharpened. As the tool kit became depleted, the group would move back toward the quarry and

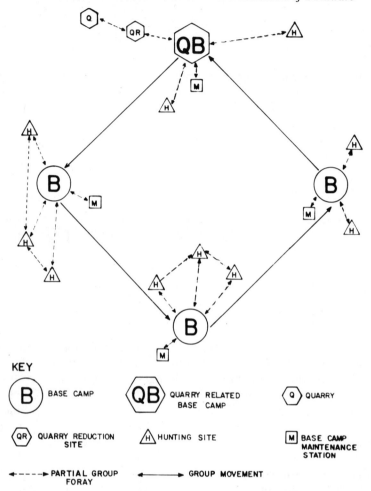

Fig. 6. Cyclical model.

would hopefully arrive before all tools were exhausted. After a refurbishing of the tool kit, the group would begin its movements anew. Continual reuse of the quarries and their related base camps made them focal points in Paleo-Indian wanderings, and probably several groups shared the same quarry.

The model presented in Figure 6 is a "cyclical model" (Custer, Cavallo, and Stewart n.d.) where groups move through a cycle of base camps with the quarry-related base camp as a focal point. The cyclical model seems most applicable to areas where lithic resources are large and dispersed. In such a resource setting, social groups were most likely to cycle their movements around a single lithic source. However, in many areas lithic resources may have been small and clustered in an area relatively close

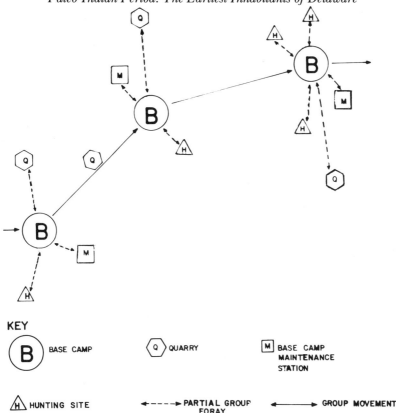

KEY

$\textcircled{B}$ BASE CAMP $\langle Q \rangle$ QUARRY $\boxed{M}$ BASE CAMP MAINTENANCE STATION

$\triangle$ HUNTING SITE   ◄- - - -► PARTIAL GROUP FORAY   ◄────► GROUP MOVEMENT

Fig. 7. Serial model.

together. In this case the cyclical model might not apply. An alternative model, Figure 7, is one in which a group would use a number of different quarry sources in a serial fashion. In this "serial model" (Custer, Cavallo, and Stewart n.d.) there are no quarry-related base camps because procurement of raw materials for tool manufacturing was carried out on an as-needed basis. As a group encountered a lithic source, it would add a few new tools to its tool kit and discard exhausted tools. In the cyclical model, lithic procurement would be a special activity or "direct procurement" with specialized sites (Binford 1979, 19–20). In the serial model, lithic procurement would not be carried out at specialized sites, but would occur in conjunction with other activities. Binford uses the term *embedded procurement* to describe similar procurement systems. In both the cyclical and serial models, the lithic resources were critical for Paleo-Indian populations. It was the structure of the lithic resource distribution that caused the different settlement systems.

Using the various models of Paleo-Indian settlement systems described above, a researcher can analyze the known Paleo-Indian sites in Delaware. The method used here is examination of the environmental settings and artifacts from concentrations of sites, as well as individual sites, to see how they fit with Gardner's model. Three major concentrations of Paleo-Indian sites are noted for the northern portion of the Delmarva Peninsula. The first concentration is located in north eastern Cecil County, Maryland, and northwestern New Castle County, Delaware. The location of this concentration of Paleo-Indian sites coincides with the location of the Delaware Chalcedony complex, a large outcrop of cryptocrystalline lithic material (Custer and Galasso 1980). Many of the fluted points from the area were manufactured from local materials. Excavations have been carried out by the Delaware Bureau of Archaeology and Historic Preservation in the vicinity of jasper outcrops on Iron Hill, Delaware, at site 7NC-D-34. Much debitage was recovered from 7NC-D-34 and the size and shape of the flakes indicates a variety of quarrying activities and early stage biface production. No diagnostic Paleo-Indian tools were recovered from the site, although a number of bifaces made from quartz were found. It is likely that these bifaces were manufactured elsewhere and discarded at the quarry site as new jasper tools were manufactured. However, the absence of diagnostic fluted points from 7NC-D-34 makes assignments of the site to the Paleo-Indian period problematic.

One additional site in the same area, the Everett site (7NC-D-21), has produced fluted points and has been subjected to subsurface testing. No diagnostic Paleo-Indian artifacts were found in an excavated context, although a number of scraping and cutting tools manufactured from local jaspers were found. The Everett site is located close to a poorly drained area that could represent a game-attractive locale. The combination of possible butchering tools and a game-attractive setting make the Everett site likely for a hunting site or camp maintenance station. Similar settings in the Pennsylvania Piedmont Uplands are locations of Paleo-Indian sites such as the Narvon Paleo-Indian site (36-AL-91) in Lancaster County and the Honey Brook Paleo-Indian Site (36-CH-131) in Chester County reported by Shrader (1978). Also, the Michell site (7NC-A-2), located near Hockessin, Delaware, provides a good association of poorly drained sinkholes and Paleo-Indian tools. Two fluted points and a wide variety of cutting and scraping tools were found on the surface of the Mitchell site. However, subsurface testing showed that all diagnostic artifacts were within a plowzone and have been disturbed from their original context.

No base camps have been identified for northern Delaware. However, because the Delaware Chalcedony complex is a large lithic source, the cyclical model no doubt applies, and quarry-related base camps should be found in the area. Further field studies are needed to test this hypothesis.

The second concentration of Paleo-Indian sites on the Delmarva Peninsula is found in the vicinity of the mouths of the Choptank and Nanticoke rivers. During the Late Pleistocene, when sea level was lower and the Chesapeake Bay was not in its present location, these areas would have

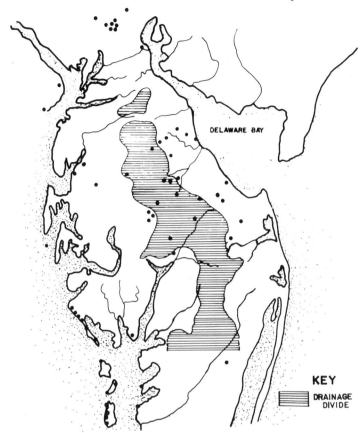

Fig. 8. Drainage divide area and Paleo-Indian sites.

been headlands overlooking the confluence of the ancestral Susquehanna, Potomac, Choptank, and Nanticoke rivers. Gardner and Haynes (1978) note that large accumulations of cobbles derived from gravel point bar deposits of the river confluences are present in the area. Custer and Galasso (1980, 8–9) have documented the high quality lithic materials that can be found in these cobble deposits; and Gardner (1979) suggests that Paleo-Indian sites in the area could have included quarries, quarry reduction stations, and quarry-related base camps, although site data are scanty. Because the cobble lithic source is quite large, these sites were probably quarry focal points within a cyclical settlement system.

The third concentration of Paleo-Indian sites is located along the Midpeninsular Drainage Divide. As noted in Chapter 1, the Midpeninsular Drainage Divide is characterized by a mosaic of poorly and well-drained settings. The extent of the interspersed poorly drained areas can be discerned using LANDSAT satellite images, and is correlated with the locations of Paleo-Indian sites. The poorly drained areas are seen as a dark red

Plate 2. Artifacts from the Hughes Early Man complex. The top two rows are notched points, the bottom row biface and flake tools. (Courtesy Delaware Division of Historical and Cultural Affairs.).

color on a simulated infrared image taken on 13 February 1973. Most of the known Paleo-Indian sites of the central peninsula are either in the poorly drained area or adjacent to it. The Hughes complex of sites in central Kent County, Delaware (7K-E-10, 24, 33), provides a good example of the Paleo-Indian sites from the drainage divide area. The Hughes complex is listed on the National Register of Historic Places and includes a series of six concentrations of surface finds located on low well-drained knolls. The knolls are located adjacent to a large freshwater swamp and several poorly drained areas. The collection from the knolls includes a fluted point (Clovis) as well as notched points (mainly Kirk and Palmer). Bifaces found at the site are mainly late stage and have been heavily resharpened and reworked. A wide variety of flake tools are also included in the assemblages and are very heavily resharpened and reworked. Multiple tools such as scrapers with graver tips and cutting edges are common. Lithic sources are very scarce in the area and the heavy reworking of the Paleo-Indian tools reflects the careful husbanding of the lithic resources.

An additional area of the Midpeninsular Drainage Divide zone that has a very high potential for Paleo-Indian sites, although no known sites have been found in the area, is in southern New Castle County. Many bay/basin features with standing water are found in this area, and studies by Rasmussen (1958) have indicated that they were probably open, holding water, and supporting swampy settings during the Late Pleistocene. These would be game-attractive areas and research in the New Jersey Coastal Plain by Bonfiglio and Cresson (1978) has located many Paleo-Indian sites in association with these features. Since the New Jersey assemblages are representative of hunting sites and base-camp maintenance stations, the Delaware sites are expected to be similar.

Because no single concentration of Paleo-Indian sites on the Delmarva Peninsula contains all the different types of sites, and each probably represents only a portion of the larger Paleo-Indian settlement system. For example, it is likely that the quarry complex of sites in northern New Castle County was the center of settlement systems that range north into the Piedmont Uplands and south into the Midpeninsular Drainage Divide zone. Similarly, the lower Choptank and Nanticoke quarry complex could have been the focal point of a settlement system that ranged northeast into the Midpeninsular Drainage Divide zone. Another possibility is a peninsular-wide system where groups would begin with a complete tool kit at either one of the quarry complexes and the move into the interior drainage divide area. As tool kits became depleted, the groups could then move to a different quarry location. For example, a group could begin at the Upper Peninsular quarry concentration near Iron Hill, move into southern New Castle County and northwestern Kent County for hunting at game-attractive locations, and then move on to the quarry locales on the lower Choptank. A similar movement from south to north would also be possible. The size of the group ranges would have varied between 60 and 170 kilometers. While this might seem like a large area, the dispersed nature of the lithic sources on the Delmarva Peninsula makes such a system understandable. Further research should be able to clarify which of the large regional movement patterns is the most probable.

Much of the discussion so far has focused on the special preference of Paleo-Indian groups for high-quality lithic materials for the manufacture of tools. The fact that almost all of the fluted points found on the Delmarva Peninsula were made from high-quality materials underscores the general applicability of this view of Paleo-Indian technology. Also, two of the three concentrations of fluted points coincide with large concentrations of high-quality lithic materials. However, by the final phase of the Paleo-Indian period—the Notched Point phase—the heavy reliance on high-quality lithic materials began to break down. Although no systematic data on notched Palmer, Amos, and Kirk projectile points on the Delmarva Peninsula are available, an initial impression, based on an examination of a number of collections in Delaware and Maryland, is that a wider variety of lithic materials of variable quality were used for the manufacture of notched points. Many materials of lesser quality such as blocky quartz and grainy quartzites, and materials from outside Delaware such as Pennsylvania rhyolite, were used, rather than the higher quality jaspers and cherts. In other parts of the Middle Atlantic where good data from excavated sites are available for the Notched Point phase, a similar pattern is noted. For example, at the Fifty site, a stratified Paleo-Indian through Middle Archaic base camp maintenance station in western Virginia (Carr 1975), a shift in lithic utilization patterns moving up from the bottom of the sequence is noted. Clovis points from the Fifty site were manufactured from high-quality local jaspers. Palmer points were mainly made from jasper with some quartzite and rhyolite used, and manufacturers of Amos points utilized a variety of materials, mainly cherts. Finally, almost half of the Kirk points were manufactured from rhyolite. Similar patterns have been noted in the New Jersey Coastal Plain (John Cavallo, personal communication) and the Pennsylvania Piedmont (Kinsey 1977a).

Changes in the lithic utilization patterns hint at changes in the lithic procurement system. Because the lithic procurement system is an important component of the Paleo-Indian adaptation, these changes indicate basic shifts in Paleo-Indian lifeways. Better evidence of these changes comes from the settlement pattern data. Although notched points and fluted points are commonly found together at sites on the Delmarva Peninsula in all three site concentrations, diagnostic artifacts from the Middle Archaic are generally absent. This is especially true of the quarry locations. Gardner (1978) has noted this same pattern throughout the Middle Atlantic and believes that the combination of lithic procurement changes and settlement pattern shifts indicate major changes in lifeways and adaptations. These changes begin to show up in the Notched Point phase of the Paleo-Indian period, as environments of the Boreal episode begin to give way to the full Holocene environments of the Atlantic episode. They reach their culmination around 6500 b.c. and mark the beginning of the Archaic period.

[3]

Archaic Period:
Hunters and Gatherers in a New
Environment

The beginning of the Archaic period coincides with the emergence of Holocene environments in Delaware and is characterized by a shift in human adaptation strategies. William A. Ritchie was the first to use the term *archaic* to refer to preceramic hunter-gatherer cultures of New York (Ritchie 1932), and since then the term has been viewed as an evolutionary stage, or level of social complexity, defined by mobile small-band organizations with simple social structuring (Willey and Phillips 1958, 107; Ritchie 1965, 32). However, in more recent studies (Griffin 1967) *Archaic* has come to represent a time period devoid of stage connotations that falls after the Paleo-Indian and before the Woodland period. It is in this more modern sense that I use the term. Nevertheless, many of the attributes of Archaic stages characterize the cultures of the Archaic period of Delaware.

As noted in Chapter 2, the emergence of Holocene environments and the shifts in human adaptation strategies date to approximately 6500 B.C. The focus on adaptation changes and use of the 6500 B.C. date as a break from Paleo-Indian adaptations departs from the traditional literature; however, recent work by Gardner (1978, n.d.) and Funk (1978) has shown that this newer approach is more useful for the Middle Atlantic region.* Diagnostic artifacts associated with the emergence of new environments and adaptations include bifurcate base projectile points such as St. Albans, LeCroy, and Kanawha (Broyles 1971; Chapman 1975). Generally, these bifurcate base projectile points (see Fig. 11) occur no later than 6000–5500 B.C. (Broyles 1971, 49; Michels 1967; Michels and Dutt 1968) and an absence of stratified sites from Delaware makes it difficult to show what sort

*Gardner and others have referred to this period as the Middle Archaic. However, because the traditional early archaic materials are included in the Paleo-Indian period, and because the traditional Late Archaic cultures will be included in the Woodland I period (see Chapter 4), the adjective "Middle" will be dropped and the period referred to as the Archaic.

of diagnostic tools come next in the chronological sequence. A similar absence of sites from this period was noted by Ritchie (1965, 32–33) for New York, and some researchers (Fitting 1968) suggested that there were very low population densities due to the low carrying capacities of post-Pleistocene environments in the Northeast and Middle Atlantic. However, more recent research has revealed a number of sites with components dated to the Archaic time period, especially the traditional Middle Archaic period.

Probably the most important site excavated from this time period was the Neville site at Manchester, New Hampshire (Dincauze 1971, 1976). A series of stemmed projectile points were excavated with associated radiocarbon dates that are similar to a series of projectile points and dates obtained from the Doerschuk site excavated by Coe (1964, 14–55) in North Carolina. Based on these similarities, Dincauze (1976, 140–42) proposes an "Atlantic Slope" culture area for the Archaic that would include the Delmarva Peninsula. Three varieties of stemmed points—Neville, Stark, and Merrimack (noted in chronological order from oldest to youngest)—with overlapping time ranges are noted. These three point types date from 6000 to 4000 B.C. throughout New England (Snow 1980, 174–75). Similar dates have been seen for Nevillelike points at the Russ site near Wells Bridge, New York, and Funk notes a similarity to Coe's (1964, 36) Stanly projectile points of the North Carolina Piedmont (Funk, 1977a, 23; 1978, 21). A reexamination of other Archaic sites in southern New England (Dincauze and Mulholland 1977; Starbuck and Bolian 1980), Long Island (Ritchie and Funk 1971), the Hudson Basin (Funk 1977b; Brennan 1977), and the Upper Delaware (Kinsey 1972, 1975; Kraft 1970, 1975) shows similar patterns; however, clearcut associations of diagnostic artifacts are not present. Therefore, because preliminary evidence from surrounding areas seems to indicate that a variety of stemmed projectile points characterize the Archaic period from 6000 B.C. to 4000 B.C., these points are suggested as indicators of similar time periods in Delaware.

Use of stemmed points seemed to continue after 4000 B.C.; in many parts of the Middle Atlantic a Late Archaic period lasted until 1000 B.C. (Snow 1980; Kinsey 1977a; Kraft 1974; Ritchie 1965). However, by 3000 B.C. in Delaware, significant changes occurred in lifeways, climate, and environment. Because of these changes the 3000 B.C. date is used as an ending date for the Archaic in Delaware.

Environmental Setting

The Archaic period was associated with the Atlantic climatic episode dated to about 6540 B.C. –3110 B.C. (Table 3) and was characterized by the appearance of Holocene environments in the Middle Atlantic area as opposed to the Pre-Boreal/Boreal periods, which were a transition between Pleistocene and Holocene environments. Carbone (1976, 75) notes that a "northern hardwood" character begins in Coastal Plain forests as early as 8500 B.C., but it was not until after 6500 B.C. that the mesic hemlock forests of the Atlantic episode became established over widespread areas. Similarly, temperate faunal assemblages essentially modern in composition, if not in distribution, were established about 7300 B.C. (Carbone 1976, 75). These environmental trends coincided with the appearance of a continental climate with marked seasonal differences in air mass distribution patterns, temperature, and precipitation (Science Applications Incorporated 1979, chap. 1:115). In many ways the floral and faunal settings found in the Early Atlantic episode were modern in character in the sense that similar communities could be found today. However, distributions and associations of floral and faunal communities were markedly different. Pronounced shifts in species distribution were brought on by changes in temperature and moisture regimes (Custer 1978; Carbone 1976, 88).

The early portion of the Atlantic, up to about 5000 B.C., was characterized by a general warming trend and an increase in precipitation. Warm moist conditions favored the expansion of mesic forests, first of hemlock and later of oak (Carbone 1976, 76). Bernabo and Webb (1977, 77–78, Figs. 12 and 13) note a pronounced oak replacement around 5000 B.C. Pine elements were strongly represented in the southern Delmarva Peninsula (Bernabo and Webb 1977, 77, Fig. 12), but oak pollen increased on the order of 10 percent. The pollen profiles summarized in Tables 4 and 5 correspond with these descriptions. By 3224 B.C. there was a perturbation in the general trend of increasing moisture throughout the Atlantic. Also, temperature began to drop. There was probably little effect on the floral and faunal distributions of the Middle Atlantic area, but the pattern of climatic perturbation begun in late Atlantic times made itself strongly felt during early Sub-Boreal time.

Because of the pollen evidence, it is most likely that the entire Delmarva Peninsula supported dense mesic forests. Swampy and boggy areas were probably widely distributed in areas of poor drainage such as floodplains, particularly flood chutes of major drainages, and bays or basins. In general, however, a mixed mesic forest was found in almost all of the Delmarva Peninsula. Throughout the Atlantic episode, faunal compositions were essentially modern, with deer and turkey as major dominants and important game animals. Distributions were similar to modern distributions in structure, but not in locations. However, even though the distributions were not in their modern locations, they would still be relatively predictable.

A consideration of estuarine resource potentials shows that their potential was probably still low. According to Belknap and Kraft's data (1977, 620, Fig. 8), sea level rise was occurring at a rate of approximately 3 centimeters per decade throughout the Atlantic climatic episode. This rate is only slightly slower than the Pre-Boreal/Boreal rate and is most likely too rapid to allow large, stable concentrations of estuarine resources. The absence of any large shell beds dating to this time period in the drill cores and cross sections reported by Kraft et al. (1976) for the Delaware Bay also supports this contention.

Nevertheless, some researchers in the Middle Atlantic (Brennan 1974, 1976, 1977; Wilke and Thompson 1977) have presented evidence for the use of shellfish during the Archaic. Brennan's data from the lower Hudson includes an approximate date of 4900 B.C. on shell trash heaps, or middens; however, Snow (1980, 181) has noted that in general Brennan's shell dates tend to be 2,000 years too old, given the associated diagnostic projectile points. In Snow's view, Brennan's data indicates some initial, nonintensive use of shellfish in the later portions of the Archaic (ca. 4000 B.C.) with intensive use coming after 3000 B.C. (Snow 1980, 182). While the Hudson estuary data has some relevance for Delaware and can be viewed as an indication that sporadic Archaic shellfish use was possible, the Hudson data is only marginally applicable to Delaware because the geologic configuration of the Hudson estuary is significantly different from that of the Delaware Bay. Snow (1980, 180) notes that the lower Hudson is a fjord with very steep sides. In contrast, the Delaware Bay is quite shallow with gently sloping sides. In the Hudson, the lateral movement of shoreline associated with post-Pleistocene sea-level rise is much less than the lateral movement experienced in the more gently sloping Delaware. Consequently, during the Archaic the lower portions of the Hudson would have provided more stable estuarine conditions for shellfish such as oysters than would the Delaware.

Wilke and Thompson (1977) have reported similar early dates from the Chesapeake Bay area of Kent County, Maryland. At site PL-1/1 Wilke and Thompson (1977, 75) note dates of about 2480 B.C.–2420 B.C. for the top of a shell midden and dates of 3135 B.C.–2995 B.C. for the bottom. Within the midden Wilke and Thompson (1977, 75) note that Marcey Creek and Mockley ceramics were recovered. Reported dates for Marcey Creek ceramics on the Delmarva Peninsula are 1200 B.C. to 900 B.C. (Artusy 1976, 2) and Mockley ceramics have been dated to A.D. 100–A.D. 485 (Artusy 1976, 4) on the Delmarva Peninsula and to A.D. 300–A.D. 485 (Wright 1973, 27) on the western shore of the Chesapeake Bay. Wilke and Thompson's dates are the only divergence from the established dates for these ceramic types and are at least 2,500 years too old, a figure remarkably similar to the discrepancies in the lower Hudson dates (Snow 1980, 181). Therefore, it is most likely that the shell used for the dates is producing inaccurate dates and that these data do not contradict the interpretations presented here.

Archaeological Data and Archaic Adaptations

The Archaic period for Delaware has been defined to include the shifts in adaptations that accompanied the appearance of Holocene environments. These shifts can be seen in a number of ways in the archaeological record. However, few Archaic sites are known for Delaware, and no intact Archaic sites have been excavated. Consequently, as was the case for the Paleo-Indian period, other areas of the Middle Atlantic must be used to amplify the Delaware archaeological record.

An important indicator of the new adaptations of the Archaic period was the addition of new tools to the tool kits associated with bifurcate points and other Archaic projectile points. Special additions to the tool kits included ground stone tools such as axes, gouges, grinding stones, and plant processing tools (Chapman 1975, 275–76). A large variety of flake and biface tools were also maintained in addition to the new ground stone tool types. Assemblages from the Upper Delaware Valley of Pennsylvania provide a good example (Kinsey 1975, 60–61) of these new tool assemblages, along with assemblages from the Harry's Farm site and Miller Field site in New Jersey (Kraft 1975, 6–28, 1970, 12–18), the Kent Hally site in the Lower Susquehanna Valley (Kinsey 1959b, 114–27), a series of sites in the lower Hudson Valley (Brennan 1977, 419–22), and a series of sites in New York State (Ritchie and Funk 1973, 38–45; Ritchie 1965, 31–36). Overall, Archaic tool kits show a higher variety of tool types than was previously experienced in the Paleo-Indian period. Even when considering the vagaries of archaeological preservation, the stone tool kit, both chipped and ground, shows a high variety of tool forms. Unfortunately, because no pure Archaic components have been excavated in Delaware, we can only hypothesize the existence of these varied tool forms in Delaware Archaic assemblages.

The use of lithic resources also changes in the Archaic. A wide variety of lithic materials was used during the Archaic and lithic-dependent settlement systems, such as those documented by Gardner (1974, 1977) for the Paleo-Indian period, were replaced by systems where a variety of lithic sources were used in a serial fashion. Direct procurement systems (Goodyear 1979) were replaced by embedded systems, and a pronounced absence of a cryptocrystalline focus was also clearly indicated during the Middle Archaic period. The work of Stewart (1980a, 1980b) near central Pennsylvania rhyolite quarries seems to indicate that exploitation of newly emerging environments led to the discovery and utilization of alternative lithic sources. Also, the increased importance of floral food resources, coupled with a decreased relative importance of hunting, reduced the importance of the staged biface tool reduction pattern (Callahan 1979) that had characterized earlier periods. In Delaware, the changing lithic use patterns are evidenced by an absence of Archaic sites close to the outcrops of the Delaware Chalcedony complex (Custer and Galasso 1980). In addition, a cursory review of bifurcate points in Delaware shows the use of a variety of noncryptocrystalline materials including quartz, quartzite, and rhyolite. In many cases these materials, in addition to cherts and jaspers, seemed to have been derived from secondary cobble sources. Specific quarry locations are difficult to identify, and the serial model of lithic use seems to apply well to the Delaware Archaic.

Probably the most important indicator of changes in Archaic adaptations that can be seen in the archaeological record of Delaware and the Middle Atlantic is a change in site location preferences. In general, Archaic sites are located in a wider variety of environmental settings and in different locations compared to Paleo-Indians sites. A number of examples of different site types in varied environmental settings can be documented for the Middle Atlantic area. Studies of upland site settings provide the best examples of varied settlement sites. Gardner and Boyer's (1978) study of site distributions in the Massanutten Mountain area of Virginia, Gardner's (1978) study of Archaic site distributions in the Ridge and Valley, Great Valley, Blue Ridge, and Piedmont physiographic provinces, Gardner and Custer's (1978; Custer 1980a) study of site distributions in the Middle Shenandoah Valley, and Stevenson's (1978) study of site distributions in the Allegheny Front of Pennsylvania all provide examples of high site location variability. Many of the new site settings are related to emerging environmental zones associated with the spread of mesic forests, variations in water table, and sea level rise. The spread of site complexes associated with emerging Coastal Plain swamps and marshes in the Middle Atlantic documented by Rappleye and Gardner (1979) for Dismal Swamp, Gardner (1976) for Mattawoman and Zekehiah swamps in the Potomac estuary, and Bonfiglio and Cresson (1978) for a series of bay/basin features in the New Jersey Coastal Plain provides an example of the use of newly emerging environmental settings.

In the overall picture the variety of site types and activities seems to represent a diffuse adaptation (Cleland 1976) to an increasing variety of environmental settings, as well as to the increasing variety of resources available due to increased seasonality. Snow (1980, 183) notes that Archaic systems probably involved more elaborate and more carefully planned seasonal scheduling than earlier systems. Linked to the variety of settlement patterns would be an increasing variety of subsistence activities. More diverse food resources—especially plants—would be available in the expanding deciduous forests, and presumably the varied site locations represent use of these new resources. Snow (1980, 183) hypothesizes that a reduction occurred in the range of activities carried out at special purpose sites, as well as an increase in the number and variety of such sites utilized by any given group.

Building from these general trends in Archaic adaptation, Gardner and Custer (Gardner 1978; Gardner and Custer 1978; Custer 1979, 1980a) have identified various types of Archaic sites that reflect the seasonal variation in Atlantic episode environments and Archaic adaptations to these environments. Descriptions of the three types of sites noted below are adapted from the work of MacNeish (1971).

Macroband Base Camps

Living areas for multiple family units, these sites are located in areas of maximum habitat overlap and are characterized by a wide variety of tool classes and large amounts of debris. Access to a number of resource zones is maximized by their location. The range of tools shows a variety of maintenance activities and the quantity of debris shows the relatively long-term occupation of the site by a fairly large group.

Microband Base Camps

These smaller base camps were occupied by small individual family units, or limited sets of family units. Locations of these sites are similar to those of macroband base camps except that the carrying capacity of environmental settings for these sites was significantly lower than those of macroband base camps and the amount of debris is much less.

Procurement Sites

These sites are characterized by a limited number of activities, which were focused upon extraction of resources and energy from the environment. The limited range of activities created fewer tool types for the archaeological record. Locations of these sites depend upon the resources procured.

The relationships among the Archaic site types can be correlated with social organization patterns. A seasonal fusion/fission social organization linked the people who inhabited the different site types. Large (fused) social groups comprised of sets of individual nuclear families inhabited macroband base camps during the seasons when those areas contained rich resources. Based on analogies to living hunters and gatherers (Steward 1955, 101–50; Lee and DeVore 1968), researchers believe that as many as 20 or 30 nuclear families consisting of parents, children, and occasionally elder grandparents might have been present at one time. Most likely these nuclear families at any given macroband base camp could have traced affinal and consaguineal kinship ties among themselves. When resources in the immediate area of a macroband base camp became depleted from overexploitation or seasonal changes, macrobands would break (fission) into smaller units and move to more marginal resource settings to inhabit microband base camps. Individual nuclear families or small sets of related nuclear families were the major social units at any microband base camp.

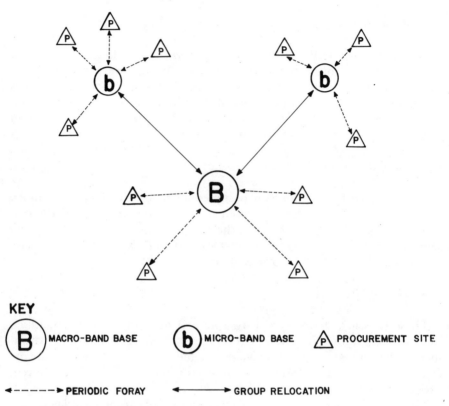

KEY

$\textcircled{B}$ MACRO-BAND BASE $\textcircled{b}$ MICRO-BAND BASE $\triangle$ PROCUREMENT SITE

◄ – – – – ► PERIODIC FORAY   ◄————► GROUP RELOCATION

Fig. 9. Archaic settlement system.

At both micro- and macroband base camps, work parties would make occasional forays from the base camps to procurement sites. These work parties would most likely be recruited on the basis of age and sex, with women and children gathering and males hunting. When resources were again available in sufficient quantities in special settings, groups would reform into the larger social units at the macroband base camps. This pattern of settlement allowed the groups to maintain appropriate population densities given the available resources. Also, the gathering of individual nuclear families into large macrobands allowed the exchange of information and mates, thereby preventing isolation and in-breeding. Again, observation of living hunters and gatherers indicates that the kinship systems were probably quite flexible, allowing movement of individuals among social units (Steward 1955, 101–50), maximizing the number of interpersonal ties that could be utilized in times of need.

The settlement pattern described above would probably be fairly consistent throughout the varied physiographic settings of Delaware during the Middle Archaic period. Some variability might be expected, however, in the Piedmont Uplands. Studies by Foss (1981; Hoffman and Foss 1980) and Stevenson (1978) in the varied topographic settings of the Blue Ridge and Ridge and Valley physiographic provinces of Virginia and Pennsylvania have shown that a more complex system of functional site types is present in these areas. A variety of site types intermediate in size and function among the sites noted above have been discovered. These more varied sites in areas with high topographic relief seem to represent an adaptation to the more varied resource settings of higher elevation areas. One might predict that when moving from the High Coastal Plain into the Piedmont Uplands of Delaware, where greater topographic relief is present, some intermediate site types might be present. The basic settlement pattern, however, remains the same.

Specific environments of the Delmarva Peninsula and surrounding areas can be used to indicate the probable site settings of the functional site types noted above. A variety of settings were likely locales for the macroband base camps, with interior swamps representing the most important location. In the Chesapeake Bay area a number of examples of the association of interior swamps and macroband base camps of the Archaic have been noted, including a series of sites near Mattawoman and Zekehiah swamps in the Potomac tidewater (Gardner 1978, 45, 48; Gardner and McNett 1971) and the Chance site, which is associated with an interior swamp on Deal Island on the Eastern Shore of Maryland (Gardner and Haynes 1978; Cresthull 1971, 1972). In New Jersey similar associations include the Indian Head site on the Maurice River (Mounier 1975, 9; Cross 1941, 44–47) and possibly the Abbott Farm site near Trenton (Cross 1956; R. M. Stewart and J. Cavallo, personal communication). In Delaware similar sites have been noted in the vicinity of Churchman's Marsh, just south of the Fall Line in northern New Castle County. Bifurcate points and some stemmed points similar to Neville points have been found in surface collections and excavated mixed plowzone assemblages from the Clyde Farm site (7NC-E-6) and the Julian Powerline site (7NC-D-42). All of these sites are located on high terraces adjacent to Churchman's Marsh and its confluence with the White Clay Creek. No earlier artifacts were recovered from these areas, and it is suggested that Churchman's Marsh was first utilized by Archaic groups around 6500 B.C.

At Churchman's Marsh, and at most of the other interior swamp sites in the Middle Atlantic, bifurcate base projectile points are correlated with the earliest relatively intensive use of these swamp settings. Although geological research has not been carried out at all of these locations, there are some indications that these large interior swamps first developed early in the Atlantic episode (Rappleye and Gardner 1979). Examination of drill records from the construction of Route I-95 reveals that in the Churchman's Marsh example the present tidal marsh deposits are underlain by impermeable Cretaceous clays and Pleistocene sands and gravels. The impermeable clays would have been the basis for swampy conditions. Once the water table reached a level above the clays, the water could not recede into the soil and became perched or stranded, with swampy conditions resulting. Although sea level rise would be the ultimate cause of the rise in the water table, the swamp itself would have been fresh water and would not have become tidal until much later, when sea level was sufficiently high to have caused brackish water to invade the swamp through the drowned Christina and White Clay drainages. Thus, Archaic use of Churchman's Marsh would seem to coincide with the initial appearance of the Marsh and is a good example of how Archaic populations were beginning to expand into the new and productive environmental settings emerging during the early Holocene. In addition, the Archaic use of Churchman's Marsh fits the new patterns of lithic resource utilization. The Churchman's Marsh headlands include large cobble deposits that are exposed in scattered locations adjacent to the marsh, and most of the bifurcate points from the area seem to have been made from cobble materials. Therefore, the serial lithic utilization pattern could be effectively carried out in the vicinity of Churchman's Marsh since the resources of the marsh itself were exploited from base camps.

Cedar and Burnt swamps on the upper Pocomoke drainage in southern Sussex County represent environmental settings similar to Churchman's Marsh. These swamps are not brackish and seem to have formed when water tables were perched on local clay deposits. Archaic base camps would be expected; however, little archaeological research has been done in the area and only one known site has been reported (7S-J-11). Nevertheless, there is an Archaic projectile point from the site, and Archaic use of these swamps is suggested as a hypothesis to be tested with future field work.

Floodplains of major drainages are also likely locations for Archaic macroband base camps. Within the Delaware River Valley a number of examples are present, including the Faucett site (Kinsey 1975), the Miller Field site (Kraft 1970, 1972), and the Raccoon Point site (Kier and Calvery 1957). Similar patterns are also noted for the lower Susquehanna Valley (Kinsey 1977a). In Delaware the most likely candidate for a macroband base camp would be the Crane Hook site (Weslager 1968, 105–14; Sweintochowski and Weslager 1942). Materials from Crane Hook were somewhat mixed except for a few discernible subsurface features; little more can be said except to note that since a substantial number of Archaic projectile points were included in the collections from the site, the existence of a macroband base camp at Crane Hook was likely. Unfortunately this statement can never be tested because most of the site has been destroyed by the construction of the Wilmington Marine complex and related industries. Further south in Delaware, from approximately the town of New Castle south, similar sites probably existed; however, these sites have most likely been inundated by sea level rise and are now buried below fairly recent sediments, or have been destroyed by dredging. Perhaps as new techniques of underwater archaeological survey and excavation are developed, more information on these potential macroband base camp locations will be revealed.

Analysis of Archaic microband base camps and procurement sites is more difficult than analysis of macroband base camp sites for a number of reasons. First, it is often difficult to differentiate between these two functional site types without controlled subsurface testing. Also, few of these sites have been excavated in Delaware or anywhere else on the Delmarva Peninsula. Therefore, I have based my discussion of their likely locations upon a review of the 42 known Delaware surface sites from the Archaic period, as well as upon a review of relevant data from other areas of the Middle Atlantic.

Microband base camp locations on the Delmarva Peninsula seem to follow the patterns noted for other areas of the Middle Atlantic, which includes locations at sheltered spots along smaller streams with maximum access to hunting and gathering areas or access to lithic sources. Studies in Virginia (Custer 1980a) and the Piedmont area of Pennsylvania (Kinsey 1977b) verify this pattern, and analysis of known Middle Archaic sites in Delaware shows some specific settings that are likely to include these microband base camps. During the initial stages of a survey of a highway corridor in northern New Castle County, Thomas (1980, chap. 2:19) has noted a number of potential Archaic microband base camps in small elevation rises near poorly drained settings away from the major drainages of the High Coastal Plain. All of these locations have been subjected only to surface collections and subsurface testing during early stages of research and no clearly diagnostic Archaic assemblages have been isolated. Further work at these sites, however, may isolate some Archaic microband base camps. Also in northern New Castle County, areas close to but not adjacent to Churchman's Marsh have produced some sites with a wider variety of tool types than that found in procurement sites, but with not quite as many artifacts as at macroband base camps. Site 7NC-E-4 is a good example; however, projectile point types are not clearly Archaic and further testing is necessary to prove that they are indeed from the Archaic period.

Within the High Coastal Plain areas south of Churchman's Marsh, researchers have found a number of potential microband base camps located in headland areas adjacent to the major tributaries of the Delaware River. In an intensive survey of a sewer line right-of-way between the towns of Middletown and Odessa, Gardner and Stewart (1978) located a number of Archaic sites that could be microband base camps along the Appoquinimink River. Because the sewer project was able to avoid most of these sites, intensive excavations were never carried out and further research will be required to more accurately identify the time period of these sites.

Data on Archaic microband base camps from Kent and Sussex counties are even more scanty than from those in northern areas of the state. One reason may be the fact that sea level rise has had greater effects on the southern parts of the state and would have inundated more sites. Upper terraces of major drainages provide a possible setting for Archaic microband base camps that have not been destroyed by sea level rise, and two sites along the upper Nanticoke (7S-E-21 and 7S-E-20) are possible candidates. Similar settings in New Castle County along the upper terraces of the Delaware have produced similar sites (7NC-E-14). Therefore, microband base camps are projected along the now-inundated upper terraces of the Delaware River in lower Kent and Sussex counties.

Archaic procurement sites, the final type of sites to be discussed, show a variety of settings that seem to be associated with game-attractive areas or specialized gathering locales. Lithic resources may also be the foci of procurement sites. In general, throughout the Coastal Plain areas Archaic procurement sites seem to be scattered on small areas of relatively higher elevation adjacent to swampy, poorly drained ground or large and small drainages. It is difficult to project exactly what resources were utilized, and often the small scattering of artifacts makes it hard to be sure if the sites are indeed from the Archaic period. However, in many cases bifurcate projectile points have been found at these sites. The largest complex of procurement sites of the Archaic period is associated with the bay/basin features and other poorly drained areas of the midpeninsular drainage divide area of the High and Low Coastal Plain. Locations and tools are very similar to Paleo-Indian period sites in the area, with the only locational difference being the existence of more Archaic sites close to the bay/basin features (e.g., 7NC-J-3,14; 7NC-G-68; 7K-C-25). The similarity in procurement sites between the Archaic and Paleo-Indian periods in this area is not surprising, considering the fact that game-attractive areas such as watering holes would continue to be good hunting locations in spite of the environmental changes accompanying the onset of the Holocene. A similar pattern is seen in the Piedmont Uplands. The limestone valleys with sinkholes and upland swampy areas at the heads of drainages that were foci of Paleo-Indian sites are also the locations of Archaic procurement sites, and use of the area seems to be very similar through the Paleo-Indian and Archaic periods (Custer and Wallace 1982). However, rarely are Paleo-Indian and Archaic procurement sites found in exactly the same location, which indicates some changes in the use of game-attractive areas (Custer and Wallace 1982). This different use could be the result of varied behavior patterns between Late Pleistocene and Holocene game animals.

Because of the nature of the data, this review of the site locations is subject to a number of qualifications. First, there is a limited number of sites to analyze. The absence of a systematic, statewide survey makes it likely that some environmental settings have been missed. This feature of the data base most strongly affects the statements about the locations of microband base camps and procurement sites. Another complicating factor is post-Pleistocene sea level rise. During the Middle Archaic period a major portion of the Delaware estuary was established, and drowning of stream mouths along the Delaware River created pronounced sedimentation throughout the estuary (Kraft 1977). Examination of some of the cross sections provided by Kraft et al. (1976) reveals that as much as 15 meters of sediments have been deposited in some areas of the Delaware estuary since Middle Archaic times. Therefore, large portions of the Archaic-age landscape and the Archaic archaeological record and settlement pattern are not . available for survey and analysis. The model of the Archaic settlement system presented here is probably biased toward the terrestrial aspect of the adaptation. Nevertheless, the basic patterns of adaptation and settlement were probably the same. Macroband base camps were probably located along confluences of the Delaware and its tributaries. Microband camp sites would most likely have been found on the medium-range terraces and procurement sites along the floodplain swamps and floodchutes. The geomorphological processes of the post-Pleistocene transgression may or may not have preserved these sites. Given present technology we can only try to predict the locations of these sites and be aware of their effects upon our statements about terrestrial sites within the same settlement system (Science Applications 1979).

The cultural complexity and regional relationship patterns that begin to emerge during the Archaic have important implications for later Woodland I groups. As noted previously, Archaic hunters and gatherers most likely had a fusion-fission social organization in which a relatively mobile lifestyle prevailed. Flexible kinship systems allowed movements of people among various social units, thereby facilitating intergroup communication. The effects of this communication can be seen in a variety of ways and have important implications for the development of regional exchange networks.

Analysis of Archaic projectile point types shows marked similarities in styles over wide areas. Chapman (1975, 248–69) has noted the widespread, pan-Eastern distribution of bifurcate point varieties, and Dincauze (1976, 140–42) notes similarities in stemmed points throughout the Atlantic Slope from New England to the Carolinas. Snow (1980, 183) notes an increasing regionalization of projectile point styles in later portions of the Archaic as adaptations adjust to local conditions. However, similar point styles can still be identified over large areas such as individual drainages and sets of drainages. When changes in styles do occur, they tend to be slow and incremental (Harrison 1974). These widespread point types and slowly changing styles have implications for social organizations and regional exchange.

Michlovic (1976) has noted that widespread distribution of diagnostic point styles such as Archaic types can be linked to fluid small-band organizations using reciprocal exchange. In the Archaic it is important to note that a variety of lithic materials were used in the far-flung distributions of diagnostic point styles. In the case of bifurcate base points, cherts were used in West Virginia (Broyles 1971, 69); cherts and jaspers in the West Branch Valley of the Susquehanna Valley (Turnbaugh 1977, 95); jaspers, cherts, and argillaceous shales in the Upper Delaware Valley (Kinsey 1972, 422); chert and rhyolite in the Shenandoah Valley of Virginia (Carr 1975); and chert, rhyolite, jasper, and quartz on the Delmarva Peninsula. When nonlocal materials were used such as rhyolite on Coastal Plain sites, the artifacts were very heavily resharpened, and rhyolite waste flakes indicative of activities other than edge maintenance are absent (Stewart and Gardner 1978). The indication is that a low level of exchange was in operation, with artifacts—rather than raw materials—moving from group to group.

The exchange of artifacts and ideas about projectile points was important beyond the immediate effect of creating regional style zones. Rappaport (1968) and Simms (1979) have noted that information concerning subsistence resources was exchanged along with the material items and that this information is often more important than the materials exchanged. Also, exchange relationships among unrelated individuals created extra ties among diverse social groups and helped to reduce the potential for conflict. Thus, the simple exchange systems of the Archaic played an important role in integrating diverse social groups. These exchange systems were also important because they provided the basis for the development of the elaborate exchange systems of the Woodland I period that spanned large areas of the Middle Atlantic. The processes that transformed the Archaic exchange systems into these elaborate systems are an important component in the development of the Woodland I period.

[4]

Woodland I Period:
The Beginnings of a Sedentary Lifestyle

The beginning of the Woodland I period marks the most pronounced change in prehistoric lifeways seen in Delaware. Although seasonal variation in resource availability and emerging Holocene environments brought about great changes in lifeways between the Paleo-Indian and Archaic periods, the change between the Archaic and Woodland I period was even greater. Custer and Wallace (1982) have noted that in the Piedmont Uplands, Paleo-Indian and Archaic cultures used the environment in very similar ways, even though the actual resources used and the locations of sites varied markedly. Both Paleo-Indian and Archaic groups seemed to have had relatively mobile lifestyles that moved them among the various locations of critical resources. Short-term forays by certain segments of local social groups procured resources that might be found in marginal areas and returned them to the complete social unit. The fusion-fission social system and settlement pattern regulated population densities and kept them within the local carrying capacities. Binford (1980, 15) has described similar adaptations among hunters and gatherers as logistical or collecting systems. Although Custer and Wallace's data are derived mainly from the Piedmont and Fall Line zones, similarities in the Coastal Plain can be seen, such as the consistent use of the Midpeninsula Drainage Divide for hunting activities through Paleo-Indian and Archaic times.

Collecting strategies were the major form of adaptation throughout Delaware during the Paleo-Indian and Archaic periods. In Delaware, these collecting adaptations seem to be associated with the flexible band organizations, mobile lifestyles, readily portable tool technologies, and simple exchange systems of the Paleo-Indian and Archaic periods. In contrast, the Woodland I period in Delaware was characterized by relatively sedentary lifestyles, less portable storage technologies and nonportable facilities, larger population aggregates, stratified societies, elaborate exchange systems, and complex burial patterns. Although some indications of environmental change seem to have important effects upon the development of the distinctive features of the Woodland I period, the major cause of the differences between the Archaic and Woodland I periods was a dramatic change in the social component of the biosocial environment. A major theme in this discussion is the examination of how this change in the social environment came about and how the distinctive features of the Woodland I period are an adaptation to this change.

The use of the date 3000 B.C. for the beginning of the Woodland I period, and indeed use of the term *Woodland I*, represent a departure from the traditional literature. As defined here, the Woodland I period includes three distinctive chronological units recognized in the traditional literature: Late Archaic, Early Woodland, and Middle Woodland. In some ways the controversy of how to divide up the chunk of time between 3000 B.C. and A.D. 1000 is a question of scale and perspective. In a review of archaeology east of the Mississippi, Griffin (1967, 178) notes that the Late Archaic period was characterized by "considerable population growth, clear regional adaptations, and interregional exchange of raw materials." It was seen as clearly distinct from the preceding Middle Archaic cultures, yet different from later Early Woodland cultures, which were characterized by ceramics, burial mounds, and agriculture (Griffin 1967, 180). Similarly, a Middle Woodland period was denoted and characterized by the appearance of a distinctive mortuary complex called Hopewell that dominated most of eastern North America (Griffin 1967, 183). In general, the main distinction between Early and Middle Woodland cultures was defined in terms of grave goods, with some attendant shifts in settlement systems. This system of classification worked well for Griffin's large-scale review; however, examination of the peculiarities of regional sequences showed that not all of the defining characteristics of these periods were present in all locations. For example, some sites from the southeast Coastal Plain showed the presence of ceramics dated to about 2500 B.C. Griffin (1978, 60–61) notes that these ceramics are included in archaeological assemblages that are otherwise typical of the Archaic. Thus, one of the diagnostic characteristics of the Early Woodland period seemed to be appearing in Late Archaic contexts, thereby blurring the distinction.

Witthoft (1953) also noted assemblages of artifacts from sites in the Middle Atlantic that seemed to be neither Archaic (they contained different styles of projectile points, stone bowls and rudimentary ceramics, and new lithic raw materials) nor Woodland (they appeared to lack agriculture, burial mounds, and a sedentary lifestyle). Witthoft called these cultures *transitional,* and many authors have since used this term to designate a developmental stage in eastern North American prehistory (Kraft 1970, 1975; Ritchie 1965). Kinsey (1971, 1972) and others have argued that the transitional sites represented a variant of the Late Archaic and they included these sites in the Susquehanna Tradition, the name of the most prolific source of distinctive projectile points and stone bowls. The controversy of terminology has not been resolved and both terms are used in the present literature (Snow 1980; Mouer et al. 1981).

A similar situation can be seen in the Early and Middle Woodland case. The initial distinction between the Adena cultures of the Early Woodland and the Hopewell cultures of the Middle Woodland worked well in the Ohio and Mississippi valleys. However, as sites from these periods were discovered in other areas it was apparent that the distinction was not so clear. Kinsey (1971, 1972, 1975) and Kraft (1970, 1975) both note continuities between the Early and Middle Woodland cultures of the Delaware Valley, as do researchers in New England (Snow 1980), the Southeast (Muller 1978, 291–307; Milanich and Fairbanks 1980, 65–88), and the Northeast in general (Tuck 1978; Fitting 1978).

The reason that the terminology controversy has not been resolved in any of the above cases is due to the fact that nearly all of the local divergences from Griffin's period definitions are correct. It should not be surprising to note that the developments in the Ohio and Mississippi are different from those of the Susquehanna River Valley. The difficulty arises when the "round" components of local sequences of cultures are forced into the "square" categories of large-scale area syntheses. The validity of the local sequences is not in question, but the frame of reference is. This is not to say that broad trends cannot be identified across North America. The important point is that the trends viewed 15 years ago must be evaluated in light of newly emerging data.

In the case of the Delaware local sequence, it is my contention that traditional Late Archaic, Early Woodland, and Middle Woodland categories should be combined into a single chronological unit based on the following similarities exhibited between 3000 B.C. and A.D. 1000:

1. The development of estuarine and riverine adaptations that were stable and intensive enough to produce large macroband base camp sites in the zone of freshwater/saltwater interface and along the major drainages;
2. Population growth at single-site locations that produced sites much larger than Archaic macroband base camps;
3. The appearance of foraging and collecting adaptations (Binford 1980) in areas less productive than the estuarine and riverine settings;
4. The participation in exchange networks that moved raw materials as well as finished artifacts across large areas;
5. The occasional participation in complex mortuary ceremonies that created cemeteries with rich grave offerings.

These similarities help to define a period of similar adaptations to rapidly changing biosocial environments.

Table 7:   Woodland I Culture Complexes

Date	Low Coastal Plain Sussex County	Low Coastal Plain Kent County	High Coastal Plain New Castle County	Piedmont/Fall Li[ne] New Castle Count[y]
AD 1000	Late Carey Complex	Webb Complex		Delaware Park Complex
AD 500				
		Carey Complex		
AD 0				
600 BC	Wolfe Neck Complex	Delmarva Adena Complex	Wolfe Neck Complex	
3000 BC	Clyde Farm Complex	Barker's Landing Complex	Clyde Farm Complex	

Because there are many more Woodland I sites known in the archaeological literature of Delaware than from other time periods, it is possible to recognize some temporal and spatial variation within Delaware (Thomas 1977). Table 7 notes the recognized Woodland I complexes of Delaware that are used to organize this chapter, along with their spatial and temporal limits. These complexes represent specialized adaptations to local biosocial environments and are part of the trend toward regionalization noted by Griffin (1967, 178). Although numerous attributes of complete lifeways are used to discriminate among the varied Woodland I complexes, projectile point and ceramic styles help identify similar points in time. The chronological distribution of these styles is discussed below.

Large, stemmed projectile points with narrow blades comprise the majority of the projectile point types for the Woodland I period of Delaware. These points resemble some of the stemmed points of the Archaic and are often difficult to distinguish without information on associated artifacts of stratigraphic context. Traditionally, large, stemmed points with narrow blades have been documented as the dominant projectile point style of the period from 3000 B.C. to at least 2000 B.C. by Kinsey (1959b, 1971, 1972, 1975, 1977a, 1977b) in the Upper Delaware Valley and southeastern Pennsylvania, especially the Lower Susquehanna Valley. These styles of points have been called by a variety of names and Kinsey (1971) groups them together under the term *Piedmont Archaic*. Research in other areas such as the Lower Potomac (Gardner 1976 and Stephenson 1963) notes similar points with similar dates. Identical styles of points are also widespread in Delaware collections and probably date to the same period, although there are some indications that they last later in time than orginally believed. However, it is somewhat misleading to call these points Piedmont Archaic because they are not found only in the Piedmont and are not part of the Archaic as defined here. The term *Bare Island/Lackawaxen* is used here to refer to these narrow-blade stemmed points and can be considered synonymous with Kinsey's Piedmont Archaic. This term is derived from the two local type names orginally used by Kinsey (Kinsey 1959b; Kinsey 1972, 408–411).

Prior to 2000 B.C., no other projectile point styles are associated with Bare Island/Lackawaxen points. However, after 2000 B.C. the situation becomes more complex with the appearance of a series of distinctive projectile point forms called broadspears. Four basic varieties of broadspear points are Lehigh/Koens Crispin, Savannah River, Perkiomen, and Susquehanna (Kinsey 1972, 423–30; Coe 1964). Another style, Long Points (Witthoft 1959; Kinsey 1971), is also an early form of broadspears. Broadspear projectile points, recognized as a distinctive technology since Witthoft's (1953) paper that described the basic varieties, have been the center of controversy ever since. While some researchers (Turnbaugh 1975) see the broadspear projectile points as indicative of special groups of people, I suggest here that broadspears represent a distinctive set of tools and knives that are in no way connected with special groups of people (Cook 1976; Custer 1978). I favor the functional interpretation for a number of reasons. First, the major difference between broadspears and Bare Island/ Lackawaxen Points is that broadspears have a much higher width/thickness ratio than the Bare Island/Lackawaxen points. Also, broadspears have much lower edge angles. These basic differences in configuration seem to be related to changes in the functions that these tools were used for. The narrow-bladed Bare Island/Lackawaxen points would be suited for penetration while the broadspears were better for use as knives. The low-edge angles would be efficient for cutting and the broad blades would allow much resharpening (Custer 1978; Cook 1967; Ahler 1971). Indeed, many broadspears show signs of resharpening and heavy edge wear (Kraft 1970, 62–64). Therefore, broadspears are here considered specialized tools added to the tool kits of Woodland I groups some time after 2000 B.C.

The chronological relationship of broadspears to Bare Island/ Lackawaxen forms is not at all clear. If broadspears are cutting tools, other projectile points would still be necessary items in tool kits, and the Bare Island/Lackawaxen points provide a possible candidate. Data from the Upper Delaware Valley provide some indications of time overlap. Kinsey (1972, 395–96) notes that Bare Island/Lackawaxen projectile points and similar Normanskill and Lagoon point types from New York date between 3430 B.C. and 1340 B.C. while varied broadspears date to between 1820 B.C., or even earlier (Kraft 1970, 55), and 1380 B.C. While the overlap is not great and is based on the extended ranges of radiocarbon dates, the Bare

Table 8: 7NC-E-6 Area 2B S2W2 Cultural and Natural Stratigraphy

SOILS	ARBITRARY LEVELS	PROJECTILE POINTS	CERAMICS
PZ .2	PZ	none	none
.4 B1	2		-.37 Darnes Quarter (71)
		-.42 stemmed (52 67) -.44 stemmed (48)	
	3		-.53 Dames Quarter (59)
.6 m.BS.	4	} stemmed	} Marcey Creek
	5		
		-.76 fishtail (12)	

Island/Lackawaxen forms and broadspears appear to be contemporaneous. Furthermore, research from a series of sites in the Lower Potomac River Valley of Maryland (Gardner 1976) has indicated the association of Bare Island/Lackawaxen forms and broadspears in large hearths. However, more careful analysis of the complex and shallow stratigraphy at these sites is necessary to completely confirm the associations. Similarly, Kinsey's (1959b) analysis of projectile points at the Kent-Hally site on Bare Island in the Lower Susquehanna Valley of Pennsylvania indicates Bare Island points with broadspearlike points. However, again the stratigraphic situation is not completely clear.

Analysis of sites more recent than 1200 B.C. also provides some useful information on the time range of stemmed points with narrow blades. Recent excavations at the Clyde Farm site (7NC-E-6) by the University of Delaware Department of Anthropology (Custer 1981) have shown the association of Bare Island/Lackawaxen points (Table 8) with Orient fishtail points, which date to between 1280 B.C. and 810 B.C. (Kinsey 1972, 395), and Marcey Creek and Dames Quarter ceramics, which have been dated to 1200 B.C. and 700 B.C. (Artusy 1976, 1–2). These associations are well defined by the natural soil horizons and indicate that Bare Island/ Lackawaxen points last up to at least 700 B.C. It is also interesting to note that resharpening has reduced the length of some of these points, although the width of the blade and the shape of the base remains the same. The inclusion of these smaller resharpened Bare Island/Lackawaxen points in association with larger, more typical point forms is significant because the points that are usually depicted in reports are the larger, more complete specimens. However, the smaller resharpened points are also part of the same tool kits and show the complete variation of sizes and shapes of Bare Island/Lackawaxen projectile points.

Small stemmed points similar to those noted in the Clyde Farm assemblages are also noted in the Wolfe Neck midden (7S-D-10) in Sussex County and are associated with radiocarbon dates as late as 375 B.C. and possibly A.D. 330 (Griffith and Artusy 1977, 6–7; Daniel R. Griffith, personal communication).* Although the stemmed points from the Wolfe Neck midden are smaller than many of the Bare Island/Lackawaxen points, they fall within the size range of the Clyde Farm data. Similar assemblages of smaller stemmed points, which have been termed Rossville and Lagoon points, are associated with a radiocarbon date of 480 B.C. in the Upper Delaware Valley (Kinsey 1972, 436), and a range of dates from 520 B.C. to 100 B.C. is noted from Martha's Vineyard (Ritchie 1969, 224). Recent excavations at the Herring Island site (18-CE-146) in Cecil County, Maryland, by Henry Ward of Elkton, Maryland, in conjunction with the University of Delaware Department of Anthropology, have shown associations of Rossville points with Mockley ceramics that have been dated to between 0 B.C. and A.D. 600 at other sites (Artusy 1976, 3–4). Finally, recent excavations at the Delaware Park Site (7NC-E-41) in northern New Castle County by Ron Thomas (1981) have revealed a series of assemblages of Rossvillelike narrow-blade stemmed points that are found within subsurface features radiocarbon dated to between 730 B.C. and A.D. 640 (Thomas 1981, chap. 9:135–41).**

The above data indicate that stemmed points with relatively narrow blades were used for a long time span in Delaware and the Middle Atlantic in general. I argued here that the narrow blade with its low width/thickness ratio is a very efficient penetrating tool and most likely functioned as a projectile point for hunting weapons. The reduction in size, mainly length, that does seem to occur through time may be related to changing resharpening technologies and is not a particularly significant variation through time. Close analysis of length and width measurements of a series of well-dated stemmed points might reveal some trends; however, with the data now available, the range of variation in size from Bare Island/Lackawaxen forms through Rossville forms seems·to overlap, indicating a similar projectile point technology throughout Delaware and the Middle Atlantic lasting from 3000 B.C. to A.D. 600 (Kinsey 1972, 367). If the stemmed points of the Archaic are also included as a part of a similar technology, the time range can be extended back as far as 5000 B.C. The similarity of these technologies is probably not significant in any evolutionary sense and it

*See UGa-1273a, UGa-1273b, UGa-1224, and UGa-1223 in Appendix 1.
**See UGa-3489, UGa-3437, UGa-3438, UGa-3498, UGa-3501, UGa-3464, UGa-3499, UGa-3499, UGa-3467, UGa-3465, UGa-3500, UGa-3466, and UGa-3469 in Appendix 1.

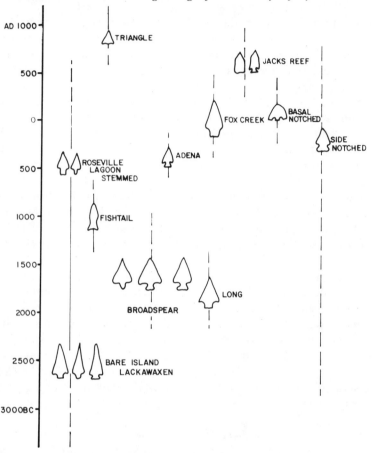

Fig. 10. Chronology of Woodland I projectile points.

most likely represents continuity in the technological requirements of penetrating projectile points for hunting weapons. Broadspear forms are special function tools that were added to tool kits in Delaware about 2000 B.C., or earlier if Kinsey's (1971) suggestions about the Long points are correct. By approximately 1000 B.C. these distinctive tools were no longer present and Orient fishtail points, a special style of stemmed points, were added to tool kits in Delaware; however, they were not as common as the broadspear forms and do not date to later than about 750 B.C. By about 500 B.C. the stemmed points with narrow blades were somewhat reduced and are termed *Rossville*, or simply *stemmed points*.

In addition to these styles, some other distinctive projectile point forms can be recognized for the Woodland I of Delaware (Figs. 18 and 19). A series of side- and corner-notched projectile points manufactured from distinctive cherts found in Ohio are found in Delaware associated with sites of the Delaware Adena Complex (Thomas 1970). These points are dated to about 500 B.C. to 0 B.C. (Y-933) and represent a very special style of projectile point that will be discussed more fully in connection with the Delmarva Adena Complex. Some small basal-notched projectile points are seen in Delaware and are similar to forms that have been found in association with Mockley ceramics at the Erb Rockshelter in southern Lancaster County, Pennsylvania (Kent and Packard 1969). A date range of 0 B.C. to A.D. 600 is projected for these basal-notched points based on Artusy's (1976, 3–4) dates for these ceramics. A similar time range is projected for a series of large broad-stemmed projectile points termed Fox Creek (Kinsey 1972, 445) and commonly found in Kent and Sussex counties. Funk (1976, 287–93) ascribes a date of A.D. 350–A.D. 700 to these points in the Hudson Valley, and Wright (1973, 27) notes a date of A.D. 300–A.D. 485 from sites on the western shore of the Chesapeake Bay. A similar range of dates is projected for Delaware. Numerous corner notched and pentagonal projectile points, called Jack's Reef projectile points (Kinsey 1972, 438–39), also comprise part of the range of points found during the Woodland I period of Delaware and are dated to around A.D. 700 at the Island Field cemetery in Kent County (Thomas and Warren 1970). Usually Jack's Reef points are associated with Hell Island ceramics, which dated to A.D. 600–A.D. 1000 (Artusy 1976, 4) (I-6338, UGa-1441, UGa-3439). Kinsey (1972, 428) reports a date of A.D. 790 from the Upper Delaware Valley, and Ritchie (1965, 234, 258) notes dates between A.D. 310 and A.D. 955. These dates include the Island Field range of dates and would seem to apply to Delaware. Some large triangular points are also found in Woodland I sites, with the clearest association coming from the Wilgus Site (7S-K-21) in southern Sussex County. Excavations by the University of Delaware Department of Anthropology and the Bureau of Archaeology and Historic Preservation found large triangular points in association with Mockley, and possibly Coulbourn, ceramics indicating a date range of at least A.D. 500–A.D. 1000. These large triangular points are quite similar to Levanna points noted in New York State (Ritchie 1961, 31; Funk 1976, 294), where they are dated to between A.D. 900 and A.D. 1350. Triangular points are also found at Woodland II sites in Delaware all the way up to European Contact (see Chapter 5) and it is likely that the triangular point style emerges in the later portion of the Woodland I period and continues into the Woodland II period. Some initial inspections of collections suggest that the earlier Woodland I triangular forms are larger than the later Woodland II forms; however, there is insufficient information to make a distinction at the present time. A final projectile point type of the Woodland I period is the generalized side-notched form. Collections throughout the state of Delaware contain a series of side-notched points that seem to vary in their shape and size, and Thomas (1981) notes a series of dates between A.D. 190 and 10 B.C. at the Delaware Park site (7NC-E-41; see UGa-3464, UGa-3499, UGa-3502, and UGa-3504 in Appendix 1). Kinsey (1972, 443–44) notes a

Table 9: Woodland I Ceramic Sequence

Date	Lower Delmarva	Southern Delaware(3)	Central Delaware	Middle Eastern Shore	Northern Delaware	Upper (15) Eastern Shore	Southeastern Pennsylvania
AD 1000			Hell Island(7)	Hell Island (11)	Hell Island(14)	Hell Island	Hell Island
AD 600	Mockley(2)	Mockley	Mockley(6)	Mockley(10)	Mockley(13)	Mockley	Mockley(17)
AD 0							
400 BC	?	Coulbourn	Coulbourn (5)	?	?	Coulbourn	?
700 BC	Wolfe Neck(1)	Wolfe Neck	Wolfe Neck(4)	Wolfe Neck(9)	Wolfe Neck(9)	Wolfe Neck	Susquehanna Series (16)
	?	Selden Island	?	?	Selden Island(12)	?	?
	Dames Quarter	Dames Quarter	Dames Quarter (8)	Dames Quarter(8)	Dames Quarter (12)	?	?
1000 BC	?	Marcey Creek	Marcey Creek (8)	Marcey Creek(8)	Marcey Creek(12)	?	Marcey Creek
?			Steatite Bowls				

Table 9: References

1. Griffith (1981:16).
2. Griffith (1981:18).
3. Entire column with radiocarbon dates taken from Artusy (1976:11) with some modifications based on unpublished data from the Wilgus Site (7S-K-21) see Artusy (1978).
4. Griffith (1981:16).
5. Griffith (1981:17) and unpublished data from the Wilgus Site (7S-K-21).
6. Griffith (1981:18).
7. Griffith (1981:19).
8. Wise (1975b:2).
9. Griffith (1981:16); Smith (1978:22–27); Handsman and McNett (1974:12–21).
10. Griffith (1981:18).
11. This listing is based on examination of ceramics from Eastern Neck Island (Thompson and Gardner 1978).
12. Wilkins (1978); recent unpublished data from Clyde Farm Site (7NC-E-6).
13. Custer (1980b:314).
14. Hell-Island-like ceramics were noted at the Delaware Park Site (7NC-E-41) by Thomas (1981).
15. The ceramics noted in this column are based on examination of a collection from Herring Island (18-CE-146) in the Elk River.
16. Smith (1978), and analysis of collections at the North Museum, Franklin and Marshall College, Lancaster, Pennsylvania.
17. Kent and Packard 1969.
18. Custer 1982.

similar phenomenon in the Upper Delaware Valley and ascribes an Archaic through Woodland age for these points; although some evidence from Martha's Vineyard (Ritchie 1969) indicates that side-notched projectile points are associated with Rossville and Lagoon components. For Delaware, it is likely that some side-notched points will be found in Woodland I associations.

In addition to projectile point styles, ceramic styles can be used as time markers during the Woodland I period in Delaware. It was during the Woodland I period that clay vessels for cooking and storage first appear; the reasons for the initial use of ceramic containers are addressed later in this chapter. Throughout the Woodland I period ceramic technology changed and developed, creating variations in ceramics that may be charted through time. Some simple decoration techniques were also used that changed through time as well, although it was not until Woodland II that decoration on ceramics provided the major source of variation through time. In general, the major variations in Delaware Woodland I ceramics were temper (the aplastic material mixed with the clay of the vessel to keep it from cracking when fired) and interior and exterior surface treatment (the scraping or impression of the interior and exterior surfaces of the vessels with fabrics, cords, or nets). Unlike projectile point styles, ceramics from the Woodland I period in Delaware have been carefully studied and an established sequence of varied ceramics is available (Artusy 1976; Griffith 1981). Table 9 notes the time space distributions of the varied Woodland I ceramic types in Delaware and surrounding areas, and the references note the sources of the information. Each of the ceramic types in Table 9 described below is based on the primary work of Griffith (1981) and Artusy (1976).

Steatite Bowls

The earliest permanent containers other than baskets or wooden boxes were not manufactured from clay, but instead were made from steatite, or soapstone. Steatite is readily found in the Piedmont areas of Maryland and Pennsylvania, with the largest outcrops and quarries near Christiana and Georgetown in Lancaster County, Pennsylvania (Holland et al. 1981). Easily carved and polished with stone tools, steatite was used to manufacture stone bowls with small lug handles. Some of the bowls, whose fragments are found throughout Delaware, are flat-bottomed, while others are more rounded. The earliest dates on stone bowls are not clear, although in North Carolina they have been dated as early as 1900 B.C. (Coe 1964, 45, 55, 118). Kraft (1970, 55, 56) suggests that stone bowls may be as early as 1700 B.C. in the Delaware River Valley, and a similar date is projected for the Delmarva Peninsula. Steatite bowls appear to be gradually replaced by similarly shaped ceramic vessels by about 1200 B.C. (Artusy 1976, 2).

Marcey Creek Plain

Marcey Creek Plain ceramics, the first true ceramics of Delaware, seem to be a copy of steatite bowls. Flat-bottomed vessels were made by modeling (sticking together large flat slabs of clay), and sometimes the small lug handles of the stone bowls are mimicked on Marcey Creek Vessels. The temper of Marcey Creek vessels is usually crushed steatite, which further underscores the technological continuity. The surfaces of the vessels are smooth and have a greasy or waxy feel (Artusy 1976, 2). Sometimes textile impressions can be seen on the flat bases of the vessels (Wise 1975a, 21). Marcey Creek vessels are widely distributed throughout the Middle Atlantic area, and in Delaware Artusy (1976, 2) projects a range of 1200 B.C. to 900 B.C.

Experimental Wares

In a review of the development of ceramic technologies in the Middle Atlantic, Wise (1975b, 2) suggests that after the initial development of ceramic technologies that produced Marcey Creek vessels, a period of experimentation ensued. A wide variety of tempers, vessel shapes, manufacturing methods, and surface treatments occurred over small areas and short time ranges. Quite often several different combinations of ceramic technologies will be manifest at a single site. Smith's (1978) analysis of ceramics of the Lower Susquehanna Valley documents this range of variation, and preliminary excavations at the Herring Island site (18-CE-146) in Cecil County, Maryland, show a similar pattern. In Delaware three major types of ceramics comprise this experimental phase: Dames Quarter Black Stone Tempered, Selden Island, and Ware Plain. Dames Quarter Black Stone Tempered ceramics are characterized by flat bottoms, tempering with crushed black hornblende or gneiss, modeled and possibly coiled construction, and in general are similar to Marcey Creek in shape, construction, and surface treatment (Artusy 1976, 2; Wise 1975b, 2). Selden Island ceramics may be either modeled or coiled and may have round or flat bases. Flat bases are associated with modeled vessels and round bases are associated with coiled vessels (Wilkins 1978). Cord impressions are common on the exterior and the temper is steatite. Artusy (1976, 2) projects a date of 1000 B.C. to 700 B.C., which matches with dates from the Loyola Retreat and Monocacy sites in the Potomac Valley noted by Gardner (1975; Gardner and McNett 1971). Ware Plain ceramics were originally described by McCann (1950), and in some ways this category has acted as a catch-all for the varied ceramic types that are now recognized as part of the experimental phase of ceramic development in the Middle Atlantic (Wise 1975b, 2). Kraft (1970, 118) has proposed a modified version of McCann's original type description and notes that Ware Plain vessels are flat-bottomed with lug handles and resemble Marcey Creek vessels. The significant feature of Ware Plain ceramics is that they are tempered with crushed sand or quartz. Kraft (1970, 119) notes that Ware Plain ceramics were found in association with Marcey Creek vessels, so a similar time range is suggested. No specific time range is specified for Delaware.

The wide range of tempers and surface treatments makes these ceramics difficult to recognize as a group. The Dames Quarter and Selden Island varieties are fairly well defined; however, the Ware Plain category remains something of a catch-all. As researchers become more sensitive to the varieties of these early ceramics, more varieties probably will be recognized in Delaware. These additional varieties will no doubt be similar to those noted by Smith (1978) for the Lower Susquehanna Valley.

Wolfe Neck Ware

Wise (1975b, 2) and Gardner (1975, 21) note that some time after 700 B.C. the period of experimentation in ceramic technology seemed to end and one dominant technology emerged. This technology produced vessels that were coiled, marked with cord and net impressions on the exterior (and sometimes the interior), bag-shaped with conoidal bottoms, and tempered with crushed rock, usually quartz. Ceramics with these attributes are known throughout the Middle Atlantic by various names, including Vinette I (Ritchie and MacNeish 1949, 100), Early Series-Exterior Corded/ Interior Smoothed (Kinsey 1972, 453), Susquehanna Series (Smith 1978), Broadhead Net Impressed (Kinsey 1972, 455–56; McNett 1967), Popes Creek Net Impressed (Stephenson 1963, 92–96), and, in Delaware, Wolfe Neck Ware (Artusy 1977, 2; Griffith 1981, 16). Wolfe Neck ceramics are tempered with crushed quartz and may be either cord-marked or net-impressed on the exterior surfaces. Vessel shape is conoidal with direct rims, and lips may be both rounded and flattened. Griffith and Artusy (1977) note that Wolfe Neck ceramics are associated with radiocarbon dates of 505 B.C. to 380 B.C. (UGa-1223, I-6891) and Artusy (1976, 3) notes that comparable ceramics in the Middle Atlantic have a time range of 700 B.C. to 400 B.C., the suggested similar range for Delaware.

Coulbourn Ware

Artusy (1976, 3) notes that Coulbourn ceramics are unique in the Middle Atlantic in that they are tempered with clay nodules or clay fragments. Otherwise, they are somewhat similar to Wolfe Neck ceramics in that they have both net and cord impressed exteriors, coiled construction, and a conoidal shape. Rims are direct and lips are smoothed, rounded, or flattened with either cord or net impressions (Griffith and Artusy 1977). A range between 400 B.C. and 100 B.C. is suggested by Artusy (1976, 3), based on a radiocarbon date of 375 B.C. from the Wolfe Neck Site (UGa-1224, UGa-1763).

Mockley Ware

Mockley ceramics have a relatively wide distribution throughout the Chesapeake area (Thurman and Barse 1974) and exhibit some varieties in surface treatment. The distinguishing characteristic of Mockley Ware is shell temper. Usually oyster shells are used, but quite often ribbed mussel *(Modiolus demissus)* is used in southern Delaware (Artusy 1976, 3). Vessel shapes are conoidal and lips tend to be either flattened or impressed. Exterior surface treatment may be either smoothed, cord marked, or net impressed.

Finds of complete vessels indicate that all three surface treatments may exist on a single vessel (Stewart and Gardner 1978). The best-defined time interval for Mockley ceramics is from A.D. 110 to A.D. 450 (Artusy 1976, 4) (UGa-1273a, UGa-1273b I-6060, UGa-1762, I-5817); however, there are some indications that in southern Kent and Sussex counties Mockley ceramics, or varieties of Mockley ceramics, last up to at least 1000 A.D. and represent the technological precursors of Woodland II Townsend ceramics (Griffith 1977, 1981). These late varieties of Mockley tend to be much thinner-walled vessels than earlier forms of Mockley ceramics and would be similar to what Thurman and Barse (1974) call Claggett ceramics of the western shore of the Chesapeake Bay. However, since insufficient analysis of these ceramics has been carried out to say for sure that they are Claggett ceramics, they will be referred to as Late Mockley ceramics in Delaware.

Hell Island Ware

The final Woodland I ceramic type discussed is Hell Island ceramics, which was originally defined by Wright (1960, 14–15) and Thomas (1966c, 10–12). Artusy (1976, 4) notes that Hell Island ceramics are tempered with finely crushed quartz with mica inclusions present in some cases. Surface treatments may be fabric and cord impressed. Vessel shapes are conoidal with direct rims and flat, corded, or fabric impressed lips (Griffith 1981, 19). Dates for Hell Island ceramics range between A.D. 600 and A.D. 1000 (I-6338, UGa-1441, UGa-3439, UGa-3437). Hell Island ceramics are distributed throughout northern Delaware and seem to be the technological precursor to the Minguannan series (Custer 1981) of Woodland II ceramics.

All of the ceramic and projectile point styles described above, in addition to other attributes, can be used to distinguish among the varied Woodland I Complexes of Delaware. Table 10 shows the relation of all of the ceramic and projectile point styles to the Woodland I Complexes in Delaware.

Table 10: Woodland I Complexes and Diagnostic Artifacts

Late Carey Complex

Mockley/Claggett ceramics
Large triangular projectile points

Webb Complex, Delaware Park Complex

Hell Island ceramics
Misc. stemmed projectile points
Jack's Reef pentagonal projectile points (Webb Complex only)

Carey Complex

Mockley ceramics
Rossville stemmed projectile points
Fox Creek projectile points (southern Delaware only)

Wolfe Neck Complex

Wolfe Neck ceramics
Susquehanna Series ceramics (northern Delaware only)
Misc. stemmed projectile points

Delmarva Adena Complex

Adena side and corner notched projectile points
Coulbourn ceramics
Misc. stemmed projectile points

Clyde Farm Complex and Barker's Landing Complex

Bare Island/Lackawaxen projectile points
Broadspears
Fishtail projectile points
Marcey Creek and Dames Quarter ceramics
Steatite bowls
Long projectile points (Clyde Farm Complex, northern Delaware only)
Selden Island ceramics (Clyde Farm Complex, northern and central Delaware
  only)

Environmental Setting

The Woodland I period is correlated with the Sub-Boreal and Sub-Atlantic Episodes (Table 3). Each episode is described below:

Sub-Boreal (3110 B.C.–810 B.C.)

The major characteristics of the Sub-Boreal episode are a pronounced warm and dry period early in the episode, around 2350 B.C., followed by a period of increasing moisture and slowly decreasing temperature. The early period of maximum warmth and dryness, called the midpostglacial xerothermic, had an important effect upon distributions of plant and animal communities, as well as on the geomorphological processes that shaped the landscapes. Several examples of the effects on geomorphological processes have been documented by Custer (1978), and many more are becoming known (Curry 1978, 1980). Midpostglacial xerothermic trends in temperature and moisture began late in the Atlantic episode but only have long-lived and dramatic effects early in the Sub-Boreal episode (Custer 1978). The midpostglacial xerothermic maximum in the Middle Atlantic area lasted approximately from 2700 b.c. to 200 b.c. (Custer 1978, 2).

Tables 4 and 5 reveal the effects of the midpostglacial xerothermic on vegetation. An increase in hickory coincided with the waning of the mesic forests, and a spread of grasslands was also evident. Hickory is noted as a dominant or accessory in 8 of the 10 pollen sequences listed. Similarly, Bernabo and Webb (1977, 79, Fig. 10) note pronounced changes in pollen distributions for eastern North America. Particularly interesting are oak decreases on the order of 10–20 percent in the southern Middle Atlantic and Delmarva Peninsula, accompanied by pine increases on the southern Delmarva on the order of 10 percent. For the Delmarva Peninsula it seems that pine was more widespread than hickory in the southern areas, while in the northern areas hickory was dominant with oak. In all areas of the peninsula pronounced changes can be seen.

Throughout the resulting xeric oak-hickory period there was a shrinking of the ranges of animal species intolerant of dry environments (Carbone 1976, 77). This shrinking would probably be most noticeable in the north, an area only recently penetrated by a northward dispersal of mesic-adapted species during the Atlantic episode (Smith 1957, 210). Accompanying the extension of the hickory forests was an eastward extension of the prairie peninsula. Smith (1957, 211) notes that at the height of the dry phase some western components could have reached as far east as the Atlantic Coast. Increased frequencies of nut-bearing trees would have favorably affected wild turkey populations, while decreased vegetation cover would have adversely affected deer populations (Carbone 1976, 78). On the other hand, climatic perturbations would have interrupted the normal sequence of forest succession and limited the extent of development of climax forests. Early seral stage vegetation communities would have had a wide distribution and would have favored the expansion of deer populations. Hydrological fluctuations due to changes in moisture regime would have affected riverine and estuarine resources, so it might be expected that the distribution of species with limited tolerances for temperature and salinity factors, such as oysters and anadramous fish (Daiber et al. 1976), would have been affected. Especially important would be the potential effects on anadramous fish such as the American shad and alewife. Upstream migrations of these fish are ultimately tied to nonsaline water and temperature conditions appropriate for spawning (Leggett 1973, 95).

Moreover, rising sea level would have caused the maximum upstream and inland penetration of these species at this time.

It is during the Sub-Boreal episode that the pattern of sea level rise and absence of estuarine resources changes. Extrapolation of Belknap and Kraft's (1977, 620, Fig. 8) sea level rise curves reveals a change in sea level from 9 meters below present to 4 meters below present, with an average rate of change on the order of 2 centimeters per decade. Throughout the episode the rate decreases so that the average rate tends to be somewhat misleading. Nevertheless, the implication is that at some point during the Sub-Boreal episode sufficient stability emerges to allow the formation of significant accumulations of estuarine resources. There is, however, some question about when these resources would have begun to be utilized by prehistoric populations. The best data come from the Lower Chesapeake Bay (Steven Potter, personal communication), where some shell middens might have been in existence as early as about 2500 b.c. These sites show a change in shellfish species composition that seem to coincide with the mid-postglacial xerothermic. Similar dates are available from the Lower Hudson (Brennan 1974, 1976, 1977; Snow 1981, 180). These dates also match drill core data from the Delaware Bay, where the earliest shell dates reported by Kraft (Kraft et al. 1976, 119, Fig. 78 and 123, Fig. 82) are between 2650 b.c. and 740 b.c.

Sub-Atlantic (810 B.C.–A.D. 1000)

The climates of the Sub-Atlantic episode can be characterized as an amelioration of the moisture stress of the Sub-Boreal, coupled with a cooling trend that leads to a close approximation of modern conditions.

Summary distributions of forests on the Delmarva Peninsula for the Sub-Atlantic episode are best characterized by the modern distributions described by Braun (1967). The northern Delaware Piedmont and Fall Line zones would fall within the Oak-Chestnut forest region defined by Braun (1967, 192). Gently sloping areas would support a mixed mesophytic association including yellow poplar, white and red oak, beech, chestnut, pig nut and shag bark hickory, red maple, white ash, wild black cherry, American hornbeam, flowering dogwood, red elm, black walnut, butternut, and bitternut. Rolling Piedmont areas would instead be characterized by a chestnut dominance (Braun 1967, 245). In some portions of the Piedmont granitic soils are interrupted by serpentine outcrops known as serpentine barrens (Braun 1967, 248), which are more common in the Maryland Piedmont. These serpentine barrens are characterized by grasslands such as *Andropogon scoparius, Bouteloua curtidendula,* and *Sorgulastrum nutans,* all of which are prairie dominants. *Phlox subulata* is also common, with scattered red cedar and groves of post oak and blackjack oak on the borders of the grasslands.

Braun (1967, 245) notes within the Coastal Plain a twofold division similar to the High/Low Coastal Plain distinction. The High Coastal Plain is equivalent to the Wicomico Terrace and is characterized by oak, chestnut, and hickory dominance. The Low Coastal Plain, equivalent to the Talbot terrace, is associated with predominantly evergreen forests. Within these broad distinctions a number of smaller types of communities can be recognized. Ravine areas within the High Coastal Plain area are dominated by chestnut and chestnut oak where the soils are gravelly. Loamy soils in these settings support a mixed mesophytic association of beech, white oak, Spanish oak, sycamore, pig nut hickory, red mulberry, wild black cherry, hackberry, and holly (Braun 1967, 246). In some areas within the High Coastal Plain setting, slope gradients, which range from steep to relatively low, may merge to produce an overlapping chestnut-pine forest type that is termed the Coastal Plain hardwood region of Delaware (Braun 1967, 246).

The Low Coastal Plain of the Delmarva Peninsula falls within the grouping of Oak-Pine forests of the Atlantic Slope (Braun 1967, 262). Loblolly pine is a dominant, but decreases in frequency moving north through Delaware. Areas of raised elevation in the Low Coastal Plain support forests more like those found further to the south, which would include loblolly pine with Virginia pine and mixed deciduous species. Flat, clayey, and poorly drained uplands usually support forests of sweet gum, willow oak, pin oak, and sour gum, with dominant white oak. Some upland swamp forests are found on both clayey and sandy soils (Braun 1967, 268). In general, the clay soil swamp forests are not sharply delimited from the mixed pine-deciduous communities of the dried clay uplands; deciduous species are more abundant and scrub pine is absent. Upland swamp forests in sandy soil may be either predominantly deciduous or coniferous, with the latter developmentally older. Included within these associations would be willow oak, white oak, sweet gum, red maple, water oak, cow oak, black gum, sweet oak, holly, and dogwood (Braun 1967, 268). It is also interesting to note that pine forests in many of the upland settings in southern Delaware are the result of modern cutting and clearing.

Forests in areas of lower elevation in the Low Coastal Plain vary in physiognomy and composition in relation to the degree of tidal overflow and the permanence of abundant water (Braun 1967, 268). The two dominant forest types of the area are the hardwood forest and the cypress swamp. Lowland hardwood forests generally have an admixture of loblolly pine and southern white cedar that in many ways approximates some of the communities found in the Pine Barrens of New Jersey (Braun 1967, 270). Sweet gum is also abundant, with red maple, willow oak, pin oak, and sour gum associates. In areas that are seldom reached by high water, tulip tree and beech may also be present. Delmarva cypress swamps, which are generally located just upstream from brackish water swamps, can be viewed as the northern outliers of the great southern cypress swamps. For example, the Pocomoke River swamp can be considered a northern outlier of the Dismal Swamp communities (Braun 1967, 269). In the Delmarva Peninsula the cypress swamps are dominated by bald cypress with associated swamp black gum or southern tupelo, and red maple. Nearly pure stands of white cedar can be found in association with the cypress swamps on the swamp borders in areas of peaty soils. In nonpeaty areas the lowland hardwood forest is in transition to upland forest types dominated by oaks such as water oak, willow oak, cow oak, and white oak, along with tuliptree, river birch, and beech.

The dominant game animals associated with these varied forests within the Delmarva Peninsula would have been the deer and the turkey (Shelford 1963). A wide variety of small mammals would also have been included, such as various species of squirrels and rabbits. Water fowl would also have been present in many areas; however, there is some debate as to the extent of migratory flocks of ducks and geese in the past.

It is during the Sub-Atlantic episode that the rate of sea level rise is drastically reduced and significant accumulations of estuarine resources occur. According to the work of Belknap and Kraft (1977, 620, Fig. 8), the sea level rise rate averages approximately 1 centimeter per decade. This rate is much lower than that of any of the previously described episodes and provides sufficiently stable salinity and temperature conditions to allow the proliferation of estuarine-adapted species. It is during the Sub-Atlantic episode that archaeological data shows the extensive use of shellfish resources. The distributions of these resources are documented in Daiber et al. (1976).

Archaeological Data and Woodland I Adaptations

In spite of the fact that a variety of different complexes are recognized for the Woodland I period in Delaware, similarities among certain complexes are evident, making it convenient to group some of them together for discussion.

Clyde Farm Complex and Barker's Landing Complex

The earliest Woodland I complexes noted for Delaware are the Clyde Farm complex (Thomas 1977, 53), named for the Clyde Farm site (7NC-E-6) in northern New Castle County, and the Barker's Landing complex, named for the Barker's Landing site (7NC-D-13) in central Kent County. Both complexes begin around 3000 b.c. and last until about 500 b.c. Sites from this pair of complexes are distinguished from earlier Archaic sites by a variety of factors, including changing tool kits, changing settlement patterns, population growth, shifts in social organization, and development of extensive trade and exchange networks.

The continuity of stemmed points from Archaic assemblages reduces the utility of projectile point types as time markers until broadspear points appear about 2000 B.C. Long points (Kinsey 1971) are more common in the Piedmont zone and are found at the Mitchell site (7NC-A-2) in New Castle County. The other varieties of broadspears are found throughout Delaware, although data from Sussex County are scanty. Stone bowls, Marcey Creek ceramics, and Experimental ceramics also mark the middle portions of the Barker's Landing and Clyde Farm complexes throughout Delaware. Additional associated technological changes include an increase in the variety of ground stone tool types after 3000 B.C. Adzes, celts, gouges, and axes increase in frequency and variety and may have been associated with the heavy woodworking necessary for the production of dugout canoes. Examples from the Middle Atlantic in general include assemblages from the Faucett site (Kinsey 1972, 361–69; 1975, 28–48), the Miller Field site (Kraft 1970, 84–115), and the Harrys Farm site (Kraft 1975, 29–48) of the Upper Delaware Valley; the Stony Brook site, the Jamesport site, and the Sugar Loaf site on Long Island (Ritchie 1959, 44, 60–62, 72–73); the West Branch Valley of the Susquehanna River (Turnbaugh 1977, 162–66); the Kent-Hally site in the Lower Susquehanna Valley (Kinsey 1959b, 117–25); and several sites in New York (Ritchie and Funk 1973, 57–95). These changes in material culture indicate alterations in adaptation and are clearly linked to shifts in settlement pattern that appear about 3000 B.C. These settlement pattern shifts represent the major feature that distinguishes the initial Woodland I complexes from the preceding Archaic period.

The major change in settlement patterns noted around 3000 B.C. in Delaware and the Middle Atlantic is a reduction in the variety of different site locations utilized. Witthoft (1953) made this observation in his study of transitional cultures, which also noted a focus on riverine environments. The reduction of variety is related to a number of factors, the most important of which is the environmental change experienced in the Late Atlantic and Sub-Boreal climatic episodes. Dry conditions were common throughout the Middle Atlantic area around 3000 B.C. to 760 B.C. and may have even lasted until later, as indicated by the Delaware Park site pollen data (Table 6). The effects of the dry episode on resource distributions have been summarized earlier in this chapter, and the overall effect seemed to be neither an enrichment nor a degradation of the environment. Instead, a shift in the distribution patterns of various resources seems to be indicated (Custer 1978). Locations that were once especially productive might have become less useful and areas that were once marginal in productivity would have been enhanced. Given dry conditions it also seems likely that surface water would become a critical resource in determining productive habitats for human settlement.

The reaction of Woodland I groups to this environmental change is difficult to reconstruct completely; however, the reduction in settlement pattern variety gives some clues to the possible trends in adaptation that emerged. From biology one knows that responses to environmental changes tend to be initially conservative (O'Kelly 1975, 104–5). Binford (1978, 496) has described similar trends in hunter-gatherer adaptations and notes that even though the organization of hunting or gathering activities may change in the overall adaptation, the activities themselves remained very much the same. In other words, one expected response to the environmental change would have been for groups to abandon areas where their traditional hunting and gathering activities no longer seemed to work in favor of areas where activities could be sucessfully carried out. In some areas such movements would not be possible, due either to competition from other groups or natural boundaries. People in these situations would be forced to turn to the exploitation of new resources, or at least new combinations of traditional resources available at different environmental zones at different times. Drastic modifications of scheduling and settlement patterns were highly likely, with consequent modifications of group size, composition, and social organization. If groups of people were successful in making these modifications, population increases might be expected. However, groups that were less successful might have had to reduce their size through fissioning and drastically alter their social organizations (Custer n.d.).

In general, archaeological evidence exists throughout the Middle Atlantic for the modifications noted above. Witthoft (1953) notes the shift toward riverine-oriented settlement systems in many areas during the peiod between 3000 B.C. and 500 B.C. Kinsey (1977b) notes a complex set of relationships between microenvironments and settlement patterns that show changes through this period. Changes in individual site use can also be seen. Michels (1967, 815–16) notes a reduction in the area of the Sheep Rock Shelter occupied during initial Woodland I times, and Kinsey (1975, 49) notes a similar pattern at the Faucett site. In Coastal Plain areas the general trend was a shift to floodplains and adjacent areas of major watercourses. An intensification in the use of marsh/swamp settings is also evident, with very large initial Woodland I sites being associated with marshes in the lower Potomac along the Piscataway Creek (Gardner 1976; Gardner and McNett 1971; Stewart and Gardner 1978; Stephenson 1963), Dismal Swamp (Rappleye and Gardner 1979), and the Abbott Farm site (Cross 1956; R. M. Stewart and J. Cavallo, personal communication). These shifts in settlement patterns, particularly in the Coastal Plain, seem to indicate an emphasis on the use of areas with predictable water resources and other faunal and floral resources in the face of the dry conditions of the mid-postglacial xerothermic. Small sites away from riverine and swamp areas

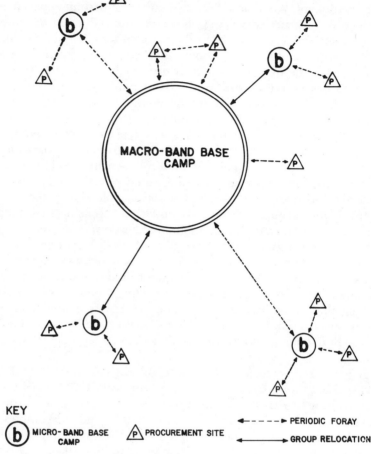

Fig. 11. Woodland I settlement system.

still existed as part of the settlement pattern; however, they were not as numerous as the nonriverine components of the Archaic settlement pattern in most areas.

In some ways, the Woodland I settlement system is similar to the preceding Archaic system in that both systems are oriented around macroband base camps making periodic forays and population movements to smaller microband base camps and procurement sites. Some population adjustments to resource variations were also probably still in existence. Nevertheless, some significant changes had happened. For one thing, macroband base camps of the Woodland I period were much larger than those of the Archaic period and were also much larger than other components of the settlement system. Also, the ratio of macro- to microband base camps would have increased and the variety of activities carried out at procurement sites decreased. The variety of activities at macroband base camps, on the other hand, would show a corresponding increase. In general, the overall tendency was toward an adaptation focusing in one a more specific range of resources and locations with a high degree of predictability.

These settlement pattern changes and the previously mentioned technological changes can be related more specifically to changes in the use of subsistence resources. Reduction of sea level rise rates would have allowed the appearance of large and stable estuarine environments that would have produced shellfish and anadromous fish resources. Freshwater floodplain settings would have produced fish, including anadromous species, deer that would have been drawn to more permanent water sources, and seed plants and other plant foods (Struever 1962, 1965). The addition of plant processing tools attests to the increased importance of plant foods, and the proliferation of broadspear knives and woodworking tools could be linked to the production of specialized tools associated with the procurement of riverine and estuarine resources such as dip nets, fish traps, leisters, and canoes. The addition of stone and ceramic containers is also linked to these general trends. Gardner (1975, 20), who notes that the earliest stone bowls and ceramic containers appeared at large base camps, sees them used for cooking and storage. Increased cooking efficiency would allow the extraction of more nutrients from food sources, and the storage of some food sources would increase the seasonal availability of certain foods. The effect would be to increase the efficiency of energy extraction from food sources and the intensification of the use of limited ranges of especially predictable resources.

Reduction of the variety of resources utilized and the intensification of the use of certain subsistence resources produced focal adaptations (Cleland 1976) and had important effects upon population growth and movement. Intensification through use of storage would allow groups to remain sedentary for longer periods of time and increased efficiency of energy extraction from food sources would allow the support of higher population densities. Consequently, as groups became more sedentary, spacing of births and population control, which are critical factors for mobile hunters and gatherers, became less important. The result, marked population growth, has been recognized in the Virginia Coastal Plain by Turner (1978). If amalgamation of several bands into single social units at large macroband base camps were combined with the population growth within individual social units, the potential for relatively high local population densities was great.

The development of these higher population densities at macroband base camps created the major modification of the social environment that distinguishes the Woodland I period from the other periods of Delaware's prehistory. Prior to Woodland I, societies in Delaware would have been classified as egalitarian (Fried 1967). If a special status was recognized, such as hunting leader, it was associated with an individual whose personal achievements qualified him for that special status. Furthermore, if there were a number of people who had the proper qualifications, there were enough special statuses so that all qualified individuals could hold a special status position. As local populations grew during Woodland I, the number of individuals qualified for special statuses would also grow. However, the number of special status positions would have been likely to decrease. Intensification of food production, use of storage, and sedentary lifestyles would require a greater coordination of efforts, and the efficiency of a coordinating system would be enhanced by a reduction in the number of conflicting managers. This is not to say that a single individual would emerge as a "chief," but the number of high status leadership positions would decrease. The decrease in the number of leadership positions and the increase in qualified individuals created an imbalance in the egalitarian organization, so additional factors came into play when individuals were selected for higher status positions. When kinship or the number of political supporters help select an individual for a high-status position, the egalitarian system is transformed into a ranked system (Fried 1967). I suggest that during the Clyde Farm and Barker's Landing complexes, societies in Delaware were in the process of making the transition from egalitarian to ranked societies, due to increased local population densities. Some groups would move farther in the transition and others would never really change their egalitarian organization. Why these differences exist presents an interesting question for anthropologists. Some of the explanations seem to be based on processes that begin during the initial portion of the Woodland I period.

One manifestation of the shift from egalitarian to ranked societies is the appearance of well-developed trade and exchange systems. Binford (1962) analyzed societies in the Great Lakes area that were subject to similar social environmental changes at a similar time period. He noted that as population grew, the degree of personal acquaintance with other members of the social group decreased and symbols became an important part of communication. Symbols were especially important in distinguishing between individuals of different statuses, and the use of raw materials not native to the local area to manufacture certain items was one way of conveying differential status. Given that groups were becoming less mobile during Woodland I, exotic raw materials would have had to be procured through trade and exchange. Custer (n.d.) provides a complete explanation of the development of this exchange elsewhere.

Winters (1968) and others (Fitting and Brose 1970) have noted the existence of widespread trade networks in the eastern United States involving materials such as native copper and marine shell. In the Middle Atlantic, many distinctive raw materials of limited natural distribution have been spread over large areas by trade and exchange. Two types of exchange patterns are evident. The first seems to be a return to a preference for cryptocrystalline materials. Certain broadspear projectile point forms were manufactured almost exclusively from special cryptocrystalline materials, with the prime example being the Perkiomen broadspear manufactured from high-quality jasper noted in general by Witthoft (1953) and documented specifically by Kraft (1970, 60–65) at the Miller Field site. A second pattern is focused on noncryptocrystalline materials for other broadspear point forms. Examples would include argillite used for the manufacture of Lehigh/Koens-Crispin points as documented at the Savich Farm site in New Jersey (Rengensburg 1970) and the manufacture of Susquehanna broadspear points from rhyolite. Special use of rhyolite has an especially widespread distribution, ranging from a south central Pennsylvania heartland (Witthoft 1953, Kinsey 1977b, 385–87, Stewart 1980a, 1980b) to the Frost Island complex of New York State (Ritchie and Funk 1973, 71–73) to the Upper Delaware (Kinsey 1972, 427) and to the Coastal Plain (Gardner 1975, 20). Also linked to the system of widespread lithic materials for the manufacture of certain projectile point styles is the common use of steatite for the manufacture of stone bowls (Ritchie and Funk 1973, 71–73).

Dating from the time of the Clyde Farm and Barker's Landing complexes, argillite, rhyolite, and steatite artifacts have been found in many areas of Delaware. Usually, these nonlocal materials are found at macroband base camps; however, their distribution is not uniform throughout the state, which provides the distinction between the Clyde Farm and the Barker's Landing complexes. The highest concentrations of nonlocal materials during the first part of the Woodland I period occur along the Saint Jones and Murderkill drainages of Kent County, whose sites comprise the Barker's Landing complex. The remaining sites in Delaware dating to between 3000 B.C. and 500 B.C. make up the Clyde Farm complex.

The Clyde Farm complex is best represented in New Castle County, where several macroband base camps are noted. The Clyde Farm site (7NC-E-6) is one of the largest extant macroband base camp sites in Delaware and provides many of the distinctive characteristics of the Clyde Farm complex, as originally defined by Thomas (1977, 53). The Clyde Farm site, located in the Interior Swamp zone adjacent to the confluence of Churchman's Marsh and the White Clay Creek, was noted in chapter 3 as a location of a macroband base camp during the Archaic period. At that time Churchman's Marsh was most likely a freshwater swamp. However, if extrapolations are made from Belknap and Kraft's (1977) sea level rise curve, it becomes apparent that Churchman's Marsh was probably invaded by saltwater some time after 2500 B.C. The estuarine tidal marsh thus created would be even more rich than the freshwater swamp and would provide a wider range of resources.

Archaeological research at the Clyde Farm site has been carried out over the years by a number of individuals and is of varied quality and usefulness. Crozier (1938b) notes that large numbers of artifacts were found at the site and indicates that it was a favorite haunt of the local Indian artifact collectors. Excavated and surface materials from the site are on deposit at the Island Field Museum, where I recently reexamined the collection (Custer 1981). My inspection showed that Clyde Farm was a large macroband base camp for most of the Woodland I period, although the heaviest occupation seemed to have been prior to 500 B.C. A wide range of tool types, including many ground stone tools, indicate many activities carried out at the base camp site. Large amounts of lithic debris and unfinished bifaces are also common, and reduction of local cobbles and manufacture of tools seemed to have been an important activity. Experimental ceramics, including Marcey Creek and Dames Quarter Black Stone Tempered, and stone bowl fragments have been reported from good stratigraphic context (Custer 1981), which further supports the macroband base camp description. Artifacts from the site also include a variety of tools made from nonlocal materials, including rhyolite from central Pennsylvania and argillite from the Triassic formations of Pennsylvania and New Jersey, which indicates participation in supralocal exchange networks.

Probably the most striking feature of the Clyde Farm site is its large size. Although some of the site has been destroyed by borrow pitting, analysis of the original field notes of some of the earlier excavations and Crozier's (1938b) description seems to indicate that the densest accumulations of artifacts are scattered over an area 2 kilometers long and .5 kilometers wide. Within this area are "hot spots" of very dense concentrations; however, throughout the entire one-square-kilometer area artifacts are abundant. Outside of the major area smaller concentrations are also noted. Reanalysis of old excavation notes and additional excavations by the University of Delaware Department of Anthropology (Custer 1981) have revealed that although much of the site has been disturbed by plowing, many areas still contain buried and intact remains. It is possible that the richest areas of Clyde Farm represent only the areas where deposits of artifacts are shallow and have been brought to the surface by plowing. Additional artifacts that are buried below the level of plow disturbance may be located outside the major concentration area. In any event, the large number of artifacts distributed over a wide area with some especially dense concentrations seems to indicate a series of periodically revisited camp sites that supported multiple social units. Even if only a small fraction of the total potential campsites were inhabited at the same time, the population would have been at least four to five times as dense as that during Archaic times.

The Delaware Park site (7NC-E-41), located approximately 3 kilometers upstream along the White Clay Creek from the Clyde Farm site, also seems to represent a macroband base camp site of the Clyde Farm complex in the Interior Swamp zone. Excavated by Ron Thomas (1981) as part of a salvage operation funded by the Delaware Department of Transportation, the Delaware Park site was occupied throughout the Woodland I period, with the heaviest use of the site after 500 B.C. Nevertheless, substantial remains from the Clyde Farm complex occupation were found. Especially interesting features were two semisubterranean pithouses that were radiocarbon dated to 1850 B.C. (UGa-3440) and 790 B.C. (UGa-3559). A ground stone grooved axe and a series of bifaces dated to 1850 B.C. were associated with the structure, and a stemmed point was associated with the 790 B.C. date. Two additional features that appear to be hearths were dated to 740 B.C. (UGa-3469) and 730 B.C. (UGa-3466). Thomas (1981, chap. 5:4) also notes that a variety of Bare Island/Lackawaxen stemmed points, broadspears, and fishtail points were found at the site, further indicating the existence of a Clyde Farm complex occupation. The presence of the pithouses is interesting because it indicates that relatively substantial investments of energy were being made to produce dwellings, which were more typical of semisedentary occupations at macroband base camps than they were of transient activities. Because only the portion of the site to be destroyed by construction of a highway bridge was excavated, the relative size and population of the site is not known.

The floodplains and upper terraces of the Delaware River at its confluences with higher order drainages in the Delaware Shore zone are also the settings of macroband base camps of the Clyde Farm complex. The largest of these sites is the Crane Hook site (7NC-E-18), which was described in chapter 3. Descriptions of artifacts from the site (Crozier 1934, 1938a; Anonymous 1939; Weslager 1941, 1968, 105–14; Swientochowski and Weslager 1942) indicate that Crane Hook was at least as large, if not larger than, the Clyde Farm site (Crozier 1934, 1938a). Many different tool types are described in the several reports, along with some indications that early ceramics were present. Further examination of the artifacts might reveal additional insights; unfortunately it comprises the only source of further data from the site, which has been destroyed by commercial development. An especially interesting feature from the site is a collection of argillite bifaces buried in a pit (Weslager 1968, 106–7). This collection, termed a *cache,* shows a special treatment of nonlocal materials different from their simple use as raw materials for tool production. This special treatment seems to underscore the symbolic role that nonlocal materials played.

A site similar to Crane Hook has been reported at the mouth of Naaman's Creek in the Delaware Shore zone of northern New Castle County (7NC-C-2). Crozier (1940) and Weslager (1968, 118–19) describe the wide range of artifacts found at the site and note the existence of a cache of argillite bifaces similar to the one found at Crane Hook. A portion of the collection from this site is housed at the Smithsonian Institution and recent examinations of the collection (Galasso 1981) seem to indicate that the cache could date to before 500 B.C., based on the similarity of the bifaces to large broadspear forms. An additional feature of the Naaman's

Creek site is its association with a series of wooden stakes found in buried marsh deposits. Hilbourne T. Cresson (1892) reported the stakes and originally viewed them as part of a series of pilings that might have supported a village that extended out into the Delaware River. Furthermore, Cresson thought that the pilings dated to the same period as his "Holly Oak pendant" with its inscribed mastodon (See chapter 2). In some ways, the circumstances of the finding of the pilings are similar to those of the shell and are therefore somewhat suspect. Reexamination of the pilings (Galasso 1981) suggests that it would be more accurate to call them stakes and that their pre-Columbian origin is not assured. However, taking the generous view that the stakes are truly prehistoric artifacts, it is possible that they were part of a fish trap, or weir. Similar weirs have been found in Woodland I contexts in New England (Johnson 1942, 1949), and it is possible that these stakes were associated with the Clyde Farm complex artifacts in the collection. Unfortunately, the site has been destroyed and the question must remain open.

South of the Chesapeake and Delaware Canal, sites that are clearly macroband base camps of the Clyde Farm complex are difficult to identify due to a lack of data. However, in a few locations some potential macroband base camps can be identified in the Mid-Drainage zone. In a recent survey of a sewer line between Middletown and Odessa, Gardner and Stewart (1978) identified several large sites that contained stemmed points and no early ceramics. These sites were quite large and contained a variety of tool types. A reexamination of these sites and others in the local area (Custer and Wells 1981; Wells et al. 1981; Wells 1981) suggested that these sites might be macroband base camps of the Clyde Farm complex. Most of the sites have not been subject to subsurface testing; therefore, further work is necessary before their identification can be completely assured. One interesting feature of the reanalysis of the sites from the Middletown-Odessa area of the Appoquinnimink drainages was a statistical analysis of site locations using a technique called a logistical regression (Wells 1981). This analysis showed that up to half of the variation in site locations was accounted for by the placement of the sites with respect to available surface water. Minor components of the variation were accounted for by variables such as soil types, slope, and gradient. The implication of the analysis is that water resources were critical during early Woodland I and that the site placement was strongly affected by the dry environments encountered during the midpostglacial xerothermic.

The recognition of Clyde Farm complex sites south of the Murderkill drainage is somewhat problematic. Some Bare Island/Lackawaxen and broadspear points and stone bowls (Hutchinson 1966) are seen in collections from Sussex County. The assignment of the sites that produced these artifacts to the Clyde Farm complex is underscored by the fact that the large quantities of nonlocal materials that characterize the Barker's Landing complex sites are not found in Sussex County. Two possible macroband base camp locations can be hypothesized, however, based on environmental analysis. The Interior Swamp zone surrounding Burnt and Cedar swamps is one possible location for Clyde Farm complex macroband base camps. The environmental setting of these swamps is somewhat similar to the Churchman's Marsh area of New Castle County (see chapter 1), and similar site distributions around the swamps might be expected. Stream confluences along interior drainages in the Chesapeake Headwater Drainage zone may also be possible settings for macroband base camps. Five sites (7S-E-2, 7S-E-32, 7S-H-1, 7S-H-2, 7S-H-3) are noted at these interior settings; however, the artifacts from the sites seem to cover the entire time range of the Woodland I period. Although these sites do seem to have a wider range of tool types than would be expected at microband base camps or procurement sites, further research is necessary to provide a clearer understanding of the area.

Microband base camps of the Clyde Farm complex, and all of the other Woodland I complexes for that matter, are difficult to identify. By definition these sites are smaller, contain fewer tool types and artifacts, and are unlikely to contain diagnostic artifacts such as ceramics. Consequently, they are not very visible as archaeological remains. Following the model of site locations described earlier, they are also fewer in number relative to base camps, further reducing their visibility. However, expected locations for microband base camps can be hypothesized, based on the previous analysis of settlement patterns from the early Woodland I period in other areas of the Middle Atlantic. Microband base camps are most likely to be located close to resource settings that are somewhat unique and located far enough from macroband base camps to make likely the development of a separate camp. These special resource settings would include rich hunting and gathering locales and lithic sources.

Some other possible Clyde Farm microband base camps can also be identified; however, they are usually multicomponent and may also date to later portions of the Woodland I period. The Green Valley sites located in the Fall Line zone (7NC-D-54, 7NC-D-55, 7NC-D-62) in New Castle County provide an especially good example of a Clyde Farm microband base camp associated with a lithic source. The complex is located adjacent to large cobble deposits and was subjected to controlled surface collections and test excavations. Although most of the sites had been disturbed by plowing, the controlled surface collection techniques allowed for the reconstruction of activity areas at the sites. Analysis of the artifacts (Custer et al. 1981) shows that the most intensive use of the site was during the Clyde Farm complex time with some later Woodland I artifacts present. Tool production areas are obvious by large amounts of lithic debris, bifaces and other tools that were broken during early stages of manufacture, and hammerstones. Living areas are characterized by hearths, discarded exhausted tools, and a generally higher incidence of varied tool classes. The Green Valley sites are distinguished as microband base camps because their size and range of artifacts is less than one-tenth that of sites like Clyde Farm.

A second series of sites that might qualify as microband base camps are sites 7NC-E-3, 7NC-E-23, and 7NC-E-24 in the Interior Swamp zone. These sites, excavated by the Delaware section of Archaeology (1975) as part of a survey of a sewer line between Newport and Christiana, are located on the north side of the Christiana River downstream from Churchman's Marsh. Researchers found hearths and some varied tool types; however, the sites seem to be quite small. They could represent microband base camps associated with fishing or gathering locales separate from the macroband base camp at Clyde Farm. Site 7NC-F-1 at the confluence of Dragon Creek and the Delaware River in the Delaware Shore zone seems to be a similar site, as are some of the sites noted by Gardner and Stewart (1978) in the Middletown-Odessa area. There are insufficient data to recognize microband base camps of the Clyde Farm complex in Sussex County, although some are projected for the Burnt Swamp/Cedar Swamp area.

Procurement sites are even more difficult to recognize than microband base camps for the Clyde Farm complex. Occupations are only ephemeral, tool types are limited, the range of artifacts would very rarely include ceramics, and only rarely would the site produce projectile points to indicate to which of the Woodland I complexes the area would belong. In general, those procurement sites of the Woodland I period that can be identified are similar in their location and composition, within the Coastal Plain zones, to Archaic procurement sites. Because there are so few procurement sites and their identification by complex is problematic, all Woodland I procurement sites are discussed here as a unit.

High Coastal Plain drainage divides contain a variety of procurement sites that show a continuity of locations with Archaic sites. Examples would include 7NC-D-3, 7NC-D-5, 7NC-D-19, 7NC-F-18, and 7NC-H-2. Upper terraces of the Delaware Shore zone, with associated marshes and swamps, also include procurement sites such as 7NC-G-2, 7NC-G-3, 7NC-G-6, and 7K-A-2 and 7K-B-8 on the Leipsic Marsh. Similarly, interior swamps include procurement sites such as 7NC-D-21, 7NC-D-27, the Woods sites near Churchman's Marsh (7NC-E-36, 7NC-E-37, 7NC-E-38), and 7K-E-43 on the Upper Choptank. Some bay/basin features in the Midpeninsular Drainage Divide zone have Woodland I procurement sites such as 7NC-J-1, 7NC-J-2, 7NC-J-3, and 7K-F-40. However, there are not as many as during preceding periods, even though continuity with Archaic patterns is seen at the Late Archaic sites noted above. Kavanaugh (1979) notes similar patterns along the upper Chester River in Maryland. The remaining location for Woodland I procurement sites is interior low order drainage floodplains of the Chesapeake Headwater zone. Examples would include 7K-E-12, 7K-G-14, 7S-J-14, and 7S-K-14.

Up to this point, I have not discussed Clyde Farm sites of the Piedmont Uplands because the shifts in settlement patterns associated with the mid-postglacial xerothermic climates of the Piedmont Uplands are somewhat different from the shifts for the Coastal Plain. Nevertheless, the process of the adaptation is the same. Custer and Wallace (1982) note that during Woodland I there were two basic site types. One corresponded to macroband base camps and was usually located on the well-drained ground closest to a sinkhole complex of a swampy floodplain. These sites are quite large, up to a hectare in area, and contain anywhere from hundreds to thousands of artifacts. The Mitchell site (7NC-A-2) is one example and has produced a wide range of tool types, a variety of projectile point forms—including stemmed Bare Island/Lackawaxen forms, Long points, and broadspears of all types—experimental ceramics, and evidence of tool production (Custer 1981). Unfortunately, most of the site has been disturbed by plowing. Two sites in Pennsylvania, the Webb site (36-CH-51) near Avondale (Custer 1982) and the Minguannan site (36-CH-3) near Stricklersville (Wilkins 1978), contain similar remains; however, at both of these sites artifacts were buried deeply enough to avoid disturbance by plowing. Since intact remains from both sites contain the same range of artifacts and ceramics reported for the Mitchell site, the two areas would also be classified as macroband base camps.

The second type of site found in the Piedmont Uplands during Woodland I includes a series of small sites with only a very few artifacts. A survey of a proposed Limestone Hills housing development in northern New Castle County (Custer 1980b) revealed a number of these sites. Locations of these sites are usually on the slopes of knolls adjacent to low order drainages. Artifact assemblages include fewer than 20 flakes, a projectile point or two, and possibly a broken ground stone tool. Excavations of a similar site with a similar inventory has been reported for the Piedmont Uplands of Lancaster County by Kinsey and Custer (1982). Custer and Wallace (1982) note that it is difficult to assign exact series of activities at these sites, and the locations probably are very ephemeral procurement sites. No microband base camps in the Piedmont Uplands have been identified for any time period.

The relationship between the two types of sites is described by Custer and Wallace (1982), who suggest that this pattern of sites is associated with what Binford (1980, 8–10) has called a "tethered nomadism," in which groups center their wandering ranges around a single fixed critical resource and make only occasional forays to other resource locations as needed. In the Piedmont Uplands during Woodland I the critical resource would have been surface water. In chapter 1, I note that since large drain-

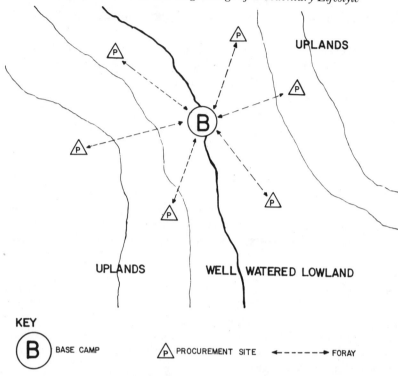

Fig. 12. Woodland I settlement system—Piedmont Uplands.

age systems are not common in the Piedmont Uplands, in the face of dry conditions many of these smaller surface water settings can be expected to carry a smaller volume of water. Higher-order drainages and sinkhole areas would have been the most predictable water sources and formed the focus of the Woodland I settlement pattern in the Piedmont Uplands. This adaptation to the dry conditions of the midpostglacial xerothermic is somewhat similar to the processes noted for the Coastal Plain in that there is an emphasis on the locations where resources are most predictable. However, the significant difference is that since in the Piedmont Uplands the interior high-order floodplains and the sinkhole settings are not as productive as those of the Coastal Plain settings, the factors that allowed population growth in the Coastal Plain would not be present in the Piedmont Uplands. Consequently, although macroband base camps of the Woodland I period in the Piedmont Uplands are larger than the preceding Archaic sites, they do not show the large population increases that mark the differences between Archaic and early Woodland I sites in the Coastal Plain areas. It is interesting to note that some of the macroband camps of the Clyde Farm complex in the Piedmont Uplands do show some indications of participation in supralocal trade and exchange networks. Rhyolite and argillite broadspears and stemmed points are noted at the Mitchell site (Custer

1981), implying that the local population densities in the Piedmont Uplands were still high enough to make participation in trade and exchange networks and use of symbolic communication of status necessary. It should also be noted that the source of much of the steatite used in the manufacture of stone bowls is found in the Pennsylvania and Maryland Piedmont (Wilkins 1962; Holland et al. 1981). The participation of Clyde Farm complex groups in exchange systems may be related to their role in procuring steatite and producing the early forms of the stone bowls.

The Barker's Landing complex shows a settlement-subsistence pattern similar to the Clyde Farm complex, from which it is distinguished by its high proportion of artifacts made from nonlocal materials. Two macroband base camps are noted in the Mid-drainage zone: the Barker's Landing site (7K-D-13), located along the Saint Jones River, and the Coverdale site (7K-F-38) on the Murderkill River. In general, the locations of Barker's Landing complex macroband base camps in the Mid-drainage zone are similar to the locations of Clyde Farm macroband base camps. If Belknap and Kraft's (1977) sea level rise curve is projected back to early Woodland I times, the locations of the Coverdale and Barker's Landing sites fall at the freshwater/saltwater interface of the Murderkill and Saint Jones drainages, respectively. This interface of different environments in the Mid-drainage zone would represent one of the most productive environmental settings in central Delaware during the midpostglacial xerothermic. Since the water resources would be highly predictable, the addition of rich estuarine resources in the immediate area would make the Mid-drainage zone portions of the Murderkill and Saint Jones rivers much richer than any surrounding areas. Consequently, the potential for population growth of local groups and in-migration of other social units during the midpostglacial xerothermic is as high as at the macroband base camps of the Clyde Farm complex in the Interior Swamp and Delaware Shore zones.

In spite of these similarities, some significant differences between macroband base camps of these complexes can be noted. For one, the Barker's Landing camps are not as large as the Clyde Farm ones. Also, the area of especially high productivity along the Mid-drainage zone of the Murderkill and Saint Jones drainages is not as large as the high productivity areas of the Interior Swamp and Delaware Shore zones. Furthermore, the difference in productivity between the rich Mid-drainage zones of central Kent County and surrounding areas is greater than the difference in productivity between high productivity areas of the Interior Swamp and Delaware Shore zones and surrouding areas. In general, the Mid-drainage zone of central Kent County is a very attractive habitat that is spatially limited and distinct from surrounding areas. This special circumscribed environmental setting helped to create a social environment slightly different from that of the Clyde Farm complex sites.

When the smaller size of the Barker's Landing complex macroband base camps and their supporting environments was coupled with the potential for population growth associated with sedentism, higher local population densities resulted. I suggest that as populations grew, intensification of food production would have been necessary. Certainly the rich estuarine environments would have supported this intensification. In the face of need for greater production, which would have been intensive shellfish harvesting and gathering, and higher population densities, the shift from egalitarian to ranked systems was probably further advanced than in Clyde Farm complex sites. In addition, the trade and exchange systems that provided the raw materials for the status symbols associated with ranking were no doubt more highly developed. Harris (1979, 2) notes that intensification of food production may have also provided temporary surpluses—for example, an especially rich collection of shellfish or plant foods—that were at the disposal of certain members of the society. These surpluses may have been used to "invest" in status symbols or accumulations of nonlocal raw materials. An elaboration of trade and exchange networks would have accompanied these changes, and a proliferation of nonlocal materials, accompanied by special treatment of these artifacts, should be seen in the archaeological record if these changes were really taking place. I contend here that at Barker's Landing complex macroband base camps the processes of production intensification and the elaboration of trade and exchange of materials that would function as status symbols had begun and developed to a point far beyond that seen at Clyde Farm complex sites. The evidence for this assertion is presented below.

The Barker's Landing site 7K-D-13 is the most thoroughly studied of the Barker's Landing macroband base camp sites. Controlled surface collections and subsurface excavations have been carried out at the site and analysis of these materials is (as of 1982) underway at the University of Delaware Department of Anthropology. Preliminary results show some interesting patterns. The most common lithic raw material found at the site is argillite, and the closest outcrops to Delaware are in the Middle Delaware River Valley, where quarry locations are well documented (Kinsey 1975). Argillite weathers very rapidly and is seldom, if ever, found in the cobble beds of the Delaware River (Custer and Galasso 1980; Spoljaric 1967; Spoljaric and Woodruff 1970). Therefore, the argillite from Barker's Landing must have been procured through trade and exchange. Even if special trips to quarry sources were made, supralocal interpersonal relationships would have played an important role in the argillite procurement. Rhyolite artifacts have also been found at Barker's Landing site and Stewart (1980a, 1980b) has documented the closest natural sources and quarries, which are in the Blue Ridge Physiographic zone of Maryland and Pennsylvania. In both cases some form of supralocal relationships with other individuals or groups would have been necessary to allow the movement of these raw materials over such great distances.

Both Bare Island/Lackawaxen and broadspear forms were manufactured from these nonlocal raw materials; however, broadspear forms, mainly Lehigh/Koens Crispin varieties, outnumber the Bare Island/Lackawaxen forms by two or three to one. Only occasionally were projectile points manufactured from anything other than argillite and rhyolite. The cobble cherts and jaspers present were primarily used for the production of flake tools from small prepared cores. Large numbers of early- and late-stage argillite bifaces, many with signs of manufacturing flaws and errors, are also present, along with large quantities of argillite chipping debris. Some large flakes removed from prepared cores are present; however, the majority of the flakes are bifacial thinning flakes that are quite thin, indicating later stages of biface production (Callahan 1979). These artifacts indicate that argillite was brought into central Delaware in the form of large primary bifaces and prepared cores. Production of late-stage bifaces and finished tools, particularly broadspears, was then carried out. Barker's Landing seems to be a production center where argillite was processed into usable forms and then redistributed.

Steatite from the Piedmont zones of Pennsylvania and Maryland (Wilkins 1962; Holland et al. 1981, 203–304) is also relatively abundant at Barker's landing. A few pieces of experimental ceramics, mainly Marcey Creek Plain, are the only other containers represented at the site, indicating a site date of about 2000 B.C. to 700 B.C. The steatite artifacts from the site are primarily fragments of finished bowls and there are no indications of stone bowl production. The processes of trade, exchange, and production of steatite artifacts, therefore, would seem to have a different organization from the argillite system. Insufficient data exist to characterize the rhyolite system.

Artifacts from the Coverdale site (7K-F-38), which includes only uncontrolled surface collection material, are similar to those from Barker's Landing. Large quantities of argillite and rhyolite are present, although no steatite was noted. The Coverdale collections are revealing in that several large early-stage argillite bifaces are present. These bifaces are up to 23 centimenters (9 inches) long and some weigh up to 3 pounds. Many have little or no modification on one face and appear to be very large flakes that were removed from very large prepared cores. Initial edging produced an oval shape and a regular edge. Since further modification of these artifacts was never carried out, I contend that they represent the form in which argillite was produced, traded, and exchanged. The absence of further modifications of these particular bifaces indicates that special treatment of argillite artifacts was beginning to appear. A number of late-stage argillite bifaces that resemble large Koens Crispin points and that show similar trends have also been found at the Coverdale site. These artifacts do not appear to have been used as tools because there are no small flakes indicating material removed from edges of these bifaces. The flakes from the final production of the edges are visible, which indicates that weathering has not artifically produced an absence of edge wear.

Examination of microband base camps and procurement sites shows some additional information concerning the use of argillite, rhyolite, and steatite. A number of sites along the Saint Jones and the Murderkill drainages that seem to be microband base camps and procurement sites of the Barker's Landing complex were discovered during an archaeological survey of the proposed Dover bypass corridor (Griffith and Artusy n.d.). Most of the examples come from the Murderkill drainages, and seven sites seem to represent microband base camps (7K-F-12, 7K-F-45, 7K-F-46, 7K-F-49, 7K-F-52, 7K-F-53, 7K-F-55). These sites are all located along the Murderkill, upstream from the macroband base camp. They are on slight rises above the old floodplains, which are now inundated marshes, and seem to represent camp sites associated with especially good hunting and gathering locations. Because they are upstream from the macroband base camps they would probably be associated with especially productive freshwater habitats. No similar sites are noted along the Saint Jones, which is due to an absence of surveys. On the other hand, systematic surveys have been carried out on Saint Jones neck downstream from the Barker's Landing site (Delaware Division of Historical and Cultural Affairs 1978), and in these areas two microband base camps of the Barker's Landing complex were discovered (K-D-42, 7K-D-52). These two sites would have been camps associated with especially productive salt or brackish water environments. No comparable sites are known for the Murderkill, but again sporadic survey coverage is the most likely explanation. A number of procurement sites are also noted for both the Saint Jones drainage (7K-C-33, 7K-C-53, 7K-C-57) and the Murderkill Drainage (7K-F-37, 7K-F-44, 7K-F-47, 7K-F-48), as well as adjacent areas of the Midpeninsular Drainage Divide zone (7K-F-40). All of these sites are upstream from the macroband base camps and seem to be associated with the hunting and gathering of freshwater resources.

Artifacts from the microband base camps do not appear in as large quantities as at macroband base camps, but they do contain a variety of tools. Procurement sites are even smaller and show fewer tool types. Argillite, rhyolite, and steatite all appear at the microband base camps. Projectile points, some bifaces, and flakes indicative of tool maintenance from argillite and rhyolite are found at microband base camps, and projectile points are the only artifacts manufactured from nonlocal materials found at procurement sites. Steatite bowl fragments are found only at microband base camps. The distribution of nonlocal materials indicates that much of the argillite that was processed at sites like Barker's Landing and Coverdale was redistributed and used for the manufacture of tools that were carried and used throughout the series of sites that comprised the settlement system. Binford (1962) proposed the term *technomic* to refer to artifacts that were created to deal directly with the physical environment; it seems clear that most of the artifacts manufactured from nonlocal materials of the Barker's Landing complex, and probably the Clyde Farm complex as well, were used for technomic functions.

Nevertheless, artifacts may also be used for other functions. Binford (1962) also notes that they may function as status symbols that help to articulate individuals into cohesive social groups capable of efficiently maintaining themselves and of manipulating technology. As was noted previously, the population pressure, intensification of food production, and shifts from egalitarian social systems to ranked social systems during early Woodland I created social environments in which symbolic communication, especially of differential status, would be useful. Artifacts manufactured from nonlocal raw materials at Clyde Farm and Barker's Landing complex sites have both technomic and sociotechnic functions. In the Barker's Landing macroband base camps, the needs for symbolic communication would have been even greater because of more use of estuarine resources and higher population densities, so sociotechnic functions would have become relatively more important than technomic functions.

Analysis of sites throughout the Middle Atlantic dating to the early Woodland I period shows how the technomic and sociotechnic functions and developing trade and exchange networks would be linked into a single system. First, broadspear projectile point styles show a surprising uniformity over most of the Middle Atlantic area (Turnbaugh 1975). The distinctive characteristic, as noted earlier, is a very high width/thickness ratio (6 or greater). It would be easiest to attain these ratios by using high-quality materials such as cryptocrystalline materials or rhyolite and argillite, as opposed to grainier materials such as quartzite or siltstones or nonhomogeneous fracture-prone materials such as quartz. Similarly, primary raw materials would more easily provide the large flakes and bifaces needed for the manufacture of broadspears, as opposed to cobble sources (Custer and Galasso 1980). Thus, participation in exchange networks would provide an adaptive advantage by providing ready access to high-quality raw materials for production of broadspear knives. These knives could then be used in the manufacture of the specialized tools needed to utilize estuarine resources. Such an advantage would be crucial among the coastal Woodland I societies of Delaware. The adaptive advantage of the exchange network participation would have also been enhanced by the fact that an increase in the availability of nonlocal materials would facilitate the symbolic communication of status. As local populations grew and food production intensified, the adaptive advantage of symbolic communication would be further enhanced (Custer n.d.). Following Harris's (1979) argument, as surpluses became available, trade would be further elaborated, ranked aspects of social organization would become more prevalent, and more complex forms of management organization would arise. In sum, the artifacts manufactured from exotic raw materials initially would be useful as technomic items, but in time they would begin to have sociotechnic significance.

I suggest here that at the Barker's Landing and Coverdale sites the transformation of artifact into symbols was taking place during early Woodland I times. The unreduced primary bifaces and unused finished tools are the first major indicators of a complete change in artifact function. An even clearer indication of the transformation from technomic functions to sociotechnic functions is evident at the Kiunk Ditch site (7K-F-18). Omwake (1955) reports that a cache of 156 primary argillite bifaces was found in an isolated pit feature. The bifaces are identical to the smaller unreduced primary bifaces found at the Coverdale site, and their deposition into an isolated feature indicates the special treatment of artifacts manufactured from exotic raw materials. The small caches also noted for Clyde Farm complex sites represent the emergence of a very specialized treatment of certain classes of artifacts. Removed from the system of tool production, the artifacts show the beginning of a new type of social status symbol. This new type of symbol was neither displayed nor was its access limited to certain people. It was completely removed from public access for variable periods of time.

Organizers of the trade and exchange networks, redistributors of non-local materials, and organizers of intensified food production were the individuals most likely to utilize the symbol systems and make the step toward removing certain goods from public access. Using analogies from living groups of similar social complexity, Harris (1979, 92–94) contends that these high-status individuals were probably adult males who acted as heads of extended families or lineages. By the end of the Barker's Landing complex these individuals had probably begun to establish regularized exchange and redistribution networks for certain classes of artifacts and raw materials. These classes of artifacts received special treatment and in many cases lost their technomic functions entirely. On the other hand, groups of the Clyde Farm complex had not developed regularized trade and exchange and symbolic communication of status, and had not moved as far toward the development of ranked social organizations. In these cases, technomic functions outweighed sociotechnic functions in importance. In one sense, societies of both early Woodland I complexes were moving along the same evolutionary pathway, making the same adjustments to changes in the bio-social environments. Barker's Landing complex societies, however, had moved farther and faster due to selective pressures provided by higher relative population densities within more circumscribed environmental settings (Carniero 1970) requiring greater intensification of production. These developments provided the foundation for the spectacular cultural expressions of the Delmarva Adena complex.

Wolfe Neck Complex and Delmarva Adena Complex

The basic adaptations developed during the Clyde Farm and Barker's Landing complexes continued through the Wolfe Neck and Delmarva Adena complexes (500 B.C.–0 A.D.). The differences between the early Woodland I complexes and the Wolfe Neck and Delmarva Adena complexes are mainly recognized by changes in diagnostic artifact styles, particularly pottery, elaboration of trade and exchange networks in some areas, intensification of food gathering, and use of estuarine resources. The Wolfe Neck complex shows continuity of social processes with the preceding Clyde Farm complex; moreover, their spatial distributions are quite similar (Table 7). Similarly, the social processes and spatial distributions of the Delmarva Adena complex (Thomas 1977) resemble those of the Barker's Landing complexes.

Table 10 shows the distribution of diagnostic artifact styles within the Wolfe Neck and Delmarva Adena complexes. The Wolfe Neck complex is distinguished by the presence of the grit-tempered cord and net-marked ceramics of the Wolfe Neck Ware category and related varieties of the Susquehanna series (Smith 1978). In general, the term *Wolfe Neck* is applied exclusively to these ceramics in the southern portion of Delaware while the term *Susquehanna series* applies to New Castle County. Rossville and other stemmed points accompany Wolfe Neck and Susquehanna series ceramics throughout Delaware. The Delmarva Adena complex is distinguished from the Wolfe Neck complex mainly by the presence of distinctive artifacts very similar in style and raw materials to Adena sites of the Ohio Valley (Griffin 1967). These artifacts are various styles of late-stage bifaces manufactured from raw materials from the Ohio Valley, copper beads, tubular pipes, pendants, gorgets, and side- and corner-notched projectile points (Thomas 1970). Thurman (1978) has noted that it is difficult to define a single ceramic style that is associated with these Adenalike materials; however, in Delaware Coulbourn ceramics and Rossvillelike stemmed points are often found at sites where small amounts of the Ohio cryptocrystalline debitage are recovered. Also, the known distribution of Coulbourn ceramics corresponds to the distribution of sites with distinctive Adena materials, which are generally restricted in Delaware to the Saint Jones and Murderkill drainages, with a scattering of sites further south. These different distributions of artifacts serve as diagnostic indicators of the Wolfe Neck and Delmarva Adena complexes; however, even more important and interesting is the cultural context in which the distinctive Adena material appears. Although some Adena materials are found on what seem to be habitation sites, the great majority of these materials have been recovered from special cemeteries, where they accompany various types of burials (Thomas 1970, 1973a). This context is as important as the distinctive nature of the artifacts themselves and will be examined later.

The settlement system noted for the initial Woodland I complexes can be applied to the habitation sites of the Wolfe Neck and Delmarva Adena complex groups. No macroband base camp sites containing only Wolfe Neck and Delmarva Adena complex artifacts have been identified as yet. On the other hand, Wolfe Neck and Delmarva Adena complex components, or occupations, are noted at most of the sites listed as macroband base camps of the Clyde Farm complex, including the Clyde Farm site (7NC-E-6), the Delaware Park site (7NC-E-41), the Mitchell site (7NC-A-2), the Crane Hook site (7NC-E-18), the Naaman's Creek site (7NC-C-2), the potential sites noted for the Appoquinnimink drainage in southern New Castle County (Gardner and Stewart 1978) and along Burnt Swamp and Cedar Swamp in Sussex County, and the Coverdale site (7K-F-38). Of these sites the Delaware Park site (7NC-E-41) provides the most interesting information concerning the Wolfe Neck complex macroband base camps (Thomas 1981). Four features produced radiocarbon dates that fall within the time range of the Wolfe Neck complex. Two shallow basin-shaped hearths containing flakes were radiocarbon-dated to 480 B.C. (UGa-3561) and 150 B.C. (UGa-3557), and two large cylindrical pits with stemmed points and flakes were dated to 425 B.C. (UGa-3560) and 10 B.C. (UGa-3500). The large cylindrical pits contained pollen from various grass seeds and some seed remains. Based on the presence of these food remains, the inferred function of the pits is storage (Thomas 1981, chap. 5:20), and the indication is that stored foods, most likely plant foods, were part of the subsistence base of Wolfe Neck complex groups at base camps. No similar features were found at other Wolfe Neck complex base camps; however, the features at the Delaware Park site were quite faint and difficult to discern. Therefore, it is possible that similar features were missed at earlier excavations.

The previous discussion of the location and composition of microband base camps and procurement sites for the Clyde Farm and Barker's Landing complexes is also applicable to the microband base camps and procurement sites of the Wolfe Neck and Delmarva Adena complexes. Many of the examples discussed earlier may indeed have been related to these later complexes, rather than to the earlier ones. Some sites that are clearly microband base camps of the Wolfe Neck and Delmarva Adena complexes can be noted. The Wolfe Neck site (7S-D-10), which provides the artifacts for the type description of Wolfe Neck ceramics, is a shell midden site in the Coastal Bay zone of eastern Sussex County (Griffith and Artusy 1977). Excavations at the site showed the use of a variety of shellfish resources (Griffith and Artusy 1977, 5), including periwinkle *(Littorina irrorata)*, mussels *(Modiolus dimissus)*, clams *(Venus mercenaria)*, and oysters *(Ostrea vir-*

giniana). Dates from the site range from 375 B.C. to A.D. 330 (see UGa-1224, UGa-1273a, UGa-1273b in Appendix 1). Griffith and Artusy's excavations were the most recent in a series of excavations at the site (Weslager 1968; Peets 1961, 1962; Marine et al. 1965a, 1966), and rather extensive midden deposits were found. Since this accumulation of shells and debris indicates something more than a procurement site yet something less than the large macroband base camp examples, a microband base camp description seems most likely.

A similar series of midden sites (7S-D-8, 9, 22, 27, 29, 30, and 34) has been noted in the vicinity of Cape Henlopen State Park (Delaware Division of Historical and Cultural Affairs 1976). A series of middens is associated with the recurved sand spits that represent the geological ancestors of Cape Henlopen (Kraft and John 1978). As the sand spits were inundated and reformed by channel currents, prehistoric groups continuously moved their sites toward the brackish water bays that would be rich in shellfish. The resulting series of microband base camps runs from oldest to youngest toward the modern bay coast. The movement of microband base camps as the estuarine environment changed underscores the focused adaptations of the Wolfe Neck and Delmarva Adena complex.

The Wilgus site (7S-K-21) represents a slightly different microband base camp site that contains material from the Delmarva Adena and later Carey complexes. Since the major part of the site seems to date from the Delmarva Adena period, it is therefore discussed here. The Wilgus site was originally tested by the Delaware Bureau of Archaeology and Historic Preservation, and a short report was prepared (Artusy 1978). Radiocarbon dates of 290 B.C. and A.D. 240 (see UGa-1762 and UGa-1763 in Appendix 1) were obtained from shell middens when the site was threatened with destruction by a proposed housing development, and intensive excavations were carried out by the Bureau of Archaeology and the University of Delaware Department of Anthropology. The artifacts are still being analyzed; however, some preliminary results can be noted. The Wilgus site is located in the Coastal Bay zone on White's Neck along a drowned tributary of the Indian River. Reconstruction of the site environment based on plant and animal remains found at the site and on extensive soil auger testing indicated that the knoll area apparently was the best-drained setting in the local area and therefore represented the living area. Broken tools and other artifacts are scattered through the plow zone. Just off the knoll's slope was a series of trash deposits, or middens, each approximately 8 meters in diameter. Some contained large quantities of oyster and clam shells, while others were defined simply by very dark-colored soil zones rich in organic materials.

Because much of the midden area was buried by slope wash over the years, many of these middens were undisturbed by modern agricultural activities. Also, the calcium from the slowly decomposing clam and oyster shells helped to preserve many organic materials including bone, antler, fish scales, and charred seed remains. Excavation techniques used within the intact middens were careful enough to identify the exact positions of all artifacts found within a .5-meter square block. Also, a record was kept of the distribution of oyster and clam shells throughout the midden. These methods were very useful because they enabled a study of the processes of how food remains and discarded artifacts found their way into the midden. One interesting pattern was that the proportion of clams to oysters changed dramatically from one end of the midden to the other. One end was mainly clams, the middle was a mixture of clams and oysters, and the other end was mainly oysters. Because these animals are available during slightly different seasons, it would seem to indicate that the site had been occupied for several seasons. Another pattern that emerged came from a careful analysis of the tools found in the midden. People living at the Wilgus site apparently used small cobbles as cores, or sources for flakes to manufacture tools. These cobbles are very distinctive in color and it is possible to identify the flakes that came from a single core. Through the careful analysis of colors of flakes and the actual piecing back together of cores, we have been able to identify six or seven distinct cores that were used to produce flake tools. Once the flake tools had fulfilled their purpose, they were discarded in the midden. For any of the given cores, the flakes are fairly evenly distributed throughout the entire midden. Because there are few lithic sources in the local area, a core would have been a valuable item, one that would not be discarded if it still were useful. Therefore, the distribution of flakes from a single core across the midden surface that spans several seasons would mean that a single group of people, using the same cores, may have inhabited the site for this period of time.

Faunal remains from the midden also revealed interesting patterns. Mary C. Stiner of the University of New Mexico analyzed all of the faunal remains and identified a number of different food sources, including freshwater fish, deer, various species of turtles, snake, and a variety of birds. The freshwater fish are interesting and indicate that Indian River was not brackish, as it is today. Deer remain were revealing because most of the bones found were skull fragments and leg bones. Body trunk parts were conspicuously absent. Stiner feels that this distribution of body parts could represent the butchering practices of the time. It is likely that trunk parts were consumed at the spot of the kill or perhaps fed to dogs, as Eskimos still do today (Binford 1978). The leg and haunch sections, rich in meat and more transportable than the trunks, would be brought back to the microband base camps. The presence of heads is interesting because the meat value would be low. It is possible, however, that the brains and/or tongue were especially desirable foods, as was the case for many Plains Indian groups, or that the brains were used for the tanning and processing of hides.

A particularly wide range of turtle species and individuals were also found in the middens. Preliminary spatial analysis of the remains also seems to indicate that the turtle remains were found clustered in one end of the midden. Perhaps winter was the best time to gather turtles because they would be buried in the mud hibernating. A wading trip through the marsh with a stick that could be poked into the mud to locate the hard shells would have been a simple food-gathering activity. The wide range of species present seems to support this contention, as does the apparent clustering of the turtle remains at the "oyster" or winter end of one of the middens. Further analysis of seed remains from the site and a closer analysis of the spatial distributions of the extensive ceramic remains should produce further information on seasonal use of the site and the span of occupation. However, it seems reasonable to assume that the Wilgus site was a microband base camp that supported a small social unit, or set of units, across several seasons of the year. Nearby related procurement sites would have been part of the system, and a variety of resources seemed to have been extensively exploited to support the group in a relatively semisedentary existence.

Other Wolfe Neck and Delmarva Adena complex microband base camps include 7NC-E-1, a small site located just downstream from Churchman's Marsh close to macroband base camps of the Clyde Farm complex. A wide range of tool types were found at the site (Custer 1980b) and many of them are ground stone tools associated with specialized plant processing activities. A similar site is the Red Lion Creek site, excavated by the Delmarva Clearinghouse for Archaeology (1975). A functional analysis of tools from this site suggests a late summer to mid-fall occupation. In Kent County, 7K-D-37 and 7NC-D-38 on the lower Saint Jones are considered microband base camps of the Delmarva Adena complex (Delaware Division of Historical and Cultural Affairs 1978) and the exploitation of special estuarine resources is projected for these sites. Finally, a series of sites along the Murderkill that were identified as microband base camp sites of the Barker's Landing complex, also contain large Delmarva Adena complex components, including 7K-F-55, 7K-F-44, 7K-F-54, 7K-F-45, 7K-F-46, 7K-F-47, 7K-F-53, and 7K-F-56 (Griffith and Artusy n.d.).

In general, when habitation and procurement sites are considered, the Wolfe Neck and Delmarva Adena complexes are very similar and show little divergence from the Clyde Farm and Coverdale complexes. There is some increased intensification of estuarine resource exploitation, and the storage features from the Delaware Park site show some intensification of food production. However, the sites from all complexes look very much the same. Even trade and exchange patterns at the habitation sites show little variance among the complexes. If anything, the trade and exchange patterns evidenced at Wolfe Neck and Delmarva Adena base camps look more like the pattern seen at Clyde Farm complex sites. Even in the Saint Jones-

Murderkill area of central Kent County, the heartland of the Barker's Landing complex, the heavy reliance on argillite was not as apparent at habitation sites during Delmarva Adena times. Rhyolite and argillite were still exchanged, and many finished tools from both of these nonlocal materials have been found throughout Delaware. However, the unutilized tools and unreduced primary bifaces of the Barker's Landing complex are no longer present. Similiar trends exist in the Middle Atlantic in general. Turnbaugh (1970) and Handsman and McNett (1974) have documented trade and exchange of rhyolite and argillite for this time period in Pennsylvania and the circum-Chesapeake region, and Stewart's (1980a, 1980b) work at the rhyolite quarry sources shows widespread activity during this period. In these cases the major emphasis seems to be on tools that are primarily technomic in function with only limited sociotechnic meaning. While the flow of material through these networks would have been great and would have helped to stimulate the flow of information (Simms 1979), the patterns of exchange revealed strictly from habitation sites seem to indicate a lower level of sociotechnic meaning and less ranking of the participant social systems than was present during the Barker's Landing complex.

Such a conclusion would be appropriate for the Wolfe Neck complex; however, it would not be accurate for the Delmarva Adena complex. By 500 B.C. a new type of site appears in the Mid-drainage zone of central Delaware associated with the Delmarva Adena complex. These new sites include graves of numerous individuals and contain few, if any, traces of domestic activities. The distinctive Adena artifacts manufactured from a variety of nonlocal materials, including cryptocrystalline lithic materials from Ohio and copper from the Great Lakes, are found at these sites, called mortuary-exchange centers. Thomas (1970, 1976) and Dunn (1966) have described these sites, briefly summarized here.

The Killens Pond site (7K-E-3) is one of the earliest of the mortuary-exchange centers in Delaware to have been discovered and is the most poorly documented. The site was discovered by accident, as is the case for all of these centers, during the excavation of a borrow pit by Delaware State Highway Department crews in 1938 (Thomas 1970, 60). Artifacts from the site were collected by the workmen and systematic data are available on only a portion of those collected. W. O. Cubbage, a member of the Archaeological Society of Delaware, was able to recover some of the artifacts and a report was eventually published (Cubbage 1941). Thomas (1970, 61) notes that the information from the site is quite vague and it seems likely that at least two concentrations of burials of various types were discovered. A variety of large late-stage bifaces manufactured from Flint Ridge Chalcedony were recovered, eight of which were included in a single cache. Gorgets and blocked-end tubular smoking pipes were also recovered (Thomas 1970, 84–85). Only 17 of the artifacts from the original excava-

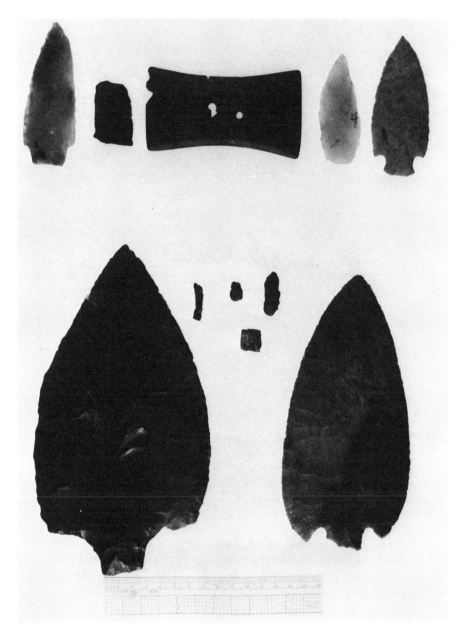

Plate 3. Delmarva Adena complex artifacts. Top row: bifaces of local materials and gorget; center: copper beads; bottom: Flint Ridge chalcedony bifaces. (Courtesy Delaware Division of Historical and Cultural Affairs.)

Plate 4. Delmarva Adena artifacts. Tubular pipes and copper beads. (Courtesy Delaware Division of Historical and Cultural Affairs.)

tions can now be located and subsequent survey of the surrounding area has not revealed any additional Adena-related artifacts. A number of living sites have been located within 2 kilometers of the site and some do contain Coulbourn ceramics, indicating a possible related habitation site. All of these sites seem to be microband base camps and it is important to note that there is no living site immediately adjacent to the cemetery.

Discovered in 1960, the Saint Jones site (7K-D-1) was subject to some controlled excavation and is better known than the Killens Pond site. Thomas (1970, 59) notes that the site was again discovered in a borrow pit. Excavation was carried out by Leon deValinger, Delaware state archivist, and two publications of the original data were produced by deValinger (1970) and Stewart (1970). Since that time, Thomas (1976) has reanalyzed the artifacts and notes from the site. Thomas (1976, 89) notes that approximately 50 burials were excavated and approximately 250 artifacts were recovered. The original notes were recorded in a narrative style and photographs were taken only occasionally; therefore, it is difficult to reconstruct the artifact associations. Nevertheless, Thomas was able to reconstruct the site map and to plot eight burial loci (Thomas 1976, 92, Fig. 2).

Several of the burial loci were inadequately recorded and many were disturbed in the midst of excavations by vandals and "pot-hunters." The more intact loci of burials do provide some contextual information, however, and associations of several large caches are noted. Locus E provided a radiocarbon date of 380 B.C. (Y-933) in association with a series of large bifaces, some of which seem to have been purposely broken. Both nonlocal and local raw materials seem to have been used for the manufacture of these bifaces. Three females and two males in both cremated and noncremated burial treatments were also noted (Thomas 1976, 94). Locus F (Thomas 1976, 94) was comprised of an oval area approximately 4 meters by 2 meters that contained up to 30 individual clusters of cremated bones. Some red ochre was present among the cremations and artifacts, although relatively scarce, included some copper beads and a broken biface. The largest number of artifacts come from Locus G, which contained the remains of at least ten distinct clusters of human bone (Thomas 1976, 94). Red ochre covered some of the numerous bifaces, copper ornaments, beads, and drilled animal teeth. A cache of 170 bifaces, most of Flint Ridge chalcedony, was also noted from Locus G (Thomas 1976, 97). The final locus that was isolated, H, included a series of locally made bifaces and stemmed points and knives (Thomas 1976, 95).

Although interpretation of the data from the Saint Jones site is difficult due to the lack of adequate controls during the excavations, some points can be noted. Thomas (1976, 96) notes that a variety of different burial treatments were noted among the loci with cremation prevalent in some areas and placement of disarticulated unburned bone common in others. Much control over the provenience of the bone specimens was lost between the field and Stewart's analysis of the materials; however, from Thomas's reconstruction it seems as if individuals of a variety of ages and both sexes were found throughout the different loci and seem to show no correlation with any particular burial treatment. Some variance of artifact associations can be seen and Thomas (1976, 96) notes that Loci G and H, which contained high percentages of unburned bone, contained the only two in-situ artifact caches, which also comprised the bulk of the bifaces manufactured from nonlocal materials. Perhaps the richness of the caches associated with the noncremated individuals indicates a higher status. The presence of females and males of various ages, including subadults (Thomas 1976, 106; Stewart 1970), shows that these various higher-status positions were not defined strictly by age and sex, as has been inferred for the Barker's Landing complex. Cremation, on the other hand, associated with a relative absence of the exotic grave goods, may indicate individuals of slightly lower status. Thomas (1973a) also notes that a complex series of stages of interments may be part of the mortuary patterns seen at the Saint Jones site. The mixed nature of some of the cremation burials and other secondary burials suggests that at one time these burials may have been found in some sort of temporary grave facility. Removal from their original graves and reinterment with the uncremated remains in other graves is suggested here. The inferred status difference may indicate that lower-status individuals were reburied and cremated in association with the noncremated burial of higher-status individuals. Similar patterns are noted among later Woodland groups in the Middle Atlantic (Ubelaker 1974).

The Frederica site (7K-F-2), located on the Murderkill River just downstream from the Killens Pond site, is the most recently discovered of the Delmarva Adena mortuary-exchange centers. The site was discovered by excavation of a borrow pit in 1964, and much of it was apparently destroyed. The discovery of the site by highway workmen came to the attention of the Delaware Archaeological Board, which recorded and photographed some of the materials (Thomas 1970, 60; Jones 1965). There were an unknown number of graves located in a circular area approximately 30 meters in diameter, and over 250 artifacts as well as 700 copper beads were found at the site. Thomas (1970, 60) notes that large and small bifaces of both exotic (Ohio Valley) origin and local derivation were present and comprised the majority of the assemblage. Gorgets, blocked-end tubular pipes, and some copper, as well as the large quantities of copper beads, were also present (Thomas 1970, 84–85).

The Adena-related sites in Delaware are not unique in the areas east of the Ohio Valley heartland. Additional Adenalike sites from the Delmarva Peninsula include the Nassawango site (Wise 1974) near Salsibury, Maryland, and the Sandy Hill site (Ford 1976) near Cambridge, Maryland. Other Adena-related sites include the West River site (Ford 1976) near Annapolis, Maryland, and the Rosencrans site (Kraft 1976) in the Upper

Delaware Valley of New Jersey. Similar complexes have also been described from New England (Snow 1980, 268–74). Also, within Delaware and Maryland, as well as surrounding states, there are a number of caches of large secondary bifaces that include artifacts made from local materials as well as Ohio Valley cryptocrystalline materials. These caches are quite different from those described for the Barker's Landing and Clyde Farm complexes in that these later caches are composed primarily of secondary bifaces rather than primary bifaces. Also, in the later caches, argillite is rarely, if ever, present. The caches noted for Delaware are distributed throughout the state and are noted by numerous authors (Weslager 1939a, 5; Marine 1966; Dunn 1966; Howard 1969; Thomas 1973b; Crozier 1934, 4; Flegel 1954; Eggen 1954).

An understanding of the cultural implication of the existence of the Delmarva Adena complex mortuary-exchange centers and the caches that seem to date from similar time periods requires a regional perspective that includes the Ohio Valley heartland for the distribution of Adena materials. In an important overview of eastern North America prehistory, Griffin (1967, 183) notes that the Adena cultures of the Ohio Valley seem to represent an outgrowth of local Archaic complexes with an elaboration of existing forms of mortuary ceremonialism and exchange. In a more recent overview, Tuck (1978, 41) makes a similar assertion and notes the appearance of mortuary ceremonialism in Archaic sites throughout areas of the far Northeast. The Adena cultures of the Ohio Valley seem to be an especially flamboyant expression of the trend toward increasingly elaborate burial treatments, which culminates in large earthen mounds and spectacular accumulations of grave goods (Tuck 1978, 43). The grave goods show a relatively limited range of styles, including large ovate late-stage bifaces manufactured of especially high-quality cherts and chalcedonies of the Ohio Valley, tubular pipes manufactured from Ohio pipestone, and copper ornaments manufactured from native copper of the Upper Great Lakes. It is the presence of these particular styles of grave furniture in Delaware and other scattered locations that justifies the use of the term *Delmarva Adena complex.* However, the cultural implications of the presence of these distinctive items and materials are not clear, unless analyzed in a local context.

In Delaware, the largest accumulations of late-stage bifaces and the other items such as copper beads and tubular pipes are found at the mortuary-exchange sites. Occasionally a side-notched point or debitage from Ohio chalcedonies will appear on a micro- (7S-K-21) or a macroband base camp (7K-F-38, 7K-D-37, 7K-D-38, 7NC-E-18), and Thomas (1970, 60) notes the appearance of an ocasional tubular pipe. Also, caches may contain some of the distinctive Adena materials (Thomas 1970, 61) and are usually associated with macro- and microband base camp sites. The significant points are that the most substantial accumulations of exotic materials occur in the context of graves and that the sites of the graves are not clearly associated with living sites from the same time period. Killens Pond is a possible exception because it is the mortuary-exchange center most closely associated with a living site among the three major sites in Delaware. Killens Pond also seems to be the smallest of the three sites. Gardner (n.d.) has suggested that the difference in size between Killens Pond and the Saint Jones and Frederica sites is significant enough to view the Killens Pond as a different type of site. In recognition of this difference, Killens Pond is here called a minor mortuary-exchange center and Saint Jones and Frederica are termed major mortuary-exchange centers. If the relative abundance of distinctive Adena artifacts and exotic raw materials such as copper and Ohio chalcedonies is considered for all occurrences of these artifacts in Delaware, the following rankings and definitions of sites can be seen:

1. *Major Mortuary-Exchange Centers* (Saint Jones and Frederica). Relatively large accumulations of Adena artifacts and exotic raw materials in association with distinctive mortuary ceremonialism.
2. *Minor Mortuary-Exchange Center* (Killens Pond). Small accumulations of Adena artifacts and exotic raw materials in association with distinctive mortuary ceremonialism.
3. *Cache Sites.* Small accumulations of Adena artifacts, almost exclusively late-stage bifaces manufactured from exotic and local materials, buried in cache pits in association with macroband base camps.
4. *Spot Find Sites.* Occurrences of single side-notched and corner-notched projectile points manufactured from Ohio chalcedonies, or small concentrations of debitage from the reduction and alteration of these tools associated with macro- and microband base camp sites (Delaware Division of Historical and Cultural Affairs 1978).

The distribution of these site types can be related to the Woodland I habitation sites previously noted. Major mortuary-exchange centers were not associated with any habitation sites and represent a dramatic change in the social organizations of the cultures that produced these sites. Minor mortuary-exchange centers were associated with a series of microband base camps and may represent localized expressions of the larger-scale social processes that produced the major centers. Caches and spot finds associated with both macro- and microband base camps may represent uses of the Adena artifacts that are more similar to the patterns seen during the Barker's Landing complex.

As was noted earlier, the absence of association between habitation sites and major mortuary-exchange centers is a significant fact that can perhaps be explained if considerations of the changes in exchange and social organization are considered. First, it should be noted that the appearance of nonlocal materials and special artifact forms in graves is a significant de-

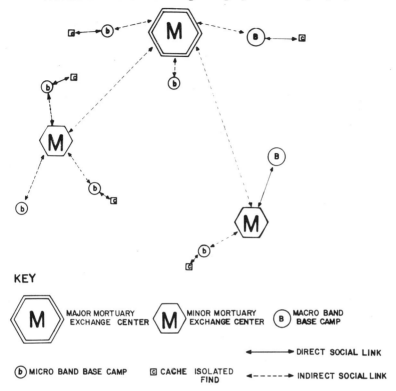

KEY

M (double hexagon)	MAJOR MORTUARY EXCHANGE CENTER
M (hexagon)	MINOR MORTUARY EXCHANGE CENTER
B	MACRO BAND BASE CAMP

▲──────► DIRECT SOCIAL LINK

b MICRO BAND BASE CAMP   **c** CACHE ISOLATED FIND

◄- - - - -► INDIRECT SOCIAL LINK

Fig. 13. Delmarva Adena complex settlement system.

velopment. Burial of items with the dead is a complete removal of the item from circulation and seems to indicate close association of the artifact with the deceased individual. As such, burial of artifacts in graves is the ultimate expression of sociotechnic functions. The artifacts are so closely linked to the individual that even though they may be used by other individuals as similar symbols, they are not. Binford (1962) also notes that artifacts may function as symbols within religious systems, and when they do they may be termed ideotechnic artifacts. The appearance of Adena materials in graves at major and minor mortuary-exchange sites is seen here as an indication of their initial use as ideotechnic artifacts. Functions of artifacts in some areas of Delaware were therefore transformed from sociotechnic functions to both sociotechnic and ideotechnic functions.

The transformation of artifact function to include ideotechnic functions is not unique to Delaware. Regensburg (1970) notes a series of burials with associated grave goods at the Savich Farm site in New Jersey, and similar data were recorded from the Koens Crispin site in New Jersey (Cross 1941, 81–90; Hawkes and Linton 1916). These sites are both dated to times that can be correlated to later stages of the Barker's Landing complex. While it is difficult to completely correlate the social processes at these New Jersey sites with events in Delaware, recent work by Regensburg (1978) suggests a circumscribed environment with attendant population growth, intensification and symbolic communication of status associated with incipient ranked societies. These variables seemed linked to the transformation of artifact functions to include ideotechnic functions.

I suggest that in Delaware between 500 B.C. and 0 B.C. similar changes in the social environments took place in the Mid-drainage zone of central Kent County. The social environments of the Barker's Landing complex sites were already favoring symbolic communication of status, and special use of artifacts and the intensification of food production in a relatively restricted environment had already started. An increase in the number of Delmarva Adena macroband base camps moving into the Delmarva Adena complex seems to indicate some degree of local population growth. In the face of this growth, the estuarine environment would grow in size due to the continued invasion of the Saint Jones and Murderkill drainages by saltwater from sea level rise. However, the especially productive freshwater/saltwater interface of the Mid-drainage zone, which is the prime location of macroband base camps and the center of the largest sites and population aggregates, would still remain limited in area. Further intensification of food production and storage would be necessary and is indicated by the appearance of food storage facilities and shell middens at sites associated with the Delmarva Adena complex. The process of intensified use of symbols and increased evidence of ranking is likely and the existence of the Delamarva Adena cemeteries and the ranking of major and minor centers reveal the effects of these evolutionary processes.

Many of the patterns of artifact distribution in the Saint Jones cemetery show the effects of the social processes of increased ranking and ideotechnic functions of artifacts. It has been noted that a series of secondary cremations in one of the loci had few if any artifacts while another burial locus contained uncremated interments associated with abundant grave goods, including several large caches. This differing treatment of bodies is here interpreted as evidence for the increased differentiation of social status, which points to increased development of ranked social systems. The presence of males and females of various ages in the special interment area, presumably the high-status area, implies that the higher-status positions in the societies of the Delmarva Adena complex were no longer limited to adult male lineage or extended family leaders, as was suggested for the high-status individuals of the Barker's Landing complex. It is likely that certain kin groups, rather than single individuals, were emerging as social units of higher status. However, the social system probably was still not divided into distinct classes, and it is unlikely that any single individual could have acted as a "chief" with any real authority.

Among living societies of similar social complexity and technology, a "big-man" organization is evident in many parts of the world (Harris 1979,

92–95) and may provide an analogy for Delmarva Adena social systems. The big-man organization is based upon certain local leaders who are able to assemble temporary surpluses of food and other goods that can be used to sponsor communal labor projects such as feasts, building projects, or religious rituals (Price n.d.). Quite often the big-man does not actually assemble the goods but rather organizes the productive capabilities of individuals, usually his relatives, to produce the surplus. The organizational abilities of the big-man are reflected in the success or failure of the group activity; if successful, the relative status of the big-man and his supporting kin group is enhanced. It is especially important to note that these big-men are usually able to only temporarily produce these surpluses in nonagricultural and nonherding societies; therefore, their enhanced status and that of their kin group may also be only temporary (Harris 1979, 92–95). However, if the special communal activities can be linked to rituals, special religious practitioners may then appear and ritual performance and group activities may take on a degree of regularity.

The Delmarva Adena cemeteries have many attributes that would seem to suggest that they were created by a big-man social organization operating on a supralocal basis. The lack of association of the cemeteries with any single village site may have been a result of the inability of any single group to produce the necessary ritual practitioner, big-man, or excess labor to organize and support the activities that created the cemetery sites and provided the exotic exchanged materials. The major mortuary-exchange sites may represent a common ground where numerous social units from a variety of macro- and microband base camps pooled their labor under a common organization to produce certain rituals. On the other hand, minor mortuary centers may have represented a local big-man organizing other smaller scale rituals. The presence of what apear to be high-status individuals in mortuary contexts at these sites suggests that special funeral services for members of the emerging higher-status kin groups were the rituals that provided the focus for the organization of labor. Using analogies to living groups, one might expect that feasting and exchange would also be a part of the activities carried out during these rituals. In many ways the system was self-perpetuating. The special funeral activities, themselves symbols of higher status for the individuals involved, were organized by the very individuals who would most benefit from them.

The co-occurrence of the different burial treatments also can be understood in this light. The secondary burials, which appear to have been exhumed from some temporary burial facility and then reburied after cremation, were noted earlier as probably lower-status individuals due to the paucity of grave goods. It is suggested here that the reinterment of these lower-status individuals with higher-status individuals may have been a part of the rituals sponsored by the higher-status groups. Among later Woodland II groups of the coastal Middle Atlantic, the practice of reinterment of individuals at certain intervals of time is well documented (Ubelaker 1974). Consequently, the Saint Jones cemetery and other major Delmarva Adena mortuary-exchange centers may have resulted from a similar practice.

It is important to note the role that exchange played in the development and maintenance of these mortuary-exchange centers as well as the role that ritual may have played in exchange. The main items of exchange during the Delmarva Adena complex seemed to be finished artifacts rather than raw materials. Although there are a few instances where Flint Ridge chalcedony debitage has been found, the incidence is much lower than that of argillite during Barker's Landing complex times. No large primary bifaces or cores are known and from this evidence it does not seem likely that Flint Ridge chalcedony entered the area as anything other than finished artifacts. These artifacts ranged from large secondary bifaces, generally associated with sociotechnic and ideotechnic functions, to possibly projectile points generally associated with technomic functions. Similarly, no large copper nuggets for the production of beads or raw quantities of Ohio pipestone have been found. In all cases the movement of finished artifacts is indicated.

Rappaport (1968) and others (Earle and Ericson 1977) note that different organizations of exchange systems were possible, based on the materials involved and the social relationships that reinforced the exchange. Simple systems, such as those involving argillite and rhyolite raw materials in the Wolfe Neck complex, were characterized by a weblike set of relationships where trading partnerships were maintained by force of personality and moral suasion. On the other hand, long-distance trade involving special commodities, such as the special finished artifact forms of the Delmarva Adena complex, tended to be characterized by a chainlike organization where ties among participating members were highly ritualized. Both systems may have been operating at the same time in a single area. Researchers studying long-distance trade networks of the Pacific note that as the distance of the trade increased, so did the complexity of the attendant ritual relationship (Gould 1971; Stanner 1933). Harding (1970, 95) notes that long-distance trade partnerships are often viewed as inherited, enduring relationships that were based on fictive kin ties and were associated with definite rules of conduct that define the conditions of the exchange. It is no accident that the ritualized use of exotic artifacts of the Delmarva Adena complex was tied to an increase in the range of the exchange network. The rituals of the mortuary systems also provided the sanctification of the exchange relationships, and it is likely that the ritual ceremony itself, with an attendant gathering of people and feasting, was a social setting where exchange could take place. Thus, the emerging ritual system that emphasized the sociotechnic and ideotechnic functions of artifacts also helped the development of more elaborate exchange networks by ritualizing the trade relationship. Similarly, the existence of special artifact forms manufactured from exotic items and procured through trade facilitated the ritual systems by providing elaborate symbols for display and use.

At this point I should comment on the form of the exchange that has been hypothesized for the Delmarva Adena complex period. The typical understanding of exchange is based on our Western conception of trade or barter where items are exchanged and values are assessed. However, in many non-Western societies the act of exchange is often more important than the items that actually change hands. In other words, the establishment of rights and obligations that accompany the acceptance of one gift and the giving of another are often more crucial than the gift itself. It is probably best to view the Delmarva Adena exchange in this fashion. Although it was useful to receive the valuable nonlocal item that could function as a symbol, the relationship between the giver and the receiver was equally important. In these sorts of exchange systems, it is also likely that recycling and circulation of special items results. The classic example is the "Kula Ring" of the western Pacific, observed in action and documented by Malinowski (1922), where ritualized trade of armbands and pendants provides for a circulation of these items through a series of societies. Special artifact forms are exchanged for other equally special items and a series of ritualized trading relationships is thus maintained. I suggest that a similar system might have existed among Delmarva Adena sites. The bifaces could have been circulated among groups for varying periods of time and then removed from the system when an individual of special importance died. The rituals of death themselves would have perpetuated the system by producing the social context for the exchange itself.

Such a system of highly ritualized exchange would seem likely also because it would not require a constant relationship to the Ohio Valley and a continual input of exotic items. A wide gap exists in the distribution of Adena artifacts between the Atlantic Coast and the Ohio Valley with no individuals in intervening areas seeming to participate in the trade. Therefore, a constant relationship between the two extremes of the distribution would have been difficult to maintain. However, in a ritualized exchange system such a constant link would not have been necessary. Once the initial stock of exotic items was obtained, it would be circulated through the system and slowly removed in conjunction with special events. Thomas's (1973a) reconstruction of funeral practices suggests the possible recycling of grave goods, and in this system the maximum utility could be gained from the minimum number of goods. Occasional replacement of items might be necessary, but a constant flow of items between the Atlantic Coast and the Ohio Valley would not be required. Although this explanation can account for some of the patterns seen in the archaeological record, it still does not answer the question of how the initial input of Ohio Valley artifacts and raw materials appeared in Delaware. The social setting that favors ritualized exchange and the possible relations among mortuary ceremonies, special burial treatments, and the exchange itself can be delineated. However, the event that brought the first ovate biface manufactured from Flint Ridge chalcedony and the first copper beads to Delaware has probably been lost forever to archaeology. We can only make conjectures about a special journey or an entrepreneur that can never be tested with hard data from the archaeological record.

Nevertheless, whatever the source of the original materials, it can be hypothesized that the distinctive social environment that had been established in central Kent County at the end of the Barker's Landing complex set the stage for the acceptance of these exotic artifacts, their incorporation into the ideotechnic and sociotechnic symbol system, and their use as grave furniture. Trade networks were already in place to redistribute the materials in various forms, ranging from the high-status items found in mortuary-exchange sites to the lower-status items such as projectile points and tool discards at base camps. The social environment also was ready for the transformation of artifact function that would accompany the development of more complex ranked systems. Outside the central Kent County area among the Wolfe Neck complex groups and among some marginal Delmarva Adena complex groups the correct conditions for complete participation did not seem to have existed and only traditional trade in technomic-sociotechnic items continued. Even within the central Kent County area the social organizations that maintained these systems of exchange and symbols seem to have been quite ephemeral, for by approximately 0 B.C. the distinctive features of the Delmarva Adena complex seemed to disappear. In sum, knowledge of the Delmarva Adena must be composed of many educated guesses about the social systems and the cultural processes that produced this interesting portion of Delaware's archaeological record. However, the educated guesses presented here are testable in the archaeological record. We can only hope for a chance at some future time to excavate an undisturbed Delmarva Adena mortuary site and, using controlled methods, refute or confirm the hypotheses presented here.

Carey Complex and Late Carey Complex

By approximately 0 B.C., the available archaeological evidence seems to indicate that the distinctive trade and exchange networks and the special ritualized treatments of the dead that characterized the Delmarva Adena complex ceased to exist. In general, the apparent disappearance of these especially flamboyant cultural expressions defines the Carey complex, which dates from approximately 0 B.C. to A.D. 600 (Table 7). During this time period, the spatial variation in the archaeological record of Delaware reaches the lowest level of the entire Woodland I period and the Carey complex (Thomas 1977) is distributed throughout at least Delaware and probably the entire Delmarva Peninsula. Table 10 shows the diagnostic artifact styles associated with Carey complex sites. Mockley ceramics are the most important diagnostic artifact type, and projectile point styles include both Rossvillelike stemmed points and a minor component of Fox Creek and large triangle forms. However, the Fox Creek artifacts from Delaware (Thomas et al. 1974) are not as numerous as are these artifact styles from other areas of the Middle Atlantic (Handsman and McNett 1974; Kinsey 1971).

The only change noticeable in the settlement patterns at the beginning of the Carey complex is the disappearance of the major and minor mortuary centers. Therefore, the Woodland I settlement system described earlier can be applied to the Carey complex. Carey complex components are seen at several of the Woodland I macroband base camps noted previously, including the Clyde Farm site (7NC-E-6) and the Delaware Park site (7NC-E-41). At the Delaware Park site are eleven features with radiocarbon dates between A.D. 65 and A.D. 455 (Thomas 1981; see UGa-3504, UGa-3465, UGa-3503, UGa-3558, UGa-3567, UGa-3502, UGa-3499, UGa-3464, UGa-3501, UGa-3498, and UGa-3438 in Appendix 1). Four large storage features with plant remains and pollen and seven hearths are included and seem to reveal use of the site that is similar to the preceding Wolfe Neck complex. Stemmed projectile points of various configurations and some side-notched points are associated with the radiocarbon dates.

An additional macroband base camp of the Carey complex is the Carey Farm site (7K-D-3). The Carey Farm site is located along the Saint Jones River in the Mid-drainage zone of central Kent County and shows the continuity of Woodland I macroband base camps in the Mid-drainage zones. A date of A.D. 200 (I-5817) was obtained from the site, which included Mockley ceramics and a limited array of Fox Creek projectile points (Delaware Division of Cultural and Historical Affairs 1977). Faunal remains recovered from refuse features included deer, shellfish, beaver, box turtle, diamond-back turtle, dog, muskrat, turkey, and woodchuck. Hickory nuts were also found in the refuse. In an analysis of these materials, Griffith (1974) suggests that the site was a base camp occupied from at least midfall to midwinter. When compared with other Carey complex sites, the Carey Farm site represents a base camp (macroband) from which occasional forays were made to surrounding areas especially high in their productivity of hunted and gathered resources. Seasonal movement to spring camps near the coast may also have been a part of the seasonal movement pattern for the exploitation of shellfish (Griffith 1974, 78–79; Delaware Division of Historical and Cultural Affairs 1978).

Microband base camps of the Carey complex play a role in Griffith's (1974) model and can be recognized in the archaeological record. In most

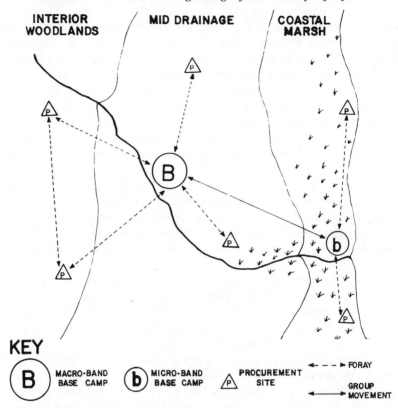

Fig. 14. Carey Farm complex settlement system.

cases the microband base camps were multicomponent and included several sites already mentioned. The Green Valley sites (7NC-E-54, 7NC-D-55, 7NC-D-62) associated with cobble deposits produced some Carey complex artifacts (Custer et al. 1981). The Wolfe Neck Midden site (7NC-D-10) included some Mockley ceramics associated with a radiocarbon date of A.D. 325 (UGa-1273b), as reported by Griffith and Artusy (1977). The Wilgus site (Artusy 1978) also includes a Carey Farm component with Mockley ceramics and a radiocarbon date of A.D. 240 (UGa-1762). Shell midden sites within the Cape Henlopen Archaeological District (Delaware Division of Historical and Cultural Affairs 1976) also contained Carey complex ceramics and showed a continuing exploitation of the embayed areas associated with the development of Cape Henlopen. Microband base camps associated with interior areas of the Drainage Divide zone were identified during the survey of the proposed Dover Bypass and include 7K-F-12, 44, 45, 46, 53, 54, 55 (Griffith and Artusy n.d.). No procurement sites that can be definitely ascribed to the Carey complex were found; however, many of the procurement sites described earlier in conjunction with other Woodland I complexes may date to this period.

In general, the Carey complex seems to be very similar to the preceding Wolfe Neck complex in terms of site distributions, subsistence, and exchange. The multicomponent nature of all of the sites comprising the settlement system show this continuity. Some movement of macroband base camps from the different complexes was required as an adjustment to the changes in the location of the freshwater/saltwater interface brought on by sea level rise. However, the basic pattern of seasonal movement seems to have a continuity that reaches back to Wolfe Neck and possibly Clyde Farm complex times. Exchange patterns also show continuities among these complexes in that the exchange networks of the Carey complex are related to relatively low levels of movements of artifacts and raw materials that are used primarily within technomic and sociotechnic contexts. There are no artifacts comparable to those of the Barker's Landing or Delmarva Adena complexes and there are few, if any, indications of sociotechnic and ideotechnic functions of nonlocal materials and artifacts.

Given the similarities of the adaptation of subsistence bases of all the Woodland I complexes discussed to this point, it is difficult to explain the disappearance of the elaborate exchange systems and mortuary ceremonialism. Two possibilities exist. One of the easiest explanations is that the elaborate exchange systems and mortuary ceremonialism did not disappear. The poorly defined Oxford complex (Thomas 1977) is a possible candidate and it is possible that archaeologists simply have not yet found these sites. While it is always possible to resort to heretofore undiscovered sites in discussing archaeological data, this approach is not particularly useful and generally leads to a conceptual deadend until more sites are discovered. Nevertheless, it is possible that Carey complex mortuary-exchange centers are waiting to be discovered. However, if elaborate exchange exists, the other habitation sites should show some of the exotic raw materials in sociotechnic contexts, as was the case for the Barker's Landing complex sites. Because Carey Farm habitation sites do not show such evidence, an alternative explanation should be offered that considers the possibility of an absence of the very elaborate exchange networks during Carey complex times.

It was noted earlier that the elaborate trade and exchange networks, the use of artifacts in sociotechnic and ideotechnic contexts, and mortuary ceremonialism were associated with the central Kent County area of Delaware where there seemed to be a certain degree of circumscription of populations, population growth, and intensified use of special food resources such as gathered plants and shellfish. The Carey Farm complex data seem to show a continuity in subsistence practices, such as intensive gathering of plant foods and estuarine resources. A continuity in site size and number indicates that populations were at least remaining stable, if not expanding. Given these continuities, the major change may be in the effects of population circumscription. During the Carey complex period the sea level continued to rise and inundate the Saint Jones and Murderkill drainages. This inundation would have increased the size of the productive estuarine settings and reduced the circumscription of the local area. I suggest that in the face of expanding estuarine environments with high productivity, Carey complex communities were not under the strong pressures to intensify production that affected the Delmarva Adena and Barker's Landing communities. Also, by the time of the Carey complexes the effects of the midpostglacial xerothermic would have been ameliorating and the difference in productivity between the estuarine settings and the surrounding area would not have been as marked as it was previously. In this case, the selective effects of the social environment would not have favored incipient ranked societies and their attendant trade and symbol systems.

The breakdown of the elaborate exchange and mortuary systems was probably not a cataclysmic event. It should be remembered that the big-man organizations that most likely formed the core of these special developments were based on the organizational skills of special individuals who could amass temporary surpluses that could support the ritualized settings of the trade and mortuary systems. Although the Delmarva Adena complex includes some ranking of kin groups, the ranking within the society was still probably very poorly developed and would represent only a minor change from egalitarian societies typical of hunter-gatherers. If the rewards of the organization and management of a complex trade and mortuary ceremonial system were outweighed by the costs involved, participation would certainly decline. Ritual interments and special trade and exchange relationships would become less frequent until they reached the point where the special supralocal relationships would cease to exist entirely. Once relationships were broken, the flow of special materials would end and the system would be finished. Given the reliance on exotic Adena materials that had to come from a great distance and that were linked with quite elaborate funeral ceremonies, the Delmarva Adena trade and mortuary relationships would be especially susceptible to disruption once the social force that favored its development was removed. From a cultural evolutionary perspective, this view of the beginning and demise of somewhat complex social organizations in Delaware would seem to indicate that Woodland I societies of Delaware were poised on a crucial dividing line between egalitarian and ranked societies. During some complexes in some areas the appropriate combination of social forces allowed the beginning of the development of complex organizations with their accompanying trade systems and status differentiations. However, these combinations of social forces were not constantly present and the relatively complex organizations that developed could not survive without the appropriate conditions.

By A.D. 500, the state-wide homogeneity of the Carey Farm complex began to break down. More complex societies begin to appear again in central Delaware and were labeled the Webb complex. Intensification of food production also appeared in northern Delaware and a distinct Delaware Park complex is noted. Both of these northern terminal Woodland I complexes are characterized by the appearance of a new ceramic type, Hell Island Ware. Hell Island ceramics, tempered with grit and crushed rock, are quite distinct from the preceding shell-tempered Mockley ceramics. In southern Delaware no such technological change is apparent. No grit-tempered ceramics later than Wolfe Neck Ware are noted; moreover, there seems to be a technological continuity between the Mockley and Townsend ceramics that characterize the Woodland II period in southern Delaware. Triangular projectile points are also found during late Woodland I and Woodland II times. Later, it will be seen that early Woodland II adaptations of southern Delaware show a certain continuity with Carey complex adaptations, and on the basis of the continuities in adaptation and ceramic technologies, a Late Carey complex that spans the period from A.D. 500 to A.D. 1000 is hypothesized for southern Delaware (Table 7). No known sites exist to be placed in this complex, and further field research will be needed to establish its validity. Nevertheless, the Late Carey complex is one way to account for the continuities in adaptations, settlement patterns, ceramic technology, and projectile point technology that cover the years between A.D. 500 and A.D. 1000 in southern Delaware.

Delaware Park Complex

The archaeological data from extreme northern Delaware from A.D. 500 to A.D. 1000 is not much better than the data for southern Sussex County. However, Thomas's (1981) excavations at the Delaware Park site (7NC-E-41) provide some indications about the adaptations in northern New Castle County between A.D. 500 and A.D. 1000. Two storage features excavated from Delaware Park revealed dates of A.D. 640 (UGa-3439) and A.D. 605 (UGa-3437) and contained stemmed points and Hell Island ceramics. The Hell Island ceramics are the major diagnostic artifact style of the Delaware Park complex, and a variety of projectile point styles are noted, including Jack's Reef pentagonal points, Rossville stemmed points, generalized side-notched points, and some large triangular points. The multicomponent nature of the Delaware Park site shows continuity of adaptation in the use of macroband base camps. The presence of the storage features, one of them quite large, seems to indicate continued intensive harvesting of plant foods. Since these patterns show a continuation of trends in adaptation seen during preceding Woodland I complexes, the Woodland I settlement system described earlier would probably apply to the Delaware Park complex.

Hell Island ceramics are noted at only two other sites in northern New Castle County. The Clyde Farm site (7NC-E-6) has a small quantity of Hell

Island ceramics and some Jack's Reef projectile points (Custer 1981). The size of the site suggests a macroband base camp and the multicomponent nature of the site is similar to that of the Delaware Park site. A few scattered Hell Island ceramic sherds are present as well at the Green Valley sites (7NC-D-54, 55, 62, Custer et al. 1981), and the site probably continued in use as a microband base camp associated with the use of cobble resources in the immediate area.

In the Piedmont Uplands occasional Hell Island ceramic sherds are present at the Mitchell site (7NC-A-2) near Hockessin (Custer 1981) and at the Webb site (36-CH-51) near Avondale, Pennsylvania (Custer 1982). These are the only Piedmont Upland sites with clearly discernible Woodland I complexes. Various Delaware Park complex projectile point styles were found in surface collections (Custer and Wallace 1982), and a similar settlement pattern for Clyde Farm complex through Delaware Park complex times is evident (Custer and Wallace 1982). The continuity shows collecting adaptations centered around predictable water resources and the low levels of exchange in nonlocal materials.

Webb Complex

The Webb complex was originally described by Thomas and Warren (1970) based on excavations at the Island Field site (7K-F-17) in Kent County. An intensive gathering subsistence base, participation in wide-ranging trade networks, Hell Island ceramics, Jack's Reef projectile points, and a mortuary complex incorporating various special grave goods were diagnostic characteristics noted by Thomas and Warren (1970a, 22–23; Thomas 1974b) that are used to define the Webb complex here. As such, the relationship between the Webb and the Delaware Park complexes would be similar to the relationship between the Delmarva Adena and the Wolfe Neck complexes and the Barker's Landing and Clyde Farm complexes. The Webb, Delmarva Adena, and Barker's Landing complexes would be similar to the Delaware Park, Wolfe Neck, and Clyde Farm complexes, respectively, in basic adaptations, settlement patterns, and tool kits. However, the Webb, Delmarva Adena, and Barker's Landing complexes can be distinguished by the presence of extensive trade networks, sociotechnic and some ideotechnic artifacts, and mortuary ceremonialism. These distinguishing characteristics indicate more complex social organizations and emerging ranked societies.

Although the basic adaptation of Webb complex groups would be generally similar to that of other Woodland I groups, site distribution data seem to indicate that some alterations of the settlement patterns had begun. Sites with recognizable Webb complex occupations are generally distributed from south of the Chesapeake and Delaware Canal to the southern Kent County area. Within this region only one true macroband base camp, the

Hell Island site (7NC-F-7), and one potential macroband base camp (7K-C-94) are noted. The Hell Island site is located on a small island in the Mid-drainage zone of the Appoquinnimink River. The Hell Island site was originally discovered and test-excavated by H. T. Wright of the University of Michigan in the early 1960s when he was a student at nearby Saint Andrews School. Wright excavated one test unit close to the bluff of the island and wrote a short report on the site (Wright 1962). Later excavations were carried out by Thomas (1966c), and, based on the results of both excavations, the site was nominated to the National Register of Historic Places. Both series of excavations recovered numerous artifacts, including a variety of ceramics, predominantly Hell Island Corded and Hell Island Fabric-impressed, Jack's Reef and Rossvillelike stemmed projectile points, and a wide range of tool types indicating the presence of a macroband base camp. Also included in the artifacts was a carved platform pipe made from nonlocal steatite.

There is some question as to whether or not the Hell Island site was stratified. Wright's short report seems to indicate that there was some stratification; however, Thomas's excavations could not verify the existence of a stratigraphic sequence. A recent examination by George Galasso (1981) of Wright's materials from the site, which are currently housed at the Smithsonian Institution, seems to support Wright's interpretation. Three basic ceramic types can be recognized from the excavations at the site: Townsend ceramics (a Woodland II variety), Hell Island wares, and a type that Wright termed "Price Farm Interior-Corded" and which Thomas did not identify. Price Farm ceramics appear to be related to Wolfe Neck/ Susquehanna ceramics and are referred to here by the later term. Because the levels used by Wright were smaller than those used by Thomas, his excavation techniques were more likely to discern slight differences in artifact distributions. The distribution of ceramics from Wright's excavation as reanalyzed by Galasso (1981) at different depths shows three major components: A Late Woodland Townsend component, a Hell Island component, and a Wolfe Neck component. The three components slightly overlap but still seem to be nicely stratified. The Hell Island site can therefore be characterized as a stratified macroband base camp, with the major component associated with the Webb complex.

Recent analysis of archaeological site distributions in the Appoquinnimink drainage using a logistical regression technique (Wells 1981; Wells et al. 1981; Custer and Well 1981) reveals an interesting feature of the Hell Island site location. By analyzing the environmental factors that correlate with archaeological site locations, Wells was able to map out locations where archaeological sites were likely to exist. When additional known site distributions were compared to the predicted locations, the match was fairly good. However, the Hell Island site was something of an anomaly in that it is located in an area that is only moderately likely to contain archaeological sites. The location of a large macroband base camp with some evidence of elaborate trade and exchange would be expected to be in the richest environmental zones, in this case the zones of highest probability. The appearance of the Hell Island site in a zone of lower probability suggests that factors other than environmental ones had a role in its location. These additional factors may be related to access to trade routes or centralized redistribution locations.

South of the Hell Island site there are no other recognizable macroband base camps of the Webb complex. However, many microband base camps have been identified. Sites 7NC-F-15 and 7NC-F-19 along the Appoquinnimink near Hell Island both appear to be microband base camps of the Webb complex and may be part of the same settlement system. On Saint Jones Neck, where a comprehensive survey has been carried out (Delaware Division of Historical and Cultural Affairs 1978), macroband base camps are absent and microband base camps of the Webb complex are abundant, including sites 7K-D-42, 47, 48, and 7K-F-86. Along the Murderkill River similar distributions were noted during the survey of the proposed Dover Bypass (Griffith and Artusy n.d.). Seven microband base camps with Webb complex components (7K-F-45, 46, 47, 53, 54, 55, 56) and one Webb complex procurement site (7K-F-48) were noted. Further south on the Mispillion drainage, two microband base camps were excavated (Delaware Division of Historical and Cultural Affairs 1980; Thomas 1966d); these appear to be part of the Webb complex. A feature related to the Webb complex was also reported from the Taylor Cedar Creek site (7S-C-17). This feature contained Hell Island net-impressed ceramics, a Jack's Reef projectile point, and a drilled shark's tooth associated with a radiocarbon date of A.D. 645 (UGa-1441). From the fairly intensive study of these areas focusing on the Saint Jones, Murderkill, and Mispillion drainages, it seems evident that a reduction in base camp size took place during the Webb complex. Therefore, the Woodland I settlement system described earlier does not apply to the Webb complex in central Delaware; however, it may apply to areas of southern New Castle County such as the Appoquinnimink Drainage. Before considering the social changes that might be related to these settlement pattern shifts, we must consider an additional site type found in the central Kent County area during the Webb complex.

The Island Field site (7K-F-17), which provided the original defining characteristics of the Webb complex, is a large mortuary center that was excavated by the Delaware Section of Archaeology in the late 1960s under the direction of Ron Thomas. A preliminary report on the site was published (Thomas and Warren 1970a) and the site has since been incorporated into a museum of archaeology and an archaeological research center. The Island Field site is located on the lower Murderkill River, well within the Delaware Shore zone. At present the site is less than one kilometer from the Delaware Bay; however, the lower Murderkill has been subjected to considerable local sea level rise due to some subsidence of the local area (Kraft 1974; Kraft et al. 1976). This subsidence is due to the compaction of old marsh deposits that underlay the present ground surface. Therefore, the Island Field site was considerably further removed from the shore at the time of its use. The site was first discovered in the late 1920s by a local farmer, who over the years collected a large number of artifacts from the site (Thomas and Warren 1970a, 2). Some excavations were planned after a thorough survey of the site by members of the Sussex Society for Archaeology and History; these are reported in their bulletin, *The Archeolog* (Austin et al. 1953). The major component of the site observable from the surface was an extensive Woodland II Slaughter Creek complex occupation, so initial intensive excavations by the Delaware Section of Archaeology in 1966 focused on these materials. The following year a Webb complex cemetery was discovered, and two more field seasons were spent investigating this area.

As of June 1970, 88 burials had been recorded from an area of approximately 80 meters square, with only about one-half of the area excavated (Thomas and Warren 1970a, 3). Later this total was expanded to 120 burials (Thomas 1973, 57). A wide variety of multiple and single burial practices are noted, including the following methods: flexed burials (62 percent), disarticulated burials (20 percent), redeposited cremations (8 percent), *in situ* cremations (2 percent) extended burials (4 percent), prone burials (2 percent), and bundle burials (2 percent) as noted by Thomas and Warren (1970, 4, Plate 1). Many of the burials cross cut one another, and in many places the burials and the associated grave goods are quite mixed. However, the homogeneity of the artifact assemblages seems to show that the graves all date to a similar time period close to A.D. 740, the only radiocarbon date noted from the site (I-6338) (Thomas and Warren 1970a, 3). In the original publication, Thomas and Warren (1970a, 3) note that no associations among burial treatments, age/sex distinctions, or grave goods were noted; however, lumping of the various graves by treatment categories probably obscured their analysis and the sophisticated analytical techniques now available were not applied to the data. Unfortunately, the limitations on the detail imposed by the format of the original report precludes the possibility of reanalyzing the association data based on the published report.

Further research with the original collections will be necessary to clarify the picture; however, some initial correlations can be noted, based on a perusal of the original excavation records and a later summary by Thomas (1974b). Six of the graves from the site are buried much deeper than the other graves and contain adult males with their bodies oriented in the same direction. Grave goods associated with these individuals range in quantity from one to 208 artifacts (Thomas 1974b). These deeply buried individuals could represent some sort of special status group whose membership was

Plate 5. Webb complex bifaces. (Courtesy Delaware Division of Historical and Cultural Affairs.)

exclusively adult males. Nevertheless, individuals of all ages and sexes are found within the cemetery (Thomas and Warren 1970a, 4, Plate 1; Neumann and Murad 1970), indicating that people of different ages and sexes had access to some sort of special burial treatment and that kinship groups were ranked rather than individuals (Thomas 1974b).

Artifacts used as grave goods include a variety of technomic, sociotechnic, and ideotechnic forms. Bone and antler tools, projectile points, celts, and pestles represent some of the utilitarian artifacts with primarily a technomic functional context (Thomas and Warren 1970a, 8–21). Some large pentagonal bifaces made from a variety of nonlocal materials (Thomas and Warren 1970a, 18) may represent sociotechnic items similar in function to the Delmarva Adena bifaces. A variety of steatite platform pipes may also have similar functions. Ideotechnic functions may also accompany the sociotechnic functions of some of these artifacts, and an antler headdress and a cup fashioned from a portion of a human skull seem to represent purely ideotechnic functions. In many ways the organization of the grave goods and their functional contexts seem to be similar to those of the Saint Jones and Frederica Adena sites. The presence of nonlocal materials also suggests a reappearance of wide-ranging trade networks (Thomas and Warren 1970a, 23).

In sum, the Island Field site seems to indicate that in central Kent County during the Webb complex social environments were again similar

Plate 6. Webb complex burial cache. Includes bone tools, biface, pestle, and whelk shell from Island Field site. (Courtesy Delaware Division of Historical and Cultural Affairs.)

to those seen during Delmarva Adena and Barker's Landing complexes. At least they were similar enough to indicate a reemergence of some similar cultural patterns. Elsewhere in the Delmarva Peninsula sites similar to Island Field also appear at this time, including the Riverton site on Marshy-hope Creek (Jackson 1954) and an unreported site near Oxford, Maryland (Thomas and Warren 1970a, Thomas 1977).

Changes in settlement pattern may be related to the reappearance of mortuary-exchange centers. It should be noted that no habitation site was ever found to be associated with the Island Field site. This pattern is similar to that noted for Delmarva Adena sites, and along with ideotechnic artifacts and ranked kin groups may indicate the reemergence of a big-man organization that provides a focus for local populations dispersed at a number of smaller sites. The reappearance of a big-man organization may be explained in light of the previously noted absence of macroband base camps in the Saint Jones and Murderkill drainages. Throughout the Woodland I period in central Delaware there seems to be evidence of a continuing population growth. Beginning with the Barker's Landing complex, semisedentary macroband base camps seem to increase in size, culminating in the relatively large macroband base camps such as the Carey Farm site. After the end of the Carey complex, the macroband base camps are no longer found and a large number of microband base camps appear.

Cohen's (1978) analysis of political evolution provides a possible explanation of the social changes that could produce such a pattern. Cohen notes that quite often human population densities may increase at certain locations to the point where there are too many people at any single location for the existing social organizations to be able to organize interpersonal relationships, food production, and redistribution. When this crucial point is reached, there are two options: either develop new and more complex forms of social organization that can accommodate the higher numbers and densities of people, or split up (fission) into smaller groups. Usually it is easier to fission and Cohen (1978) notes numerous examples. If population densities in surrounding areas are sufficiently low and if there are sufficient resources available in other areas, the fissioning is easily accomplished. However, in some cases populations are circumscribed by other groups of people or differential resource distributions (Carniero 1970), so fissioning cannot take place. The change in the Webb complex settlement system from one that included macroband base camps to one that did not could have been the result of fissioning of the Carey complex population aggregates of central Delaware. The size of the largest Cary complex macroband base camp may be the threshhold where it is necessary to fission into separate communities or develop new and more complex social organizations. In central Delaware, circumscription had been reduced since Carey complex times and the easy option, fissioning, could take place. The Webb complex microband base camps throughout the Saint Jones and

Murderkill drainages represented the new communities that resulted. However, in northern reaches of the Webb complex area, fissioning did not take place and macroband base camps such as the Hell Island site were still in existence.

The existence of the Island Field site as a major mortuary-exchange center seems to present an anomaly if the view of reduced circumscription and fissioning is accurate, because circumscription was seen as a part of the social environments of Delmarva Adena complex societies that produced similar sites. However, if fissioning took place in late Carey complex and early Webb complex times, the newly fissioned communities could have been subject to a new set of local environmental conditions that could have established circumscribed environments in certain areas. These new communities that resulted from the fissioning of the large macroband base camps would have faced the same biosocial environments that the early Barker's Landing complex communities in the estuarine zones would have faced. They would have a productive environment to use and the initial low population density within the community would have favored population growth. Increased population would have necessitated intensification of food production, and the whole cycle of factors that produced the initial ranked societies with trade and exchange and ultimately mortuary ceremonialism would have been reproduced. Big-man organizations that would have spanned more than one community would have been easy to develop because it is likely that microband base camps that had fissioned from the same macroband base camp would have retained some social or perhaps kinship ties. Therefore, an underlying set of links among villages would have been available in the big-man organizations. Similar developments may be expected in other zones of the Delmarva Peninsula, where similar biosocial environments were created by fissioning in terminal Woodland I times. The presence of some indications of elaborate exchange networks at the Hell Island site, a macroband base camp, suggests that similar biosocial environmental pressures existed in these zones as well.

Woodland I Period in Retrospect

Because the Woodland I period as defined here for Delaware includes several chronological periods that are usually viewed as distinct entities, I offer a few concluding remarks to underscore the validity of lumping together these archaeological periods. In the first place, the Woodland I period is defined on the basis of overall continuities of adaptations to quite similar biosocial environments. The biotic portion of the environment includes the distinctive conditions brought on by the appearance of the mid-postglacial xerothermic. The social component of the environment, which is even more important than the biotic component, is composed of the new

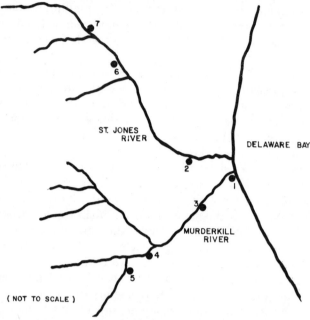

Fig. 15. Woodland I sites of central Delaware. 1 = Island Field (7K-F-17); 2 = Barker's Landing (7K-D-13); 3 = Coverdale (7K-F-38); 4 = Frederica Adena (7K-F-2); 5 = Killens Pond (7K-E-3); 6 = St. Jones Adena (7K-D-1); 7 = Carey Farm (7K-D-3).

social relationships that arise in the face of semisedentary lifeways and population growth within certain circumscribed environments. These similarities are considered much more important for the distinction of culture periods than are the presence of attributes such as ceramics and burial complexes. The ceramics and mortuary systems are important features of Woodland I life; however, they are merely symptoms of more important changes in the adaptations to the biosocial environment.

The common characteristics of the Woodland I adaptations to the biosocial environments that existed between 3000 B.C. and A.D. 1000 in Delaware were the emergence of a focal adaptation and the appearance of a settlement system that was centered on large macroband base camps. The multicomponent nature of Woodland I macroband base camp sites such as Clyde Farm, Crane Hook, and Delaware Park, which span the entire Woodland I period, testifies to the continuity of adaptation. In the central Kent County area, the continuity of adaptation can be seen by considering the distribution of the macroband base camps along the Saint Jones and Murderkill drainages. From 3000 B.C. to A.D. 1000 the sites seem to follow the freshwater/saltwater interface right up the drainages until the fissioning of the Webb complex occurs. Even the fissioning of macroband communities in terminal Carey and initial Webb complex times attests to the continuity of cultural processes because the fissioning is the result of continued population growth at the macroband base camps.

The presence of elaborate exchange networks and mortuary ceremonialism, attributes that were often used to exclude the Late Archaic cultures from the Early and Middle Woodland periods in the traditional literature are related to the important changes in biosocial environments that emerge in Delaware as early as 3000 B.C. In fact, the trade and exchange networks that appear in the Barker's Landing complex, which would be classified as a Late Archaic complex in the traditional literature, are more extensive than the trade and exchange networks that are found during the Wolfe Neck, Carey, Late Carey, and Delaware Park complexes, which would be classified as Early and Middle Woodland in traditional studies.

The confusion that results is due to the fact that the basic cultural processes that produced trade and mortuary ceremonialism have not been considered in past studies. When the biosocial adaptations that ultimately caused the existence of features like extensive trade and mortuary ceremonialism are studied, as was the case in the Woodland I analysis presented here, more meaningful results are obtained.

[5]

Woodland II Period:
Agriculture and Village Life

By A.D. 1000 numerous important changes occurred in the archaeological record of Delaware that indicate important alterations of the lifestyles of prehistoric peoples. The basic changes noted in Delaware include the breakdown of trade and exchange networks, alterations of settlement patterns, the development of sedentary lifestyles, and the appearance of agricultural food production to varying degrees in different areas. These changes are noted throughout the eastern United States, although the timings vary slightly, and the Woodland II period corresponds to the Late Woodland Period noted in the traditional literature (Willey 1966, 267–86; Griffin 1967, 189–91).

The post-A.D. 1000 disappearance of the trade and exchange systems that characterized the Woodland I period was linked to events that were happening during the later portions of the Woodland I period throughout the Middle Atlantic. In Delaware, the process of fissioning of large macroband base camps noted during the Webb complex disrupted traditional patterns of exchange in nonlocal materials. Even when nonlocal materials were procured through trade after the apparent fissioning of some local communities such as at the Island Field site, the materials were not as distinctive and the trade was not as intensive as in earlier complexes such as the Delmarva Adena complex. Even though some social environments favored the development of intensive trade in certain specialized items for use of grave goods, the disruptions of social networks caused by the fissioning of communities weakened the potential trade relationships. The networks of trade and exchange that distributed the rhyolite and argillite used to manufacture technomic artifacts also broke down after A.D. 1000. Stewart's (1980b, 394–95) research in the vicinity of the rhyolite outcrops

146

and quarries in western Maryland indicates that by A.D. 1000 there was a shift in settlement pattern associated with the development of agriculture. This shift created a situation where groups became more sedentary and made less use of the upland environments where rhyolite is found. Consequently, procurement of rhyolite decreased and the supply for trade and exchange was limited. In fact, the use of rhyolite in areas within 50 kilometers of the quarries and outcrops almost disappeared. Similar patterns may be projected for the quarry outcrops in south central Pennsylvania. Disruption of argillite procurement may have been produced by similar patterns of settlement change; however, data are not available to say for sure. In any event, the raw materials that flowed through trade and exchange networks in the Woodland I period were no longer flowing and the exotic raw materials were not found in any appreciable quantities on the Delmarva Peninsula after A.D. 1000. Consequently, the use of exotic raw materials and special artifact forms as grave goods also ended by A.D. 1000.

The alterations of settlement patterns, appearance of sedentary lifestyles, and use of agricultural food production systems are all linked together. There is evidence of domesticated plants in eastern North America prior to the beginning of the Woodland II period (Adovasio and Johnson 1981; Yarnell 1976); however, the effects of the use of these food sources on lifestyles appear to be minimal prior to A.D. 1000 (Ford 1979). In many ways, it is difficult to distinguish between the intensive gathering of selected plants and the harvesting of early domesticated plants because the change from gathering of plant foods to actual food production was a slow and gradual process (Flannery 1968). In Delaware it might have been very difficult to tell the difference between the intensive gathering of plant foods carried out during the Woodland I period and the early forms of agriculture practiced during the Woodland II period. Analysis of food remains from sites in the Middle Atlantic that date to the Woodland II period shows the extent of the use of domesticated plants. In a detailed analysis of the food remains from the Woodland II occupations of the Faucett site in the Upper Delaware Valley of Pennsylvania, Moeller (1975) notes a wide variety of wild plant foods accompanying the remains of corn in trash features. Ameringer (1975) notes similar plant food remains from a Woodland II Susquehannock site in Lancaster County, Pennsylvania, and Kinsey and Custer (1982) note the use of wild plant foods from sites as late as the beginning of the eighteenth century A.D. The implication of these findings is that even though domesticated plants such as corn, beans, and squash might have been introduced into the Middle Atlantic area, few, if any, Woodland II groups ever became fulltime farmers. Wild plant foods continued to provide a major portion of the diet and farming was a secondary food production activity. Nevertheless, the addition of domesticated food sources provided the basis for surpluses that allowed the establishment of sedentary lifestyles. The extent to which Delaware Woodland II populations became sedentary is discussed in more detail later in this chapter.

The addition of agriculture to the subsistence base of prehistoric groups also brought about settlement pattern changes including changes in site locations and site sizes. As groups became more sedentary, use of storage facilities became more important for preserving surpluses of either gathered or cultivated plant foods. As energy was invested in storage facilities and lifestyles became more sedentary, more permanent house structures appeared. With increased sedentism, birth spacing could be even further reduced and local populations would begin to grow. The result of this growth was the appearance of semisedentary villages that would house multiple social units and that would be larger than any of the earlier macroband base camps. As populations continued to grow, further emphasis would have been placed on stored surpluses and cultivated plant foods. The result would have been an intensification of agricultural systems. This intensification could have been carried out most effectively in the fertile floodplains of the major drainages, and a shift to these locations is indeed noted in many areas of the Middle Atlantic during Woodland II times. This shift often entailed the abandonment of productive estuarine settings. Good evidence of such an abandonment and shift to other floodplain locations is noted for the lower Potomac River Valley (Gardner and McNett 1971, 48–50). The extent to which these shifts occurred in Delaware is quite variable and is discussed later in this chapter.

In sum, the major changes in lifestyles that are evident throughout the Middle Atlantic around A.D. 1000 involve the development of agricultural food production systems, the establishment of relatively sedentary lifestyles, changes in settlement patterns, and disruptions of Woodland I trade and exchange systems, which are mainly related to alterations of the social environment. All of these shifts are manifest in the archaeological record of Delaware to varying degrees and eventually culminate in the Native American communities and societies observed by the first Western Europeans to visit the Middle Atlantic seaboard.

Changes in ceramic technologies and projectile point styles accompanied the changes in adaptations and lifestyles noted above and can be used to recognize archaeological sites from the Woodland II period. It was noted in chapter 4 that toward the end of the Woodland I period triangular projectile points appeared in the lithic tool kits. Use of these triangular points continued into the Woodland II period and by A.D. 1000, triangular projectile projectile points were the only styles seen in prehistoric tool kits (Kinsey 1972, 441–43; Ritchie 1961, 31–33). The appearance of the exclusive use of triangular points, which seem to be smaller than previous projectile points, is believed to be related to the appearance of the bow and arrow in the Middle Atlantic and Northeast. Triangular points usually have high width/thickness ratios and are usually manufactured from higher-grade cryptocrystalline materials.

Woodland II ceramics show certain technological similarities to the preceding terminal Woodland I ceramics; however, the appearance of more complex decorations, including incised lines and cord-wrapped stick impressions, distinguished the later Woodland II ceramic styles. Two basic varieties of Woodland II ceramics are noted for Delaware: Townsend Ware and Minguannan Ware. Townsend Ware ceramics have been extensively studied by Daniel Griffith (1977) and are described as tempered with crushed shell with fabric-impressed exterior surfaces (Griffith 1981). Although Townsend ceramics are more finely made and the vessels have thinner walls, similarities to later varieties of Mockely ceramics can be noted and the distributions of Townsend and late Mockley ceramics seem to be coterminous (Table 8). A variety of design motifs are present on Townsend ceramics and have been systematically described by Griffith (1977). Griffith (1977) was able to discern some chronological variation in the use of the various designs, with incised designs coming earlier than the cord-wrapped stick and direct cord designs.

Minguannan ceramics have been recognized as a distinctive form of Woodland II ceramics only recently (Custer 1981). These ceramics are tempered with sand, grit, and crushed quartz. Their exterior surface treatment may include smoothed surfaces, corded surfaces, and smoothed-over corded surfaces. Decorations are similar to Townsend designs and include incising, cord-wrapped stick, and direct cord impressions. The only difference observed is that Minguannan ceramics may have somewhat more complex design motifs. One variety, Minguannan Compound Decorated, includes both incised and cord-wrapped stick impressions in the same design element. Such combinations are rare in Townsend ceramics. The distribution, temper, and general technology of Minguannan ceramics in Delaware is similar to that of Hell Island ceramics.

Both Minguannan and Townsend ceramics have been found in well-defined associations with triangular points in Delaware and are good indicators of Woodland II occupations. The different ceramics may also be used to define two separate Woodland II complexes for Delaware. In an earlier paper, Thomas (1977) defined a Slaughter Creek complex based on the appearance of Townsend ceramics and large habitation sites in southern Delaware. The distribution of the Slaughter Creek complex was coterminous with that of Townsend ceramics and lasted from A.D. 1000 to European Contact in the seventeenth century A.D. For the purposes of this study, a Minguannan complex is defined as a habitation site in northern Delaware with Minguannan ceramics. The different settlement patterns for both groups are discussed later in this chapter.

The definition of the spatial boundaries for Woodland II complexes in Delaware is not completely clear. Townsend ceramics have been recog-

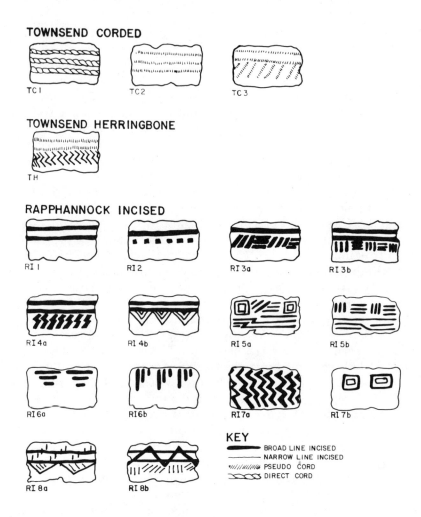

Fig. 16. Townsend Ceramic Design motifs.

Key to Figure 16*

Townsend Corded: Cord-wrapped stick-impressed (pseudo-cord) and direct-cord impressed.

TC1 = Direct-cord impressed, horizontal bands as the only motif.

TC2 = Pseudo-cord impressed, horizontal bands as the only motif.

TC3 = Pseudo-cord impressed, horizontal bands surmounting pseudo-cord impressed oblique lines.

Townsend "Herringbone": Pseudo-cord impressed horizontal lines surmounting incised herringbone or zigzag patterns (TH).

Rappahannock Incised: Broad- and narrow-line incised.

RI1 = Horizontal bands as the only motif.

RI2 = Horizontal bands surmounting single, discrete lines.

RI3 = Horizontal bands surmounting any combination of two or more discrete lines of any type.

RI4 = Horizontal bands surmounting complex geometrics consisting of at least zigzags, squares, or triangles and associated filling elements.

RI5 = Squares, horizontal lines and vertical lines surmounting horizontal and vertical lines in field 2.

RI6 = Discrete horizontal and oblique lines as the only motif.

RI7 = Complex geomotric designs (squares, triangles, zigzags) as the only motif.

RI8 = Horizontal lines with overlying embellishments of other elements; this motif may or may not be surmounting another motif.

*From Griffith 1981, 22.

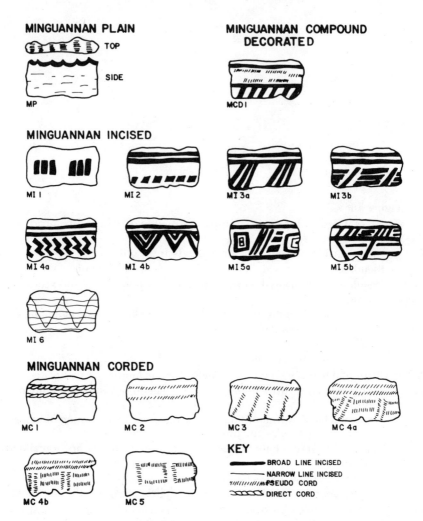

Fig. 17. Minguannan Ceramic Design motifs.

Key to Figure 17

Minguannan Plain: No decoration other than cord-wrapped stick impressions on the lip. There are no recognized varieties.

Minguannan Incised: Predominantly broad-line incised with occasional narrow-line incising. The recognized varieties are described below to correspond to Townsend motifs described by Griffith (1981).

MI1 = Discrete horizontal and oblique lines as the only design motif. Corresponds to RI6 (Griffith 1981, 22).

MI2 = Horizontal bands surmounting single, discrete lines. Corresponds to RI2 (Griffith 1981, 22).

MI3 = Horizontal bands surmounting any *combination* of two or more discrete lines of any type. Corresponds to RI3 (Griffith 1981, 22).

MI4 = Horizontal bands surmounting complex geometrics consisting of at least zigzags, squares, or triangles, and associated filling elements. Corresponds to RI4 (Griffith 1981, 22).

MI5 = Squares, horizontal and vertical lines surmounting horizontal and vertical lines in field 2. Corresponds to RI5 (Griffith 1981, 22).

MI6 = Horizontal bands with overlying embellishments of other elements; this motif may or may not be surmounting another motif. Corresponds to RI8 (Griffith 1981, 22).

Minguannan Corded: Predominantly cord-wrapped stick (pseudo-cord) impressions with some direct-cord impressions.

MC1 = Direct-cord impressed, horizontal bands as the only motif. Corresponds to TC1 (Griffith 1981, 22).

MC2 = Cord-wrapped stick-impressed (pseudo-cord), horizontal bands as the only motif. Corresponds to TC2 (Griffith 1981, 22).

MC3 = Cord-wrapped stick-impressed (pseudo-cord), horizontal bands surmounting pseudo-cord impressed oblique lines. Corresponds to TC3 (Griffith 1981, 22).

MC4 = Horizontal bands of direct-cord and pseudo-cord impressions surmounting any combination of two or more discrete linear sets of pseudo-cord impressions. Similar to RI3, except executed in pseudo-cord and direct cord (Griffith 1981, 22).

MC5 = Complex geometric designs (squares, triangles, zigzags) as the only motif. Corresponds to RI7 (Griffith 1981, 22), except executed in pseudo-cord.

Minguannan Compound Decorated: Both incised and corded designs are combined in several sets of elements. Only one recognized variety described below.

MCD1 = Horizontal bands surmounting any combination of two or more discrete lines of any type. Horizontal elements usually executed in pseudo-cord and incised. Oblique elements executed in broad line incisings. Similar to RI3 (Griffith 1981, 22).

nized for a long time and the range of their distribution is relatively well defined and extends from central Kent County southward (Griffith 1981, 20). On the other hand, Minguannan ceramics have only recently been recognized as a distinctive Woodland II ceramic variety and their distribution is not well known. Preliminary studies (Custer 1981) indicate that these ceramics are found throughout northern New Castle County and into Maryland and Pennsylvania along the Delaware, Brandywine, and Susquehanna drainages. However, the southern boundary is not clearly known. No Minguannan ceramics are known from areas south of the Chesapeake and Delaware Canal, although the distribution of Hell Island ceramics, which seem to be the technological precursors of Minguannan ceramics, continues well into southern New Castle County and northern Kent County. Indeed, there seems to be an absence of Woodland II sites in southern New Castle and northern Kent County. This absence is partly related to the frequency of archaeological surveys, and few, if any, systematic surveys have been carried out in Smyrna and Leipsic drainages. However, in the few cases where surveys have been done in southern New Castle and northern Kent counties (Gardner and Stewart 1978; Rappleye and Gardner 1980), Woodland II sites are not common. Therefore, the existence of a region with relatively low population density between the main population concentrations of the Minguannan and Slaughter Creek complexes is a possibility. However, further testing will be necessary to confirm the existence of such an area.

Environmental Setting

The environmental setting of the Woodland II period was essentially modern in character and would correspond to the description of the Sub-Atlantic episode described in chapter 4. Some researchers (Goudie 1977; Carbone 1976) note that some perturbations in global climate can be noted over the past 1,000 years and may have had dramatic effects upon societies with agricultural food production systems (Griffin 1961). However, the paleoenvironmental record for Delaware for the more recent periods of time is poorly understood and the recognition of these late Holocene climatic changes is somewhat problematic. Therefore, until better data are available on late Holocene climatic changes in the Middle Atlantic, it is best to view the environments of the Woodland II period as similar to the modern environments encountered by the first west Europeans to arrive in Delaware. Consequently, this study's search for the causes of change in Woodland II societies will focus on changes in the social environment attendant with the emergence of true food production systems.

Archaeological Data and Woodland II Adaptations

Minguannan Complex

The most distinctive characteristic of the Minguannan complex adaptations is their similarity to Woodland I adaptations of the Delaware Park complex. Triangular projectile points and Minguannan ceramics are found at many of the macroband base camps of the Delaware Park complex in northern New Castle County, including the Clyde Farm site (7NC-E-6) and the Crane Hook site (7NC-E-18) in the Fall Line zone and High Coastal Plain. At these sites Minguannan complex materials are almost always included in plowzones mixed with older materials; therefore, it is difficult to be sure of the tool associations. However, large quantities of Minguannan ceramics recovered at sites like Clyde Farm (Custer 1981) seem to indicate that the occupations were fairly large and can be considered as macroband base camps. No traces of permanent structures and storage features are noted. Recent test excavations at the Julian Powerline site (7NC-D-42) by the University of Delaware's Department of Anthropology recovered Minguannan ceramics and triangular projectile points in a rare undisturbed context (Custer 1981). Further excavations are planned, and tool kit associations should be found at this important site. The Hollingsworth Farm site near Elkton, Maryland (18-CE-129) recently excavated by Ron Thomas (1982) also appears to be a base camp site of the Minguannan complex. Storage features with some preserved plant remains were excavated; however, as of 1982 analysis of these ecofacts has not yet been completed. A number of enigmatic features that may have been semisubterranean pit houses were also noted; however, analysis of the soils of these features suggests that they might be tree falls. Whatever the case, the Hollingsworth Farm site seems to show intensified use of stored resources similar to the patterns seen at the Delaware Park site during Delaware Park complex times.

Minguannan complex sites of the Piedmont Uplands also show continuity of settlement pattern and general adaptations. The Mitchell site (7NC-A-2) near Hockessin contains a substantial Minguannan complex occupation within the plowzone (Custer 1981) and was also the focus of one of the tethered-nomadism subsistence patterns noted for the Woodland I period (see chapter 4). Custer and Wallace (1982) note that throughout the Woodland II period in the Piedmont Uplands of northern Delaware, northeastern Maryland, and southeastern Pennsylvania settlement patterns remained focused on areas of predictable and reliable surface water resources. Examples of sites outside of Delaware that show multicomponent macroband base camps containing Woodland I and Woodland II materials include the Minguannan site (36-CH-5) excavated by Elwood

Wilkins and members of the Archaeological Society of Delaware and the Webb site (36-CH-51) excavated by the University of Delaware Department of Anthropology (Custer 1982), both of which are along the White Clay Creek, and the Conowingo site excavated by Joseph McNamara and the Archaeological Society of Maryland. Areas distant from the predictable water resources contain scattered concentrations of artifacts that often incude triangular projectile points. These sites were also seen in the area during the Woodland I period and are thought to represent very short-term forays away from macroband base camps (Custer and Wallace 1982).

The presence of numerous multicomponent macroband base camp sites that include Woodland I materials and Minguannan complex artifacts seems to underscore the similarity of Woodland I and Minguannan complex adaptations. There is no real settlement shift to areas with extensive arable land, and large, sedentary villages with well-developed house structures have not been noted. The absence of these sites, however, is not a result of differential survey coverage. Custer and Wallace (1982) have studied more than 300 sites in the Piedmont Uplands and no large village sites were noted, except on the northern fringes of the Piedmont Uplands in the Pequea and Conestoga drainages of Lancaster County, Pennsylvania (Kinsey and Graybill 1971; Graybill 1973). However, these sites are far removed from northern Delaware and are part of the Shenks Ferry complex, which is adapted to markedly different biosocial environments. The general Woodland I settlement pattern described earlier can therefore be applied to the Minguannan complex. Apparently, the introduction of agricultural food production systems had little effect on the lifestyles of native American groups in northern Delaware. From an ecological perspective, agriculture requires rather large investments of labor to supply a surplus. In order for a society to become involved in agricultural food production, the payoff of energy resources from the harvests and stored foods must be greater than the energy costs of the initial labor. Numerous social and natural environments can produce situations where this happens, and the most common is a rapidly expanding population in a marginally productive environment for hunting and gathering. Northern Delaware fulfills neither of these conditions. There is no evidence of increased population beyond the levels seen during Woodland I, and the hunting and gathering potential of most of the area is quite high. Although some social pressures for the establishment of semisedentary communities and intensive food gathering existed during Woodland I times accompanied by population growth, there were sufficient wild food resources to supply the populations. Consequently, agriculture was not really necessary and represented only a very minor portion of the food resources utilized, if indeed they were utilized at all.

This view of the Woodland II adaptations in northern Delaware corresponds to patterns noted for the era of European Contact (Weslager 1972;

Table 11: Slaughter Creek Complex Settlement Models (Thomas et al 1975:60-65)

Model	Winter	Spring	Summer	Fall
1	micro-band base camp; interior	micro-band base camp; mid-drainage	micro-band base camp; coastal	micro-band base camp; mid-drainage
2	→ macro-band base camp; interior	micro-band base camp; mid-drainage	macro-band base camp; coastal	macro-band base camp; interior →
3	macro-band base camp; interior	macro-band base camp; coastal ——————————————→		macro-band base camp; interior
4	→ macro-band base camp; mid-drainage	——————————→	micro-band base camp; coastal	macro-band base camp; mid-drainage →
5	→ macro-band base camp mid-drainage ——————————————————————————————→			

Becker 1976, 1980a, 1980b, 1981a, 1981b, 1981c) and may be generalized for the historic Lenape (Unami) Delaware Indians.

Slaughter Creek Complex

The Slaughter Creek complex was originally noted by Thomas (1973, 1977) based on the work of Weslager (1939b, 8) and is defined by the presence of Townsend ceramics, triangular projectile points, large macroband base camps, and possibly sedentary villages with high densities of storage features. The distribution of the Slaughter Creek complex runs from central Kent County south into Sussex County. In many ways, the Slaughter Creek complex is the most intensely studied of all of the prehistoric archaeological complexes noted for Delaware. The sites are quite large and are easily recognized and the artifacts can be rather spectacular, including complete ceramic vessels. As such, the sites attracted many early investigators and over the past fifty years many Slaughter Creek complex sites have been excavated.

The adaptations of the Slaughter Creek complex have also been subjected to intensive study (Thomas et al. 1975). Building from a careful analysis of the potential food sources found in the different environmental zones of southern Delaware, Thomas and his associates were able to develop a series of models of archaeological site distributions for the groups of people that would be exploiting these food resources. They noted two basic site types, including seasonal camps and base camps (Thomas et al. 1975, 62). Base camps would correspond to macroband base camps as defined here, and seasonal camps would correspond to microband base camps. No projections were made about individual procurement sites. Five basic models of the settlement patterns were generated from the analyses of potential food sources and each model projected different combinations of microband base camps in different environments during different seasons. Table 11 summarizes each model. Each settlement model assumes a

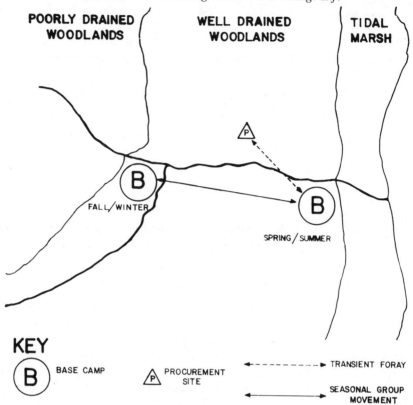

Fig. 18. Woodland II—Model 3 (from Thomas et al. 1975, 63).

different degree of residential stability, ranging from groups of transient microband base camps to single sedentary macroband base camps or villages. After the models were developed, the expected artifact distributions were noted. In other words, they listed the types of artifacts that one would expect to find if any given model were true. In this manner the expectations of each model of prehistoric activities could be compared to the actual distributions of artifacts recovered. The model whose expectations were most similar to the observed artifact distributions would be the most accurate picture of the prehistoric adaptations.

When the various settlement models were compared to known sites, Models III, IV, and V (see Table 11) were seen to be the most accurate. These models have the highest degree of residential stability and correspond to the view that when moving from the Woodland I to the Woodland II period, lifestyles became more sedentary. Unfortunately, the available data are not really sufficient to discriminate among the most accurate and the three most sedentary models; however, further work should be able to provide a clearer picture.

Macroband base camps and villages of the Slaughter Creek complex are noted at a number of locations throughout southern Delaware. A series of macroband base camps and small village locations along Slaughter Creek provided the original data for the description of the Slaughter Creek complex. The earliest work at Slaughter Creek was directed by D. S. Davidson (1935a, 1935b, 1936), and a summary of the circumstances of this early work is provided by Weslager (1968, 58–61). Davidson was working at the University of Pennsylvania and was contacted when artifacts and some human bones were recovered by workers on a Civilian Conservation Corps road-building project along the south side of Slaughter Creek. Subsequent archaeological research, aided by the newly organized Archaeological Society of Delaware, uncovered the remains of a relatively large site (7S-C-1) with many storage features. A large number of tool types seem to be indicated and ceramics were abundant. Plant-processing tools also seem to have been quite common. Faunal remains included deer, bear, and other small

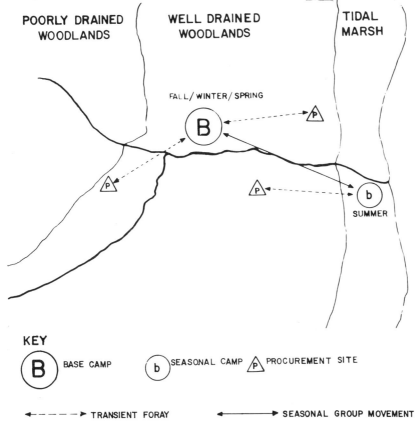

KEY

Ⓑ BASE CAMP   ⓑ SEASONAL CAMP   ◬ PROCUREMENT SITE

◄ – – – – ► TRANSIENT FORAY   ◄――――► SEASONAL GROUP MOVEMENT

Fig. 19. Woodland II—Model 4 (from Thomas et al. 1975, 64).

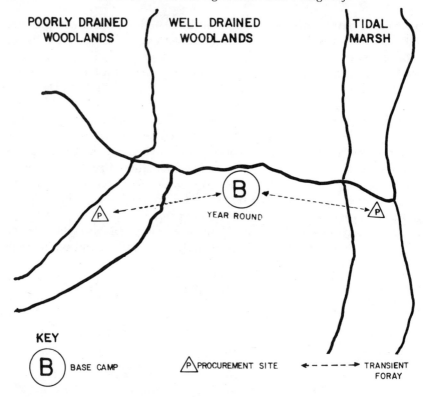

POORLY DRAINED WOODLANDS	WELL DRAINED WOODLANDS	TIDAL MARSH

B YEAR ROUND

P   P

KEY

B   BASE CAMP   P PROCUREMENT SITE   ◄ ─ ─ ─ ─ ► TRANSIENT
FORAY

Fig. 20. Woodland II—Model 5 (from Thomas et al. 1975, 64).

mammals (Davidson 1936). Notes from these early excavations are difficult to interpret; however, it seems likely that at least one of the larger features reported was a semisubterranean pit house. Later work at the nearby Draper site (Purnell 1958) showed similar patterns, and the Delaware Bureau of Archaeology and Historic Preservation carried out some additional test excavations in the early 1970s near the site of Davidson's earlier work. More recently, a field school from New York University under the direction of Bert Salwen and Karen Zukerman made a comprehensive survey of most of the Slaughter Creek drainage. Preliminary reports (Zukerman 1979a, 1979b) show a series of similar sites in the area. Sites 7S-C-8, 9, and 29, found along the south side of Slaughter Creek, seem to be smaller versions of the main 7S-C-1 area originally excavated by Davidson. On the north side of Slaughter Creek several site locations (7S-C-7, 30) seem to be smaller concentrations of shell-filled features and possibly a pithouse feature (Daniel Griffith, personal communication). These sites may be separate microband base camps, or hamlets, or may be outlying activity areas associated with the main site at 7S-C-1. The Slaughter Creek area thus seems to be a setting of very high population density during

Woodland II times and contains a variety of types of sites, including a large macroband base camp, or small village, and a series of outlying hamlets or microband base camps. These varied sites may or may not be contemporary with each other. Radiocarbon dates from later excavations seem to indicate that some time variation is evident and range between A.D. 975 and A.D. 1345. (See SI-4946, SI-4944, and SI-4943 in Appendix 1.)

Of interest is an additional feature type found in the original excavations noted by Davidson (1935a, 1935b). In one area of the site a number of human skeletons were found. Some of the skeletons seem to have been single fully articulated burials, while others were in groups and appear to be secondary burials with many disarticulated individuals. Davidson (1935b) described this burial feature as similar to an "ossuary," which is currently defined as a "collective secondary deposit of skeletal material representing individuals initially stored elsewhere" (Ubelaker 1974, 8). Similar burials are noted elsewhere in southern Delaware during the Slaughter Creek complex time, including a series of burials near Rehoboth Beach excavated by Wigglesworth (1933), Thompson's Island burials excavated and reported by Weslager (1942) and Stewart (1945), and a series of sites along the Choptank on the Eastern Shore of Maryland (Weslager 1942). Thomas (1973) has reviewed many of these burials and notes that many seem to show some secondary treatment of the skeleton to produce the disarticulated remains. In a more recent review, Ubelaker (1974) notes that these sites on the Delmarva Peninsula are probably not true ossuaries like the large accumulations of individuals seen at sites in the lower Potomac River Valley and recorded among various Algonkian groups of the eastern seaboard (Feest 1973). Nevertheless, some special reburial of individuals after their first interment seems indicated by the Slaughter Creek complex data and should be considered as part of its cultural system.

The Townsend Site (7S-G-2) near Lewes, Delaware, is another large Slaughter Creek complex macroband base camp or village. Originally discovered in 1947, the Townsend site was excavated for several seasons by the newly formed Sussex Society for Archaeology and History (Omwake and Stewart 1963). More than 90 shell-filled pits were excavated and a disturbed grave feature including approximately 19 individuals in both bundles and disarticulated burials were found (Omwake and Stewart 1963, 4–5). In many ways, the distribution of the features and the burials look very similar to the main area of the Slaughter Creek site. A large number of artifacts were recovered from the features and the ceramic sample provided the basis for Blaker's (1963) original analysis and definition of Townsend ceramics. A variety of stone tool types were found, including triangular projectile points made from cobble cherts and jaspers and many plant processing tools. Shells from the features included oysters, clams, conch, and mussel (Omwake and Stewart 1963, 6). Numerous bone specimens, including tools, were recovered; however, no comprehensive analysis is available to note what species were used. One interesting find from the site was the discovery of 12 dogs that were included in pit features and possibly prepared burials. All of the dogs were mature (Omwake and Stewart 1963, 54) and the skeletons articulated. This suggests that these animals were not dismembered and butchered for food, but were domesticated for use in hunting, or possibly just for pets.

The dating of the Townsend site is something of an enigma. The ceramics described by Blaker (1963) include both Townsend-corded and Townsend-incised designs, indicating that the entire time range of the Slaughter Creek complex is present (Griffith 1977). Some artifacts from early colonial years are noted from the site and a historic well feature was excavated (Omwake and Stewart 1963). Also found in the feature fill were some roulette decorated pipes, which are often found at sites that date to the post-European Contact period (post-1620). In a series of interpretations of the Townsend site included in the Omwake and Stewart volume, Witthoft (1963, 61) suggests a post-1550 A.D. date for the site. Based on new information, such a date would be inconsistent with the presence of the Townsend-incised ceramic designs. Griffith's (1977) analysis of Townsend ceramics has recently shown that these incised designs are relatively early in the sequence of the development of Townsend design motifs, probably occurring before A.D. 1300 (Griffith 1977, 19). Plotting of the distribution of the Townsend designs across the site did show that there seem to be two distinct clusters of features (Daniel Griffith, personal communication). One group of features included the earlier Townsend designs and another set of features included the later corded designs and the roulette decorated pipes. Thus, there seems to be two occupations of the Townsend site: one prior to A.D. 1300 and another that may be as late as the A.D. 1550 date proposed by Witthoft, if not later. The later occupation of the Townsend site will be discussed in more detail in chapter 6.

The Mispillion site (7S-A-1) represents another large Slaughter Creek complex macroband base camp, or possible village, and is very similar to the Townsend and Slaughter Creek sites. The Mispillion site has a long history of excavation and is noted in articles by numerous authors (Hutchinson 1955a, 1955b; Hutchinson et al. 1957; Omwake 1954a; Flegel 1959; Thomas and Warren 1970b; Tirpak 1978). It is difficult to pull together the varied reports, although Thomas and Warren (1970b) and Hutchinson et al. (1957) make a valiant effort. A large number of shell-filled pits were noted and the wide variety of tool types and the large number of ceramics seem to represent a situation similar to the other large Slaughter Creek complex sites. In a reevaluation of features from a number of Slaughter Creek complex sites, Artusy and Griffith (1975) note that a semisubterranean house feature was present at Mispillion. Lopez's (1961) report on the ceramics seems to show a predominance of incised designs, so the site probably dates to the earlier part of the Slaughter Creek complex. Seriations of Townsend ceramics also place this site early in the sequence of the Slaughter Creek complex sites (Griffith 1977, 129–30) and a single radiocarbon date of A.D. 1085 (UGa-923) seems to support this contention. The early dating of Mispillion is significant because it indicates that the social processes linked to the appearance of population concentrations much larger than any seen during the Woodland I Webb complex began fairly early during the Woodland II period, at least in northern Sussex County.

One of the more recently excavated Slaughter Creek complex macroband base camps is the Hughes-Willis site (7K-D-21) in central Kent County. The Hughes-Willis Site is the northernmost site of the Slaughter Creek complex and was excavated by the Delaware Bureau of Archaeology and Historic Preservation in conjunction with the Kent County Archaeological Society. Some Carey complex components are noted at the site; however, the major part of the occupation seems to have taken place during Slaughter Creek complex times. The Hughes-Willis site is one of the sites used to test the various settlement models for Woodland II groups (Thomas et al. 1975, 70–78) and its description is drawn mainly from the summary presented by Thomas et al. (1975). A detailed analysis of the tool categories was carried out and a wide variety of tools are noted. Only ten features were excavated, representing about 20 percent of the total site, indicating that Hughes-Willis is somewhat smaller than the Slaughter Creek complex sites discussed previously. Faunal and floral remains from the site included a large number of wild species including deer, birds, turtles, hickory nuts, black haw, and American lotus (Thomas et al. 1975, 76). A fall through midwinter occupation is suggested (Thomas et al. 1975, 77), since extensive hickory nut processing seems to have taken place at the site itself. The relatively short-term occupation of this rather extensive site could suggest that different social processes were at work in the northern fringes of the Slaughter Creek complex distribution. The smaller size of the site and the limited nature of the seasonal occupation could indicate that Woodland II groups in central Kent County were not as sedentary as groups farther south.

Also located toward the northern end of the distribution of the Slaughter Creek complex is the Island Field site (7K-F-17), which in addition to being the site of a Webb complex cemetery is the location of a Woodland II macroband base camp or village site. No description of the Woodland II components was ever published, although Artusy and Griffith (1975) did note the presence of a semisubterranean pit house feature at the site. Recent excavations by the University of Delaware Department of Anthropology, still in progress, have revealed the presence of a sheet midden adjacent to the house structure. Extensive flotation of the midden has recovered a large number of plant remains, many of which appear, on the basis of initial inspection, to be wild plant foods. Plotting of the exact position of artifacts within the sheet midden deposit also seems to reveal a number of activity areas, including a small feature composed of resharpening flakes. The implication of the presence of activity areas within the sheet midden suggests that many of the deposits of living debris found at Woodland II sites are not trash accumulations that represent extensive single-event garbage deposits. They may be just small accumulations of living debris, scattered around house structures, that slowly accumulate through time. As new vegetation covers the small accumulations of debris, activities such as tool resharpening may take place, and be preserved in the archaeological record. More careful analysis of living debris at other Woodland II sites, therefore, seems to be warranted.

A number of macroband base camps and villages have been discovered further south on the Delmarva Peninsula; however, most of these sites are poorly known archaeologically. The Russell site (7S-D-7), located near Lewes and the Townsend site, is reported by Marine (1957), and some excavations were carried out. The quantity of artifacts and the varied tool forms and features seem to indicate the presence of a macroband base camp, although there is insufficient evidence to say much more. The Moore site (18-DO-13), located on the Nanticoke River in Maryland, also seems to be a macroband base camp, based on the description offered by Callaway et al. (1960). The presence of the Moore site is important because it documents the existence of macroband base camps in drainages away from the Delaware Bay shore within the southern portions of the Slaughter Creek complex.

A very large number of microband base camp sites of the Slaughter Creek complex are noted in Delaware and some provide the focus of the earliest archaeological work in Delaware (Weslager 1968, 10–30). A series of small shell middens in the vicinity of Rehoboth Beach and Lewes were discovered in the nineteenth century by Leidy (1865) and Jordan (1880, 1895, 1906). Very little is known about these early sites although the ceramics described seem to fall within the Townsend description. The small size of some of the sites attests to the fact that they are quite different from the larger Slaughter Creek complex sites described earlier. Over the years, various similar sites have been discovered in approximately the same area, including the Rehoboth midden (7S-G-3) reported by Marine et al. (1965b) and the Lighthouse site (Weslager 1968, 26; Delaware Division of Historical and Cultural Affairs 1976). Especially interesting is the Lighthouse site, which is part of the previously described Cape Henlopen Spit set of sites. The Lighthouse site and an additional shell midden (7S-D-22, 9) represent the final series of microband base camps, or especially large and intensive procurement sites, that were associated with the changing estuarine environment behind the Cape Henlopen Spit. The continuity of site locations in these brackish water environments underscores the similar nature of at least some aspects of the subsistence activities between Woodland I and

Woodland II times. In general, the discussion of microband base camps of the Slaughter Creek complex can be organized on the basis of the similarities of Woodland I locations to Woodland II locations.

A close correspondance of locations and apparent function between Woodland I and Woodland II microband base camps is seen at a number of sites in southern Delaware. At the Millman sites (7K-E-4, 23) Thomas (1966d) and others (Delaware Division of Historical and Cultural Affairs 1980) note the presence of microband base camps with multiple components of the Webb complex and the Slaughter Creek complex. The overlap of locations shows the continuity of Woodland I and Woodland II adaptations in this particular area of the northern portion of the Slaughter Creek complex, as do the similar tool forms found at the sites. Similar continuities of multicomponent occupations are noted at sites 7K-D-45 and 7K-D-48 on Saint Jones Neck (Delaware Division of Historical and Cultural Affairs 1978), also in the northern portion of the distribution of the Slaughter Creek complex. The Wilgus site (7S-K-21), which was noted as the location of a Delmarva Adena and Carey complex macroband base camp in chapter 4 and which is located in the central portion of the distribution of the Slaughter Creek complex, also has a Slaughter Creek complex occupation. A large storage feature that contained stratified remains was excavated. A small quantity of artifacts was found within the feature, along with abundant faunal and floral remains including deer, fish, and turtles. A variety of wild plant foods was also found. The similarity of these faunal remains to the earlier components at the same site underscores the similarity of the subsistence activities between Woodland I and Woodland II times.

Microband base camps of the Slaughter Creek complex also appear as single component sites. A number of these sites are reported in the older literature and about all that can be done with the data, as it exists now, is to list these sites and their references. Intensive work with the old collections and some limited testing may provide further information. Included among these microband base camps are the following sites: Lewes High School site (7S-D-5) reported by Omwake (1948) and others (Anonymous 1951a); the Ritter site (7S-D-2, 3), which produced the only corn remains in Delaware, reported by Omwake (1951, 1954b, 1954d); the Derrickson site (7S-D-6) reported by an unknown author (Anonymous 1951b); and the Miller-Toms site reported by Omwake (1954c). These sites are all similar in configuration to the Slaughter Creek components noted at the multicomponent microband base camps.

More recent excavations have also been carried out at single component microband base camp sites of the Slaughter Creek complex that reveal more about the functions of these sites in Woodland II adaptations in southern Delaware. The Indian Landing site (7S-G-1) along the north shore of Indian River Bay represents one of the best-studied of these sites (Thomas et al. 1975). Thirteen storage and refuse pits were excavated and

Plate 7. Semisubterranean pit house, Poplar Thicket site. (Courtesy Delaware Division of Historical and Cultural Affairs.)

a variety of floral and faunal remains were noted including shellfish, deer, turtle, small mammals, birds, fish, and some hickory nuts (Thomas et al. 1975, 83–84). A summer and fall occupation is inferred. A variety of tool forms are noted and an interesting component of the tool kit is a series of bone tools that seem to be related to weaving, or perhaps the production of textiles such as nets or mats. The site is nowhere near as large as the macroband base camps and sees to be related to a variety of food production activities. Similar sites have been noted, including the Warrington site (7S-G-14) reported by Marine et al. (1964) and Griffith (n.d.a.), the Poplar Thicket site (7S-G-22) reported by Griffith (n.d.b.) and the Bay Vista site (7S-G-21). The Warrington and Poplar Thicket sites are interesting in that both contained semisubterranean pit house features (Artusy and Griffith

1975), documenting the presence of these house forms at microband base camps as well as at macroband base camps and villages. Radiocarbon dates from Poplar Thicket (UGa-924), Warrington (UGa-925), and Bay Vista (UGa-1440) range between A.D. 1100 and A.D. 1370 and are correlated with the varying designs of Townsend ceramics noted by Griffith (1977). As noted previously, these sites appear to be similar to Indian Landing, although the seasonal usages may not be the same. Nevertheless, they all represent smaller social units than those seen at macroband base camps and villages. Some small changes in internal site patterning can be seen at the later Poplar Thicket site, dated at A.D. 1370, which looks like a more tightly defined small cluster of dwellings and features (Griffith n.d.b.). Griffith (personal communication) has suggested that this site may be representative of a small, nuclear-family-based hamlet rather than a microband base camp with a less structured social unit composition.

As was the case for the macroband base camp sites, microband base camp sites are found in the Nanticoke drainage as documented by the Prickly Pear Island site (7S-H-18), which contained a number of shell-filled features and which produced a radiocarbon date of A.D. 1015 (UGa-1760) associated with Townsend ceramics. Similar sites are also noted throughout the southern portion of the Slaughter Creek complex distribution in Maryland, including the Willin site (18-DO-1) reported by Bryant et al. (1951) and Hutchinson (1967); the Chicone No. 1 (18-DO-11) and the Chicone No. 2 (18-DO-10) sites reported by Hutchinson et al. (1964), and a number of sites along the Marshyhope Creek (Corkran and Flegel 1953; Flegel 1978).

The problems in identifying procurement sites that were evident in earlier periods of Delaware prehistory are also present in the Woodland II period. Only five Woodland II Slaughter Creek complex procurement sites can be noted with certainty and these all come from the Saint Jones Neck area, including 7K-D-42, 45, 49, 52, and 7K-F-86. All of these sites seem to be associated with saltwater or brackish water environments and may represent special gathering locations. Tool forms and numbers of artifacts are very limited (Delaware Division of Historical and Cultural Affairs 1978).

From the description of the Slaughter Creek complex sites noted above, it is apparent that there is a range of variation in settlement patterns and adaptations during the Woodland II period in southern Delaware. It is not surprising that Thomas et al. (1975) were unable to distinguish a single model of Slaughter Creek settlement and subsistence patterns. Depending on the site location, any one of the three models (Models 3, 4, 5—Table 11) may be applicable. Adaptations may also vary through time. Luckily, the large amount of data available for varied Slaughter Creek complex sites makes it possible to make some preliminary statements about spatial and temporal variation in adaptations.

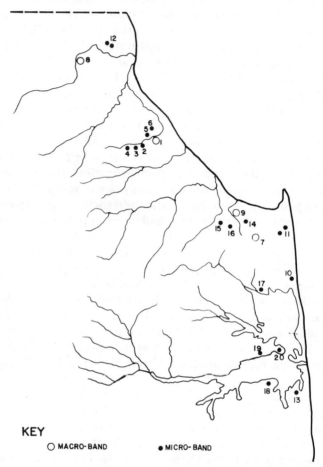

Fig. 21. Slaughter Creek complex site locations. 1 = Slaughter Creek (7S-C-1); 2 = 7S-C-8; 3 = 7S-C-9; 4 = 7S-C-29; 5 = 7S-C-7; 6 = 7S-C-30; 7 = Townsend (7S-G-2); 8 = Mispillion (7S-A-1); 9 = Russell (7S-D-7); 10 = Rehoboth Midden (7S-G-3); 11 = Lighthouse sites (7S-D-9,22); 12 = Millman sites (7K-E-4,23); 13 = Wilgus (7S-K-21); 14 = Lewes High School (7S-D-5); 15 = Ritter (7S-D-2,3); 16 = Derrickson (7S-D-6); 17 = Warrington (7S-G-14); 18 = Bay Vista (7S-G-21); 19 = Poplar Thicket (7S-G-22); 20 = Indian Landing (7S-G-1).

Significant spatial variation in settlement patterns and adaptations can be seen when various portions of the Slaughter Creek complex are compared to one another. North of the Mispillion River, only two Woodland II macroband base camps are noted, the Hughes-Willis and Island Field sites, which are significantly smaller than the large macroband base camps or villages located south of the Mispillion River. The Hughes-Willis site especially looks very much like a Woodland I macroband base camp except for its high concentration of storage features, especially with its Mid-drainage zone location. Model V (Table 11) as described by Thomas et al. (1975, 64) seems to best approximate the Slaughter Creek complex settlement pattern in Kent County. Continuity with Woodland I adaptations in the Kent County area is noted and underscored by the distribution of microband base camps in the Delaware Shore zone on Saint Jones Neck and at the Millman sites. The absence of macroband base camps in the Saint Jones Neck area, as revealed by comprehensive survey (Delaware Division of Historical and Cultural Affairs 1978), also shows the continuity with Woodland I adaptations and social environments. The fissioning of macroband base camps that occurred during the Woodland I Webb complex apparently continued into the Woodland II period in this area. Intensified use of storage in the Mid-drainage zone may be correlated with increased sedentism and population growth; however, these processes are not strongly developed in this northern portion of the Slaughter Creek complex distribution.

South of the Mispillion River different settlement systems are present. The area of interface between the Mid-drainage and the Delaware Shore zones between the Mispillion River and Cape Henlopen includes the largest Slaughter Creek complex macroband base camp sites. Model 5 (Table 11) described by Thomas et al. (1975, 64) best approximates the site distributions in this area. The large size of the macroband base camps and the high density of storage features indicate an increase in population and/ or sedentism beyond the levels seen at Woodland I sites. Similarly, the location of these large sites at the interface of the Mid-drainage and Delaware Coastal zones represents a break from Woodland I patterns. The location at this interface and the high incidence of shellfish remains found at the sites demonstrates the fact that intensive utilization of shellfish and gathering of plant foods and possibly agriculture were the major subsistence activities. Exploitation of these resources from the interface of the Delaware Shore and Mid-drainage zones in an essentially brackish water environmental zone rather than from the middle of the Mid-drainage zone at the saltwater/freshwater interface may be explained by the configuration of the local drainages. The drainages of northern Sussex County between Cape Henlopen and the Mispillion River are shorter, and somewhat truncated, compared to the drainages to the north and to the south. As such, the effects of sea level rise would be more pronounced and the size of the productive resource zone smaller. In these settings, groups would be forced to intensify food procurement, use storage facilities, and possibly even add agricultural food production to their subsistence base. As these changes were made, population could grow and groups would become sedentary. Similarly, increasing population growth and sedentism would create a greater need for increased use of storage and agricultural food production systems. In spite of the high local population densities, which seemed to be even greater than levels seen during Woodland I times, there is no evidence of ranked societies such as elaborate burials or exchange networks. Although disarticulated burials and ossuarylike features seemed to be present at some of the larger Slaughter Creek complex sites, they cannot be clearly related to attributes of ranked societies and, as Ubelaker (1974) notes, they are not at all similar to the true ossuaries seen in the lower Potomac River Valley. As such, these sites appear to represent villages of relatively constant egalitarian social group composition. Interaction among social units through exchange seemed to be minimal, although there was enough interaction to produce similar ceramic design motifs throughout the Slaughter Creek complex sites. It is particularly interesting to note that these large sites seemed to appear in a zone of marginal productivity. However, the appearance of agricultural food production systems in marginal environments occurs in numerous areas throughout the world (Binford 1968; Flannery 1968; MacNeish 1971). In southern Delaware the marginal environments of the truncated drainages may have initially provided a biosocial environmental setting that favored some intensification of food production; however, the necessary social environments for the development of more complex ranked societies were not present and extensive trade and exchange and mortuary complexes, such as were seen during the Woodland I period, do not develop. The crucial variation in the social environments between Woodland I and Woodland II groups may be related to the fact that Woodland I groups were circumscribed in highly productive environments where intensification of food production generated temporary surpluses that could be stored by some individuals and "invested" in symbols of status that could be exchanged or in the sponsorship of ritual events that verified the high status of the participating individuals (Harris 1979). In contrast, the Woodland II groups of the lower Delaware Bay were not able to generate a true surplus, even with agricultural food production, that could be used for anything beyond normal subsistence needs. Therefore, there was nothing to "invest" in the accoutrements of ranked societies and these more complex social organizations never developed.

The area south of Cape Henlopen that includes the Coastal Bay zone is similar to the area north of the Mispillion River in that no large macroband base camps are noted in this area. The wide range of microband base camps in this area indicates that Model 3 (Table 11) as noted by Thomas et al. (1975, 63) best applies to the Slaughter Creek complex south of Cape Henlopen. The large extent of highly productive estuarine settings in the Coastal Bay zone precluded the use of agricultural food production systems and reduced potential circumscription so that a constant fissioning of groups was likely as critical local population densities were reached. Consequently, intensification of food production, use of storage, and group size could be maintained at low levels comparable to those of Woodland I times. A high degree of continuity seems to exist in settlement patterns from Late Carey and Carey complexes.

In addition to the spatial variation, temporal variation in site distributions can be related to larger trends throughout the Delmarva Peninsula and the Middle Atlantic. As noted earlier, during the Woodland II period ceramic design similarities were evident among Townsend and Minguannan ceramics (Griffith 1977, 145–50; Custer 1981; Lopez 1961), which span most of Delaware. By about A.D. 1300 (Griffith 1977, 148) ceramic styles changed in southern Delaware, with the corded horizontal motifs similar to designs found on Potomac Creek ceramics of the western shore of the Chesapeake Bay (Stephenson 1963) becoming more common. At the same time, there seemed to be a southward shift of populations using Townsend ceramics (Griffith 1977, 145–50). Accompanying this southward shift was the appearance of nonlocal Woodland II ceramics such as Potomac Creek and Keyser Farm varieties at the Robbins Farm site in central Kent County (Stocum 1977). The location of these nonlocal ceramics is especially interesting in that they were found at the southern margin of the area of Delaware that seemed to have a low population density during Woodland II times. This possible low-population zone, mentioned in the discussion of ceramic distributions, extends from the Chesapeake and Delaware Canal at least to the headwaters of the Saint Jones drainage. The apparent southward shift of the Slaughter Creek complex populations could have extended this zone as far south as the Mispillion drainage by A.D. 1300. The presence of nonlocal ceramics may have represented an initial expansion of nonlocal populations using markedly different ceramics into this low-population density zone. Gardner (n.d.) believes that numerous population disruptions were apparent throughout the Woodland II period in the Middle Atlantic and that the appearance of Potomac Creek ceramics in central Delaware may have been correlated with one of the later population disruptions in the lower Potomac River Valley. Future fieldwork should be able to test the validity of this hypothesis.

[6]

European Contact Period: Cultures in Conflict

The seventeenth century marks the beginning of the European Contact period, the final episode in the long story of native American cultures in Delaware. Throughout the entire time range of Delaware prehistory discussed up to this point, native American populations were able to adjust their lifestyles to accommodate major changes in their biosocial environment. The major alterations of the biotic environments accompanying the shift from Pleistocene to Holocene environments were accommodated by changes in settlement-subsistence systems, and although important cultural changes took place, native American societies maintained a relatively continuous population throughout Delaware before, during, and after this biotic environmental change. Similarly, the major alterations of the social environments associated with the new settlement patterns of the midpostglacial xerothermic were accommodated through the development of new and more complex social organizations that were based upon existing social systems. In general, no matter how drastic the biosocial environmental change, native American populations of Delaware were flexible enough to maintain their existence. However, beginning in the middle of the sixteenth century, the native American populations of eastern North America were exposed to drastic changes in their social environment that would culminate in the virtual extinction of their unique way of life. Throughout the seventeenth and eighteenth centuries, the native American societies of Delaware would be drawn ever more tightly into the western European sociopolitical system that would eventually exterminate their way of life.

Up to this point, the absence of writing systems in North America made the archaeological record the only source of information about native American societies. However, when western Europeans arrived in Delaware, a body of written references and descriptions of native American populations began to develop. These historical documents provide an additional source of information on native American populations in Delaware. Thorough analyses of these records have been carried out (Weslager 1978, 1972, 1961; Porter 1979; Goddard 1978b) and will not be repeated here. Nevertheless, it should be noted that archaeology and history represent two separate lines of evidence that should converge to produce a single reconstruction of past native American societies and the social processes affecting them. However, this is not always the case. Just as the archaeological record is incomplete and its interpretation subject to error, so also is the early historic record. Not only is the historical record incomplete, but grossly distorted views of native American societies resulted from the prejudiced and ethnocentrically biased accounts produced by Europeans. Similarly, the manipulation of native American societies by western European colonial powers often produced a series of purposefully distorted views of native American life (Jennings 1966, 1968, 1975). Thus archaeology and history often produce contradictory views of the European Contact period, and crossing from one discipline to the other can be somewhat difficult. In some areas, such as the lower Susquehanna River Valley, abundant finds of European trade goods in native American sites allows the development of explicit linkages between the historical and archaeological record (Hunter 1959; Witthoft 1959a; Kinsey 1977a; Jennings 1978). However, a similar situation does not exist in Delaware and linkages between the records are not readily apparent. A brief review of some of the processes associated with the European Contact period, presented below, will develop a context for the understanding of the archaeological record for the European Contact period in Delaware and its relation to similarly dated archaeological complexes in the surrounding area.

The search for sites of the European Contact period is at first complicated by the processes of interaction between native American and western European societies. For example, since the beginning of the European Contact period cannot be linked to any single event at a single point in time, there is some question as to when the earliest direct contact between native Americans and western Europeans took place in Delaware. Two opinions dominate the answers to this question. Weslager (1961) takes a conservative view and places the earliest *documented* European contact around 1609, the date when Henry Hudson entered the Delaware Bay, or even as late as 1616 when records specifically note that Cornelius Hendricksen traded with native American groups along the Delaware Bay (Weslager, personal communication, 1981). Other researchers (Thurman 1974; Goddard 1978b) have suggested that contact could have taken place earlier, such as during Verazano's 1524 voyage along the Middle Atlantic coast. However, there is no hard evidence for these earlier direct contacts between native American and western European populations in Delaware. Further complications are introduced by the fact that the effects of interaction with western Europeans spread far beyond the native American groups who were actually involved in face-to-face contact with the Europeans. These indirect effects were recognized by the presence of European trade goods in archaeological assemblages or in descriptions of native American groups by early explorers. For example, Witthoft (1959a, 22) notes that European goods have been found in Susquehannock middens at the Schultz site in Lancaster County, Pennsylvania, around 1580. The ultimate source of the European goods is not known and probably never will be; however, their presence indicates the existence of an intricate set of trade relationships that spread the effects of European contact far and wide fairly rapidly.

Trade for furs, especially beaver pelts, provided the mechanism whereby these European goods came into the possession of native Americans in the Middle Atlantic region. The fashion trends of Europe provided an almost insatiable market for furs and the lure of the immense profits from trade in furs drew many European commercial enterprises to eastern North America. Weslager (1961), Jennings (1966, 1968, 1975, 1978), and Hunter (1959) note how the Dutch, Swedish, and English traders were drawn into the Delaware and Susquehanna drainages to participate in this trade. Competition among the various European trade companies, exacerbated by political clashes among the colonial powers, combined with competition among native American groups for access to European goods, such as guns and metal tools, to produce a complex sociopolitical conflict (Hunt 1940). In the lower portion of the Susquehanna and Delaware drainages, the Susquehannocks emerged as the dominant native American group in the fur trade during the seventeenth century. Trading with both the Dutch, Swedish, and English, the Susquehannocks provided procurement, processing, and transportation services (Kinsey 1977a; Witthoft and Kinsey 1959; Jennings 1966, 1968, 1978; Weslager 1972, 98–104). As intensive hunting rapidly depleted the populations of fur-bearing animals of the eastern seaboard, the production area for furs shifted progressively westward throughout the seventeenth century. Native American societies in Delaware, blocked to the west by the Susquehannocks, were therefore closed out of intensive participation in the emerging trade by at least the middle part of the seventeenth century. The implication regarding the archaeological record for the European Contact period in Delaware is that large quantities of European trade goods, the only good indicators of European Contact period sites, were never present in Delaware. Therefore these sites are more difficult to recognize archaeologically than European Contact period sites in other areas such as the Susquehannock sites of southeastern Pennsylvania.

The fur trade had numerous disruptive effects upon native American societies. Competition for access to the fur trade centers and sources of pelts increased the incidence of intertribal warfare (Jennings 1975) and enabled the European colonial powers to play one native American group against another. The flood of European tools into native American material cultural assemblages caused the abandonment of traditional ceramic and lithic technologies and created a dependence on European goods that was manipulated to the Europeans' advantage. Although dependence on European trade goods and intertribal warfare caused serious disruptions of native American societies, even more serious were the diseases that were transmitted to native American groups. Lacking natural immunities to diseases such as influenza and smallpox, native American populations were decimated by disease. Building from the work of Cook (1976) and others, Jennings (1975) notes that a 90 percent population reduction occurred among native American groups for each century of contact. Disease spread well ahead of face-to-face interactions and in many areas depopulation had occurred before the Europeans arrived. Indeed, Jennings (1975) suggests that it is better to think of North America as a "widowed" land rather than a "virgin" land. Although there is no firm evidence available, native American groups in Delaware were probably subject to the same processes of depopulation during the seventeenth and eighteenth centuries.

A significant byproduct of the depopulation and the competition for access to the fur trade was the dislocation of native American populations. One of the best-documented cases was the movement of the Susquehannocks from their homeland in the upper Susquehanna Valley to their seventeenth-century location at the headwaters of the Chesapeake Bay (Hunter 1959; Witthoft 1959a; Jennings 1978). The Susquehannock movement probably began prior to 1580, and other group movements continued well into the late eighteenth century (Kinsey and Custer 1982; Weslager 1972, 1978; Porter 1979). These population disruptions and the possible earlier population movements of the Woodland II period make it very difficult to apply the direct historical approach (Wedel 1938; Strong 1935, 1940; Steward 1942) and to link Woodland II archaeological complexes with the known ethnohistoric groups (Goddard 1978b; Feest 1978; Weslager 1972, 1978; Porter 1979). However, the Woodland II material culture similarities, especially ceramics, do seem to fit well with the Central Algonkian subarea defined by Flannery (1939, 190–97) and may also be related to language distributions (Goddard 1978a).

In reality it is not critically important to know the exact ethnic identification of the native American groups that might be linked to any specific European Contact period site in Delaware. For this review, we need know only that the Unami Delaware, Choptank, Nanticokes, and other ethnic groups of the Delmarva Peninsula seemed to share a common egalitarian band-level or simple tribal-level organization that lacked any large-scale supralocal organizations, although intercommunity interaction was present (Becker 1976, 1980a, 1980b, 1981a, 1981b, 1981c; Weslager 1972, 1978; Feest 1978; Goddard 1978b; Porter 1979). Also, communities were small and extended family organizations did not seem to have operated as corporate units in large-scale cooperative labor ventures, especially in the organization and support of long-term military-trading ventures. In contrast, the large communities and corporate lineages of the Susquehannocks (Trigger 1978) carried out such expeditions and ensured that no matter what ethnic groups from the Delmarva Peninsula were involved, the Susquehannocks would have been dominant. Thus, in considering the archaeological record of the European Contact period in Delaware, we can assume that throughout Delaware all groups were marginal participants in the fur trade and victims of Susquehannock hegemony.

Given the importance of the Susquehannocks in the fur trade, the period of their domination of the Delmarva Peninsula groups can be viewed as a special complex of the European Contact period (Early European Contact complex). This complex began around 1600 and lasted until 1675, when the Susquehannocks left Lancaster County, Pennsylvania, for Maryland (Jennings 1968). When they left Lancaster County, the Susquehannocks ceased to effect native American groups in Delaware and a new complex of the European Contact period, the Refugee complex, began. The Refugee complex has been defined by Kinsey and Custer (1982) as a portion of the European Contact period when native American populations began to leave areas of relatively high European population density and opted for asylum with other native American groups. The result was a complete disruption of traditional communities and cultural institutions. This complex began around 1675 and lasted until the present time. Pennsylvania colonial policies (Jennings 1966) made Lancaster County an area where many refugee groups settled. Examples of these sites include Conoy Town (Kent 1971), Conestoga Town (Kinsey 1977a), and the Lancaster County Park site (Kinsey and Custer 1982). The major effect of these movements was a depopulation of the state by native Americans. In a recently published book Weslager (1983) documents the movements of the Nanticoke out of Delaware after the early part of the eighteenth century. Similar patterns have been noted for the Delaware during approximately the same time period (Weslager 1972). The archaeological sites that have been assigned to these complexes are reviewed below.

Early European Contact Complex Sites

A number of archaeological sites in Delaware have been ascribed to the native American populations that would have coexisted with Europeans prior to 1675, the date that seems to mark the end of Susquehannock domination. The largest grouping of these sites occurred in the Cape Henlopen area and is often viewed as associated with the early Dutch whaling station at Swanendael, which was settled in 1629 and destroyed by the local Indians in April 1632 (Weslager 1961, 86–95). The early Dutch map (De-

Vries 1909) of the Cape Henlopen area produced after 1609 notes the location of several native American villages (Weslager 1961, 60); however, the archaeological data from the known archaeological sites in the area do not clearly indicate that these sites are the same native American villages noted on the DeVries map.

One of these Cape Henlopen area sites is the Townsend site (7S-G-2). I noted earlier that the Townsend site was considered by Witthoft (1963) as a possible European Contact period site and that two separate occupations of the site seemed to be present based on the analysis of the ceramics. The main evidence for a European Contact period occupation of the site is the presence of some later seventeenth-century European pipes on the site (Omwake and Stewart 1963, 40) and a number of roulette decorated pipes that were found within shell-filled pit features with Townsend ceramics, usually late varieties (Daniel Griffith, personal communication, 1982). The association of the European pipes with native American groups at the Townsend site is not clear because a historic well feature was present at the site and excavated. The European pipes were not clearly associated with the Slaughter Creek complex features and may have been originally associated with the later historic well and had nothing to do with the native American occupation of the site. The roulette decorated pipes are different in that they seem to have been found within the features. These distinctive pipes are found in European Contact period contexts throughout the Chesapeake Bay area; however, the date of their initial use is not known. The pipes may have been a Woodland II artifact style that lasted into the European Contact period or they may be strictly a European Contact period phenomenon. Thus, the evidence from the archaeological record to support the existence of a European Contact period occupation of the Townsend site is not clear-cut and the later occupation of the site remains something of an enigma.

The excavations of the locations of the bastion of the original Swanendael site (7S-D-11) provided another possibility for the discovery of archaeological evidence for native American-Dutch interaction (Peets 1952; Bonine 1956, 1964). However, no associaton of native American artifacts and Dutch artifacts were found. Similarily, the Old House site, which appears to be a late-seventeenth-century site near Lewes (Peets 1951) and which is often suggested as a possible European Contact period site, contains no clear association of native American artifacts and European trade goods. The Russell site (7S-D-7) is also noted as a possible European Contact period site near Lewes (Marine 1957), but again no clear association of native American and European materials were found. Peets (1962) and Parsons et al. (1962) also note some isolated occurrences of seventeenth- and eighteenth-century trade goods in the general location of Woodland II Slaughter Creek complex sites, but again clear-cut associations of native American and European artifacts are lacking.

Further north in Kent County, only one possible European Contact period site is noted, site 7K-D-48, located during the Saint Jones Neck Comprehensive Survey (Delaware Division of Historical and Cultural Affairs 1978). This site contained Potomac Creek ceramics that indicate the late Woodland II population disruptions in the central part of the state (see chapter 5). Although the ceramics may be associated with the very end of the Woodland II period, there are no associated European goods to assure a European Contact period occupation.

New Castle County contains no sites from the European Contact period. However, recent research by the University of Delaware Department of Anthropology (Custer 1981) has located a historic structure adjacent to an undisturbed Woodland II Minguannan complex site along the lower White Clay Creek. The Woodland II site (7NC-E-42) was described in chapter 5 and its date within the Woodland II period is not at all clear. Approximately 20 meters downstream from the undisturbed Woodland II remains a brick hearth foundation was found below the plowzone. Only a few test units were excavated and further research at the site is scheduled. However, it should be noted that Woodland II Minguannan ceramics were found in the plowzone disturbed area at the site of the historic hearth and a triangular projectile point and Minguannan ceramics were found in among the bricks and in a soil discoloration associated with the brick hearth. No diagnostic European artifacts were recovered and the bricks are not diagnostic of early Dutch constructions. Two possibilities exist for the site. On the one hand, the structure may be quite old and the Woodland II artifacts in the building features may indicate the presence of a European Contact period site. On the other hand, the structure may date from the eighteenth century and the builders may have inadvertently dug through sections of the adjacent Woodland II site without knowing it, leaving the artifacts in their feature fill. More research at the site should clarify the situation.

As can be seen from the above discussion, there are no clear-cut examples of archaeological sites that belong to the Early European Contact complex of the European Contact period in Delaware. However, given the processes of European fur trade that could have affected native American populations in Delaware, perhaps the criteria for recognizing European Contact sites should be reevaluated. As was noted earlier, European Contact period sites in Delaware are unlikely to contain the wide range and quantity of trade goods that are found at Susquehannock sites because the native American groups of Delaware were at a geographical and sociopolitical disadvantage when competing for access to trade centers and, more importantly pelts. Consequently, there were no surpluses of trade goods to be expended in lavish burials or discarded in midden contexts. Perhaps the scraps of brass, the occasional glass beads, or the pewter buttons that show up in surface collections and sites in Delaware and Pennsylvania (Weslager 1953) may be the only indication we will ever have of the interaction of native American groups and European groups in Delaware prior to 1675, or even throughout the Refugee complex as well. Thus, our research may be biased toward not recognizing these fragile sites. More research, both archaeological and historical, will be necessary to resolve this issue.

Refugee Complex Sites

After the removal of the Susquehannocks as a dominant power in the central Middle Atlantic in 1675, the processes of population disruption accelerated throughout the Delmarva Peninsula. Also, as more organized bureaucracies developed to administer the affairs of the English colonies, the historical records grew in importance as a source of information on native American populations in Delaware. In fact, there are no known archaeological sites from Delaware that can be assigned to the Refugee complex, Therefore, the historical record is the only source of direct information on the complex in Delaware at the present time. Nevertheless, a brief review of some sites outside of Delaware may indicate what one might expect to find in the archaeological record of Delaware for the Refugee complex.

Recent work by Becker (1976, 1980a, 1980b, 1981a, 1981b, 1981c), Kinsey and Custer (1982), and Custer (1982), as well as Weslager's (1953) earlier work, has shown that Refugee complex sites are not as rich in trade goods as the Susquehannock sites of the pre-1675 period and show a mixing of burial customs that indicate a blending of ethnic groups and cultural traditions. In most cases, historical records that mention the sites can be found. Therefore, future research investigating Refugee complex sites in Delaware should begin with an examination of the available historic records on land sales, treaty grants of reserved lands, and surveyors' records. Some of these records have been compiled (Hutchinson 1961; DeValinger 1940, 1941; Mayre 1936a, 1936b, 1937, 1938, 1939, 1940). Archaeological investigations of the potential site locations indicated from the historical records will have to be especially sensitive for subtle traces of these sites because the paucity of trade materials will be similar to that of the Early European Contact complex.

By the middle part of the eighteenth century, the archaeological record no longer can produce any information on native American groups in Delaware. Indeed, the contribution of archaeology to knowledge of these peoples drops dramatically as soon as Europeans make their first appearance in Delaware. However, the prehistoric archaeological record of Delaware provides the only source of information on the 15,000-year occupation of Delaware before western Europeans ever even knew that a "New World" existed. As such, this record should be preserved so that future generations may come to learn more about this unique and extinct way of life.

Appendix 1
Radiocarbon Dates from Delaware and the Eastern Shore of Maryland

This appendix lists the known radiocarbon dates for Delaware and selected dates from the Eastern Shore of Maryland that pertain to the study of prehistoric archaeology. Dates older than 15,000 B.C. are excluded, as are dates that are not associated with prehistoric cultural material. Dates are listed from youngest to oldest and include lab number, standard deviation, associated cultural materials, and references.

Lab #	Date		Site, associated materials
UGa-924	580 ± 60 BP	(A.D. 1370)	Poplar Thicket site (7S-G-22); Townsend ceramics (corded horizontal); triangular points; semisubterranean house (Artusy 1976; Thomas 1977).
SI-4943	605 ± 60 BP	(A.D. 1345)	Slaughter Creek site (7S-C-30a); Feature 2—Townsend ceramics (Karen Zukerman, personal communication).
UGa-925	665 ± 75 BP	(A.D. 1285)	Warrington site (7S-G-14); Townsend ceramics (Artusy 1976; Thomas 1977).
SI-4944	680 ± 50 BP	(A.D. 1270)	Slaughter Creek site (7S-C-30b); Feature 1—Townsend ceramics (Karen Zukerman, personal communication).
UGa-1761	750 ± 55 BP	(A.D. 1200)	Robbins Farm site (7K-F-12); Feature 1—Potomac Creek and Keyser Farm ceramics (Stocum 1977).
UGa-1440	850 ± 55 BP	(A.D. 1100)	Bay Vista site (7S-G-21); Townsend ceramics (Artusy 1976).
UGa-923	865 ± 75 BP	(A.D. 1085)	Mispillion site (7S-A-1); Townsend ceramics (Artusy 1976; Thomas 1977).
UGa-1760	935 ± 55 BP	(A.D. 1015)	Prickly Pear Island site (7S-H-18);

Lab #	Date		Site, associated materials
			Feature 3—Townsend corded horizontal ceramics.
SI-4946	975 ± 60 BP	(A.D. 975)	Slaughter Creek site (7S-C-30c); Feature 2—Townsend ceramics (Karen Zukerman, personal communication).
SI-4942	1175 ± 75 BP	(A.D. 775)	Slaughter Creek site (7S-C-1b); Feature 6—Mockley and Coulbourn ceramics (Karen Zukerman, personal communication).
I-6338	1210 ± 90 BP	(A.D. 740)	Island Field site (7K-F-17); Hell Island ceramics; in situ cremation (Thomas and Warren 1970a).
UGa-1441	1305 ± 55 BP	(A.D. 645)	Taylor Cedar Creek site (7S-C-17); Hell Island ceramics (Artusy 1976).
UGa-3439	1310 ± 155 BP	(A.D. 640)	Delaware Park site (7NC-E-41); stemmed points and Hell Island ceramics (Thomas 1981).
I-6868	1325 ± 85 BP	(A.D. 625)	Red Lion site (7NC-D-36); hearth (Thomas 1977).
UGa-3437	1345 ± 400 BP	(A.D. 605)	Delaware Park site (7NC-E-41); stemmed points and Hell Island ceramics (Thomas 1981).
UGa-3438	1495 ± 160 BP	(A.D. 455)	Delaware Park site (7NC-E-41); stemmed points (Thomas 1981).
UGa-3498	1590 ± 75 BP	(A.D. 360)	Delaware Park site (7NC-E-41); stemmed point (Thomas 1981).
UGa-1273a	1620 ± 65 BP	(A.D. 330)	Wolfe Neck site (7S-D-10); Mockley ceramics (Artusy 1976; Griffith and Artusy 1977; Thomas 1977).
UGa-1273b	1625 ± 160 BP	(A.D. 325)	Wolfe Neck site (7S-D-10); Mockley ceramics (Artusy 1976; Griffith and Artusy 1977; Thomas 1977).
I-6060	1650 ± 110 BP	(A.D. 300)	Hughes-Willis site (7K-D-21); Mockley ceramics (Artusy 1976; Thomas 1977).
UGa-3501	1675 ± 100 BP	(A.D. 275)	Delaware Park site (7NC-E-41); stemmed point (Thomas 1981).
UGa-1762	1710 ± 70 BP	(A.D. 240)	Wilgus site (7S-K-21); Mockley ceramics (Artusy 1978).
I-5817	1750 ± 90 BP	(A.D. 200)	Carey Farm site (7K-D-3); Mockley ceramics, miscellaneous side-notched points (Artusy 1976; Thomas 1977).
UGa-3464	1760 ± 75 BP	(A.D. 190)	Delaware Park site (7NC-E-41); side-notched point (Thomas 1981).
UGa-3499	1765 ± 95 BP	(A.D. 185)	Delaware Park site (7NC-E-41); side-notched and stemmed points (Thomas 1981).

Lab #	Date		Site, associated materials
UGa-3502	1775 ± 85 BP	(A.D. 175)	Delaware Park site (7NC-E-41); side-notched point (Thomas 1981).
UGa-3467	1850 ± 80 BP	(A.D. 100)	Delaware Park site (7NC-E-41); stemmed point (Thomas 1981).
UGa-3558	1855 ± 65 BP	(A.D. 95)	Delaware Park site (7NC-E-41); no diagnostics (Thomas 1981).
UGa-3503	1865 ± 75 BP	(A.D. 85)	Delaware Park site (7NC-E-41); untyped ceramics (Thomas 1981).
UGa-3465	1879 ± 85 BP	(A.D. 80)	Delaware Park site (7NC-E-41); stemmed point and untyped ceramics (Thomas 1981).
UGa-3504	1885 ± 170 BP	(A.D. 65)	Delaware Park site (7NC-E-41); side-notched point (Thomas 1981).
UGa-3500	1960 ± 80 BP	(10 B.C.)	Delaware Park site (7NC-E-41); stemmed and side-notched points (Thomas 1981).
UGa-3557	2100 ± 80 BP	(150 B.C.)	Delaware Park site (7NC-E-41); no diagnostics (Thomas 1981).
UGa-1763	2240 ± 60 BP	(290 B.C.)	Wilgus site (7S-K-21); Coulbourn and Wolfe Neck ceramics (Artusy 1978).
UGa-1224	2325 ± 60 BP	(375 B.C.)	Wolfe Neck site (7S-D-10); Coulborn ceramics (Artusy 1976; Griffith and Artusy 1977; Thomas 1977).
I-6886	2330 ± 85 BP	(380 B.C.)	Dill Farm site (7K-E-12); pollen data (Thomas 1977).
Y-933	2330 ± 80 BP	(380 B.C.)	Saint Jones site (7K-D-1); Delmarva Adena burial (Thomas 1970, 1976, 1977).
UGa-3560	2375 ± 60 BP	(425 B.C.)	Delaware Park site (7NC-E-41); no diagnostics (Thomas 1981).
UGa-3561	2430 ± 60 BP	(480 B.C.)	Delaware Park site (7NC-E-41); no diagnostics (Thomas 1981).
I-6891	2450 ± 85 BP	(500 B.C.)	Dill Farm site (7K-E-12); Wolfe Neck ceramics (Artusy 1976; Griffith and Artusy 1977; Thomas 1977).
UGa-1223	2455 ± 60 BP	(505 B.C.)	Wolfe Neck site (7S-D-10); Wolfe Neck ceramics (Artusy 1976; Griffith and Artusy 1977; Thomas 1977).
UGa-3466	2680 ± 575 BP	(730 B.C.)	Delaware Park site (7NC-E-41); stemmed point (Thomas 1981).
UGa-3469	2690 ± 80 BP	(740 B.C.)	Delaware Park site (7NC-E-41); stemmed point (Thomas 1981).
UGa-3559	2740 ± 65 BP	(790 B.C.)	Delaware Park site (7NC-E-41); no diagnostics (Thomas 1981).

Lab #	Date		Site, associated materials
UGa-3440	3800 ± 100 BP	(1850 B.C.)	Delaware Park site (7NC-E-41); grooved axe and biface cache (Thomas 1981).
UGa-4322	7790 ± 340 BP	(5840 B.C.)	Mitchell Farm site (7NC-A-2); Pollen suite (Custer 1981).
I-6045	9890 ± 140 BP	(7940 B.C.)	Dill Farm site (7K-E-12); pollen data.
UGa-4323	11,480 ± 400 BP	(9530 B.C.)	Mitchell Farm site (7NC-A-2); Nondiagnostic flakes (Custer 1981).

Dates from the Eastern Shore of Maryland

Lab #	Date		Site, associated materials
SI-2188	715 ± 60 BP	(A.D. 1235)	Lankford No. 2 (18-DO-43), Townsend ceramics (Thomas 1977).
SI-2684	905 ± 60 BP	(A.D. 1045)	Lankford No. 1; Townsend ceramics (Thomas 1977).
SI-2686	950 ± 60 BP	(A.D. 1000)	Lankford No. 2 (18-DO-43); Townsend ceramics (Thomas 1977).
SI-2793	1195 ± 85 BP	(A.D. 755)	Site Co-1/1 (18-KE-3); Accokeek ceramics in shell midden (Wilke and Thompson 1977).
SI-2189	2190 ± 70 BP	(240 B.C.)	Nassawango site (18-WO-23); Delmarva Adena (Bastian 1975).
SI-2190	2190 ± 100 BP	(240 B.C.)	Nassawango site (18-WO-23); Delmarva Adena (Bastian 1975).
SI-2188	2445 ± 100 BP	(495 B.C.)	Nassawango site (18-WO-23); Delmarva Adena (Bastian 1975).
SI-2191	2735 ± 75 BP	(785 B.C.)	Nassawango site (18-WO-23); Delmarva Adena (Bastian 1975).
SI-2794	3070 ± 75 BP	(1120 B.C.)	Site Co-1/1 (18-KE-3), Accokeek ceramics in shell midden (Wilke and Thompson 1977).
SI-2802	4450 ± 80 BP	(2500 B.C.)	Site P1-1/1 (18-KE-17); Marcey Creek and Mockley ceramics in shell midden (Wilke and Thompson 1977).
SI-2803	4030 ± 80 BP	(2080 B.C.)	Site P1-2/1 (18-KE-18); no diagnostics in shell midden (Wilke and Thompson 1977).
SI-1907	5015 ± 70 BP	(3065 B.C.)	Site P1-1/1 (18-KE-17); Marcey Creek and Mockley ceramics in shell midden (Wilke and Thompson 1977).

Appendix 2
Site Listings

This appendix lists all of the archaeological sites listed in the text by state identification number and notes the presence or absence of paleoenvironmental data, radiocarbon dates, and various prehistoric cultural periods and complexes for each site. Blanks indicate an absence of information, "x" indicates its presence, and "?" notes that the information is somewhat questionable. The site listing is organized by county.

Key

PE—Paleoenvironmental data
PI—Paleo-Indian period
WI—Woodland I period
BL—Barker's Landing complex
WN—Wolfe Neck complex
C—Carey complex
DP—Delaware Park complex
SC—Slaughter Creek complex
EC—European Contact period
RC—Radiocarbon date
A—Archaic period
WII—Woodland II period
CF—Clyde Farm complex
DA—Delmarva Adena complex
LC—Late Carey complex
W—Webb complex
M—Minguannan complex

New Castle County

Site	PE	RC	PI	A	WI	BL	CF	WN	DA	C	LC	DP	W	WII	SC	M	EC
7NC-A-2	x	x	x	x	x		x	x		x		x		x		x	
7NC-C-2					x		x	x				x		?		?	
7NC-D-3				x	x												
7NC-D-5				x	x												
7NC-D-19				x	x												
7NC-D-21			x		x												
7NC-D-27																	
7NC-D-34			?														
7NC-D-36			x														
7NC-D-54					x		x	x		x		x					
7NC-D-55					x		x	x		x		x					
7NC-D-62					x		x	x		x		x					
7NC-E-1				x	x		x	x		x		x					
7NC-E-3					x												
7NC-E-4				?													
7NC-E-6				x	x		x	x		x		x		x		x	
7NC-E-14				?													
7NC-E-18				x	x		x	x	?			x		x		x	
7NC-E-23					x												
7NC-E-24					x												
7NC-E-36					x									x		x	
7NC-E-37					x									x		x	
7NC-E-38					x									x		x	
7NC-E-41	x				x		x	x		x		x		x		x	?
7NC-E-42		x		x									x	x		x	
7NC-F-1					x								x				
7NC-F-7					x			x				x		x	x	?	
7NC-F-15					x										x		
7NC-F-18				x													

186

Site	PE	RC	PI	A	WI	BL	CF	WN	DA	C	LC	DP	W	WII	SC	M	EC
7NC-F-19					x												
7NC-G-2					x												
7NC-G-3					x												
7NC-G-6					x												
7NC-G-68				x													
7NC-H-2				x	x												
7NC-J-2					x												
7NC-J-3				x	x												
7NC-J-14				x													

Kent County

Site	PE	RC	PI	A	WI	BL	CF	WN	DA	C	LC	DP	W	WII	SC	M	EC
7K-A-2					x												
7K-B-8					x												
7K-C-25				x													
7K-C-33					x	x											
7K-C-53					x	x											
7K-C-57					x	x											
7K-C-94					x								x				
7K-D-1		x			x				x								
7K-D-3		x			x					x							
7K-D-13					x	x											
7K-D-21		x				x								x	x		
7K-D-37					x				x								?
7K-D-38					x			x									
7K-D-42					x	x							x	x	x		
7K-D-45					x								x	x	x		
7K-D-48					x								x	x	x		
7K-D-49													x	x	x		
7K-D-52					x	x							x	x	x		
7K-E-3					x				x								
7K-E-10	x		x	x													
7K-E-12		x		x				x		x							
7K-E-24			x	x													
7K-E-33			x	x													
7K-E-43					x												
7K-F-2					x				x								
7K-F-4					x								x	x	x		
7K-F-12		x			x	x											
7K-F-17		x			x								x	x	x		
7K-F-18					x	x											

188

Site	PE	RC	PI	A	WI	BL	CF	WN	DA	C	LC	DP	W	WII	SC	M	EC
7K-F-23					x								x	x	x		
7K-F-37					x	x											
7K-F-38					x	x			x	x							
7K-F-40				x	x	x											
7K-F-44					x	x			x	x			x				
7K-F-45					x	x			x	x			x				
7K-F-46					x	x			x	x			x				
7K-F-47					x	x			x	x			x				
7K-F-48					x	x							x				
7K-F-49					x	x			x	x							
7K-F-52					x	x			x	x			x				
7K-F-53					x	x			x	x			x				
7K-F-54					x	x			x	x			x				
7K-F-55					x	x			x				x				
7K-F-56					x				x				x				
7K-F-86					x								x	x			
7K-G-14					x										x		

Sussex County

Site	PE	RC	PI	A	WI	BL	CF	WN	DA	C	LC	DP	W	WII	SC	M	EC
7S-A-1		x												x	x		
7S-C-1														x	x		
7S-C-7														x	x		
7S-C-8														x	x		
7S-C-9														x	x		
7S-C-17		x			x								x				
7S-C-29														x	x		
7S-C-30														x	x		
7S-D-2														x	x		
7S-D-3														x	x		
7S-D-5														x	x		
7S-D-6														x	x		
7S-D-7														x	x		?
7S-D-8					x			x									
7S-D-9					x			x						x	x		
7S-D-10		x			x			x		x	?						?
7S-D-11																	
7S-D-22					x			x						x	x		
7S-D-27					x			x									
7S-D-29					x			x									
7S-D-30					x			x									
7S-D-34					x			x									
7S-E-20			?	?													
7S-E-21					?												
7S-E-32							?										
7S-G-1														x	x		
7S-G-2														x	x		?
7S-G-3														x	x		
7S-G-14		x												x	x		
7S-G-21		x												x	x		

Site	PE	RC	PI	A	WI	BL	CF	WN	DA	C	LC	DP	W	WII	SC	M	EC
7S-G-22		x												x	x		
7S-H-1					?		?										
7S-H-2					?		?										
7S-H-3					?		?										
7S-H-18		x												x	x		
7S-J-11				?													
7S-J-14					x												
7S-K-14					x				x	x	x						
7S-K-21		x			x									x	x		

191

References

Abbott, C. C.
   1872   The stone age in New Jersey. *American Naturalist* 6:144–60, 199–209.
   1876   On the discovery of supposed paleolithic implements from the glacial drift in the valley of the Delaware River, near Trenton, New Jersey. *Tenth Annual Report of the Trustees of the Peabody Museum* 2:30–40.

Adovasio, J. M., J. D. Gunn, J. Donahue, and R. Stuckenrath
   1977   Meadowcroft Rockshelter: Retrospect 1976. *Pennsylvania Archaeologist* 47(2–3):1–93.

Adovasio, J. M., J. D. Gunn, J. Donahue, R. Stuckenrath, J. E. Guilday, and K. Volman
   1980   Yes Virginia, it really is that old: A reply to Haynes and Mead. *American Antiquity* 45:588–95.

Adovasio, J. M., and W. C. Johnson
   1981   The appearance of cultigens in the Upper Ohio Valley: A view from Meadowcroft Rockshelter. *Pennsylvania Archaeologist* 51:63–80.

Ahler, S. A.
   1971   *Projectile point form and function at Rodgers Rockshelter, Missouri.* Missouri Archaeological Society Research Series, no. 8. Columbia: Missouri Archaeological Society.

Ameringer, C.
   1975   Susquehannock plant utilization. In *Proceedings of the 1975 Middle Atlantic Archaeological Conference,* ed. W. F. Kinsey, 58–63. North Museum, Franklin and Marshall College. Lancaster, Penn.

Anonymous
   1939   Crane Hook excavations: Preliminary notes. *Bulletin of the Archaeological Society of Delaware* 3(2):8–11.
   1951a   Aboriginal evidence from the grounds of the Lewes School. *The Archeolog* 3(1):3–4.
   1951b   The Derrickson site "worked" conchs. *The Archeolog* 4(1):9–16.

Artusy, R. E.
   1976   An overview of the proposed ceramic sequence in southern Delaware. *Maryland Archaeology* 12(2):1–15.
   1978   The Wilgus site. *The Archeolog* 30(2):4–11.

Artusy, R. E., and D. R. Griffith

2 AD

Find final pub. w/ mary C. Stiner, U of NM Reviewed

1975 A brief report on the semi-subterranean dwellings of Delaware. *The Archeolog* 27(1):1–9.

Austin, F. B., C. A. Bonine, P. S. Flegel, and H. H. Hutchinson
1953 The Webb site. *The Archeolog* 5(1).

Bastian, T.
1975 New radiocarbon dates from a Maryland Adena site. *Newsletter of the Archaeological Society of Maryland* 1(2).

Becker, M. J.
1976 The Okehocking: A remnant band of the Delaware Indians. *Pennsylvania Archaeologist* 46(3):24–61.

1980a Lenape archaeology: Archaeological and ethnohistoric considerations in light of recent excavations. *Pennsylvania Archaeologist* 50(4):19–30.

1980b A preliminary review of historic references to Lenape and related burial customs. Paper presented at the 1980 meeting of the Eastern States Archaeological Federation, Albany, New York.

1981a The Lenape bands prior to A.D. 1740: The identification of boundaries and processes of culture change leading to the formation of the Delaware. Paper presented at the Second Delaware Indian Symposium, Seton Hall University, South Orange, New Jersey.

1981b Lenape settlement patterns: "Villages" and cemeteries. Paper presented at the 1981 Middle Atlantic Archaeological Conference, Ocean City.

1981c The Lenape-Minisink relationship: Historical, linguistic, and archaeological evidence. Paper presented at the 1981 meeting of the Society for Pennsylvania Archaeology, Lionville.

Belknap, D. F., and J. C. Kraft
1977 Holocene relative sea-level change and coastal stratigraphic units on the northwest flank of the Baltimore Canyon geosyncline. *Journal of Sedimentary Petrology* 47:610–29.

Bernabo, J. C., and T. Webb
1977 Changing patterns in the Holocene pollen record of northeastern North America: A mapped summary. *Quaternary Research* 8:64–96.

Binford, L. R.
1962 Archaeology as anthropology. *American Antiquity* 28:217–25.

1965 Archaeological systematics and the study of culture process. *American Antiquity* 31:203–10.

1968 Post-Pleistocene adaptations. In *New perspective in archaeology,* ed. S. R. Binford and L. R. Binford, 313–41. Chicago: Aldine.

1978 *Nunamiut ethnoarchaeology.* New York: Academic Press.

1979 Problems and solutions. *Flintknappers' Exchange* 2(1):19–25.

1980 Willow smoke and dogs' tails: Hunter-gatherer settlement systems and archaeological site formation. *American Antiquity* 45:4–20.

Blaker, M. C.
1963 Aboriginal ceramics from the Townsend site. *The Archeolog* 15(1):14–39.

Bonfiglio, A., and J. Cresson
1978 Aboriginal cultural adaptation and exploitation of periglacial features in southern New Jersey. Paper presented at the 1978 Middle Atlantic Archaeological Conference, Rehoboth Beach, Delaware.

Bonine, C. A.

1956   Archaeological investigation of the Dutch "Swanendael" settlement under DeVries, 1631–1632. *The Archeolog* 8(2).

1964   The south bastion of the DeVries pallisade of 1631 (7S-D-11). *The Archeolog* 16(2): 13–18.

Braun, E. L.

1967   *Deciduous forests of eastern North America.* New York: Hafner.

Brennan, L.

1974   The lower Hudson: A decade of shell middens. *Archaeology of Eastern North America* 2: 81–93.

1976   Coastal adaptation in prehistoric New England. *American Antiquity* 41: 112–13.

1977   The lower Hudson: The Archaic. *Annals of the New York Academy of Sciences* 288: 411–30.

Brown, J., and C. Cleland

1968   The late glacial and early postglacial faunal resources of midwestern biomes newly opened to human adaptation. In *The Quaternary of Illinois*, ed. R. E. Bergstrom, 114–22. University of Illinois, Urbana.

Brown, L.

1979   Fluted projectile points in Maryland. Section of Archaeology, Maryland Geological Survey, Baltimore. MS on file.

Broyles, B. J.

1971   *The St. Albans site.* West Virginia Geological Survey, Morgantown.

Bryant, C. L., R. C. Rosser, Henry Hutchinson, and Helen Hutchinson

1951   The Willin Farm site. *The Archeolog* 3(3): 1–3.

Callahan, E.

1979   The basics of biface knapping in the eastern fluted point tradition. *Archaeology of Eastern North America* 7: 1–180.

Callaway, W., H. Hutchinson, and D. Marine

1960   The Moore site. *The Archeolog* 12(1): 1–8.

Carbone, V. A.

1976   *Environment and prehistory in the Shenandoah Valley.* Ann Arbor, Mich.: University Microfilms.

Carniero, R. L.

1970   A theory of the origin of the state. *Science* 169: 733–38.

Carr, K. W.

1975   The Fifty Site: A Flint Run Paleo-Indian Complex processing station. Master's thesis, Department of Anthropology, Catholic University of America.

Chapman, J.

1975   *The Rose Island site.* University of Tennessee Department of Anthropology Report of Investigations no. 14, Knoxville.

Cleland, C. E.

1976   The focal-diffuse model: An evolutionary perspective on the prehistoric cultural adaptations of the eastern United States. *Midcontinental Journal of Archaeology* 1: 59–75.

Coe, J. L.
  1964   Formative cultures of the Carolina Piedmont. *Transactions of the American Philosophical Society* N.S. 54(5).

Cohen, R.
  1978   State foundations: A controlled comparison. In *Origins of the state: The anthropology of political evolution,* ed. R. Cohen and E.Æervice, 141–60. Institute for the Study of Human Issues, Philadelphia.

Cook, S. F.
  1976   *The Indian population of New England in the seventeenth century.* University of California (Berkeley) Publications in Anthropology no. 12. Berkeley: University of California Department of Anthropology.

Cook, T. G.
  1976   Broadpoint: Culture, phase, horizon, tradition, or knife? *Journal of Anthropological Research* 32 : 337–57.

Corkran, D. E., and P. S. Flegel
  1953   Notes on Marshyhope Creek sites (Maryland). *The Archeolog* 5(1) : 46.

Cresson, H. T.
  1888   Early man in the Delaware Valley. *Proceedings of the Boston Society of Natural History* 14(2) : 141–50.

  1892   *Report upon a pile structure in Naaman's Creek near Claymont, Delaware.* Peabody Museum, Boston.

Cresthull, P.
  1971   Chance (18SO5): A major Early Archaic site. *Maryland Archaeology* 7(2) : 31–52.

  1972   Chance (18SO5): A major Early Archaic site, part 2. *Maryland Archaelogy* 8(2) : 40–53.

Cross, D.
  1941   *Archaeology of New Jersey, Vol. I.* Archaeological Society of New Jersey, Trenton.

  1956   *Archaeology of New Jersey, Vol. II: The Abbott Farm Site.* Archaeological Society of New Jersey, Trenton.

Crozier, A.
  1934   Notes on the archaeology of New Castle County. *Bulletin of the Archaeological Society of Delaware* 1(4) : 1–6.

  1938a   Indian towns near Wilmington. *Bulletin of the Archaeological Society of Delaware* 2(6) : 2–4.

  1938b   An early Indian town on the White Clay Creek. *Bulletin of the Archaeological Society of Delaware* 2(7) : 4–7.

  1940   Archaeological notes on Claymont, Delaware, and vicinity. *Bulletin of the Archaeological Society of Delaware* 3(3) : 3–6.

Cubbage, W. D.
  1941   Killens Mill Pond. *Bulletin of the Archaeological Society of Delaware* 3(4) : 23–24.

Curry, D. C.
  1978   An archaeological investigation of site 44WR59, Warren County, Virginia. Master's thesis, Department of Anthropology, Catholic University of America.

1980 Burial of Late Archaic Coastal Plain sites as a result of aeolian deposition. Paper presented at the 1980 Middle Atlantic Archaeological Conference, Dover, Delaware.

Custer, J. F.

1978 Broadspears and netsinkers: Late Archaic adaptations indicated by depositional sequences from four Middle Atlantic archaeological sites. Paper presented at the 1978 Middle Atlantic Archaeological Conference, Rehoboth Beach, Delaware.

1979 Settlement-subsistence systems in the Blue Ridge and Great Valley sections of Virginia: A comparison. Paper presented at the 1979 Middle Atlantic Archaeological Conference, Rehoboth Beach, Delaware.

1980a Settlement-subsistence systems in Augusta County, Virginia. *Quarterly Bulletin of the Archaeological Society of Virginia* 35(1): 1–27.

1980b Report on archaeological research in Delaware FY 1980 by the Department of Anthropology, University of Delaware. Bureau of Archaeology and Historic Preservation, Division of Historical and Cultural Affairs, Dover. MS on file.

1981 Report on archaeological research in Delaware FY 1981 by the Department of Anthropology, University of Delaware. Bureau of Archaeology and Historic Preservation, Division of Historical and Cultural Affairs, Dover. MS on file.

1982 Report on excavations at the Webb site (36CH51), Chester County, Pennsylvania. Section of Archaeology, William Penn Memorial Museum, Pennsylvania Historical and Museum Commission, Harrisburg. MS on file.

n.d. Paleoecology of the Late Archaic: Exchange and adaptation. *Pennsylvania Archaeologist.* In press.

Custer, J. F., J. Cavallo, and R. M. Stewart

n.d. Paleo-Indian adaptations on the Coastal Plain of Delaware and New Jersey. Department of Anthropology, University of Delaware. MS on file.

Custer, J. F., and G. J. Galasso

1980 Lithic resources of the Delmarva Peninsula. *Maryland Archaeology* 16(2): 1–13.

Custer, J. F., J. H. Sprinkle, A. H. Flora, M. C. Stiner

1981 The Green Valley site complex: Lithic reduction base camp sites on the Delaware Fall Line. *Bulletin of the Archaeological Society of Delaware* 12.

Custer, J. F., and E. B. Wallace

1982 Patterns of resource distribution and archaeological settlement patterns in the Piedmont Uplands of the Middle Atlantic region. *North American Archaeologist* 3(2): 139–72.

Custer, J. F., and I. Wells

1981 Remote sensing applications to the Middle Atlantic archaeological site form. Paper presented at the 1981 Middle Atlantic Archaeological Conference, Ocean City, Maryland.

Daiber, F. C. O. W. Crichton, L. L. Thornton, G. L. Esposito, K. A. Bolster, D. R. Jones, T. G. Campbell, and J. M. Tyrawski

1976 *An atlas of Delaware's wetlands and estuarine resources.* Delaware Coastal

Management Program, Technical Report no. 2. Newark: College of Marine Studies, University of Delaware.

Davidson, D. S.

1935a   Notes on Slaughter Creek. *Bulletin of the Archaeological Society of Delaware* 2(2):1–5.

1935b   Burial customs in the Delmarva Peninsula and the question of their chronology. *American Antiquity* 1(1:84–97.

1936   Notes on the faunal remains from Slaughter Creek. *Bulletin of the Archaeological Society of Delaware* 2(4):29–34.

Delaware Division of Historical and Cultural Affairs

1976   National Register nomination for the Cape Henlopen Archaeological District. Division of Historical and Cultural Affairs, Dover. MS on file.

1977   National Register nomination for the Carey Farm site. Division of Historical and Cultural Affairs, Dover. MS on file.

1978   National Register nomination for the St. Jones Neck Archaeological District. Division of Historical and Cultural Affairs, Dover. MS on file.

1980   National Register nomination for the Millman site complex. Division of Historical and Cultural Affairs, Dover. MS on file.

n.d.   An archaeological survey of Delaware. Island Field Museum, South Bowers, Delaware. MS on file.

Delaware Geological Survey

1976   *Geologic map of Delaware.* Newark: Delaware Geological Survey.

Delaware Section of Archaeology

1975   Archaeological investigations in the Newport-Christiana River force main right-of-way. Island Field Museum, South Bowers, Delaware. MS on file.

Delmarva Clearinghouse for Archaeology, Inc.

1975   Investigations of the Delmarva Power and Light site (7NC-E-33), Red Lion Creek, Delaware. Island Field Museum, South Bowers, Delaware. MS on file.

De Valinger, L.

1940   Indian land sales in Delaware. *Bulletin of the Archaeological Society of Delaware* 3(3):29–33.

1941   Indian land sales in Delaware, part II. *Bulletin of the Archaeological Society of Delaware* 3(4):25–33.

1970   *Report on the excavation of the St. Jones River site near Lebanon, Delaware.* Delaware State Museum Series Bulletin no. 3. Dover.

De Vries, D. P.

1909   From the "Korte historiael ende journaels aenteyckeninge," 1633–1634 (1655). In *Narratives of New Netherland 1609–1644,* J. F. Jameson, 181–234. New York: Scribner's.

Dincauze, D. F.

1971   An Archaic sequence for southern New England. *American Antiquity* 36:194–98.

1976   The Neville site: 8,000 years at Amoskeag. Peabody Museum Monographs No. 4. Boston.

1981   The Meadowcroft papers. *Quarterly Review of Archaeology* 2(1):3–4.

Dincauze, D. F., and M. T. Mulholland
1977   Early and Middle Archaic site distributions and habitats in southern New England. *Annals of the New York Academy of Sciences* 288:439–56.

Dunn, M. L.
1966   A general survey of the Adena culture on the Delmarva Peninsula. *The Archeolog* 18(2):1–10.

Earle, T. K., and J. E. Ericson, eds.
1977   *Exchange systems in prehistory*. New York: Academic Press.

Edwards, R. L., and A. S. Merill
1977   A reconstruction of the continental shelf areas of eastern North America for the times 9500 BP and 12,500 BP. *Archaeology of Eastern North America* 5:1–43.

Eggan, F.
1954   Social anthropology and the method of controlled comparison. *American Anthropologist* 56:743–63.

Eggen, J. B.
1954   Corrections and additional information about cache blades from Mispillion Creek. *The Archeolog* 6(3):17–18.

Eisenberg, L.
1978   *Paleo-Indian settlement pattern in the Hudson and Delaware river drainages.* Occasional Publications in Northeastern Anthropology no. 4. Rindge, N.H.: Franklin Pierce College.

Feest, C.
1973   Southeastern Algonquian burial customs: Ethnohistoric evidence. Paper presented at the 1973 Middle Atlantic Archaeological Conference, Penns Grove, New Jersey.
1978   Nanticoke and neighboring tribes. In *Handbook on North American Indians, Vol. 15: The Northeast,* ed. B. Trigger, 240–52. Washington, D.C.: Smithsonian Institution.

Fenneman, N. M.
1938   *Physiography of eastern United States.* New York: McGraw-Hill.

Fitting, J. E.
1968   Environmental potential and postglacial readaptation in eastern North America. *American Antiquity* 33:441–45.
1978   Regional cultural development, 300 B.C.–A.D.1000. In *Handbook of North American Indians, Vol. 15: The Northeast,* ed. Bruce Trigger, 44–57. Washington, D.C.: Smithsonian Institution.

Fitting, J. E., and D. S. Brose
1970   The northern periphery of Adena. In *Adena: The seeking of an identity,* ed. B. K. Swartz, 29–55. Muncie, Ind.: Ball State University.

Flannery, K. V.
1968   Archaeological systems theory and early Mesoamerica. In *Anthropological archaeology in the Americas,* ed. B. J. Meggers, 67–87. Anthropological Society of Washington, Washington, D.C.

Flannery, R.
1939   *An analysis of coastal Algonquian culture.* Catholic University of America

Anthropological Series no. 7. Washington, D.C.: Catholic University Press.

Flegel, P. S.

1954   Cached blades from Marshyhope Creek. *The Archeolog* 6(2): 14–15.

1959   Additional data on the Mispillion site. *The Archeolog* 11(2): 1–16.

1978   The Marshyhope Creek: Its Indian places, pottery, points, and pipes. *The Archeolog* 30(1): 13–59.

Florer, L. E.

1972   Palynology of a postglacial bog in the New Jersey Pine Barrens. *Bulletin of the Torrey Botanical Club* 99: 135–38.

Ford, R. I.

1979   Gathering and gardening: Trends and consequences of Hopewell subsistence strategies. In *Hopewell Archaeology*, ed. D. Brose and N. Greber, 234–38. Kent, Ohio: Kent State University Press.

Ford, T. L.

1976   Adena sites on the Chesapeake Bay. *Archaeology of Eastern North America* 4: 63–89.

Foss, J. E., D. S. Fanning, F. P. Miller, and D. P. Wagner

1978   Loess deposits of the Eastern Shore of Maryland. *Journal of the Soil Science Society of America* 42: 329–33.

Foss, R. W.

1981   Blue Ridge prehistory: A perspective from the Shenandoah National Park. Paper presented at the U.S. Forest Service Upland Archaeology Symposium, Harrisonburg, Virginia.

Fried, M. H.

1967   *The evolution of political society.* New York: Random House.

Funk, R. E.

1976   *Recent contributions to Hudson Valley prehistory.* New York State Museum and Science Service Memoir no. 22. Albany.

1977a   Early to Middle Archaic occupations in upstate New York. *Research and Transactions of the New York State Archaelogical Association* 17(1): 21–29.

1977b   Early cultures in the Hudson Basin. *Annals of the New York Academy of Sciences* 288: 316–32.

1978   Post-pleistocene adaptations. In *Handbook of North American Indians, Vol. 15: The Northeast*, ed. Bruce Trigger, 16–27. Washington, D.C.: Smithsonian Institution.

Funk, R. E., D. W. Fisher, and E. M. Reilly

1970   Caribou and Paleo-Indian in New York State: A presumed association. *American Journal of Science* 268: 181–86.

Galasso, G. J.

1981   An analysis of artifacts from Delaware at the Smithsonian Institution Museum of Natural Sciences. Department of Anthropology, University of Delaware. MS on file.

Gardner, W. M.

1974   The Flint Run Paleo-Indian complex: Pattern and process during the Paleo-Indian to Early Archaic. In *The Flint Run Paleo-Indian Complex: A preliminary report, 1971–1973 seasons.* Occasional Publication No. 1,

Catholic University Archaeology Laboratory, ed. W. M. Gardner, 5–47. Washington, D.C.

1975   Early pottery in eastern North America: A viewpoint. In *Proceedings of the 1975 Middle Atlantic Archaeological Conference,* ed. W. F. Kinsey, 13–26. North Museum, Franklin and Marshall College, Lancaster, Pennsylvania.

1976   Excavations at 18PR141, 18PR142, and 18PR143 near Piscataway, Maryland. Department of Anthropology, Catholic University of America. MS on file.

1977   Flint Run Paleo-Indian complex and its implications for eastern North American prehistory. *Annals of the New York Academy of Sciences* 288:257–63.

1978   Comparison of Ridge and Valley, Blue Ridge, Piedmont, and Coastal Plain Archaic period site distribution: An idealized transect (preliminary model). Paper presented at the 1978 Middle Atlantic Archaeological Conference, Rehoboth Beach, Delaware.

1979   Paleo-Indian settlement patterns and site distributions in the Middle Atlantic (preliminary version). Paper presented at the January 1979 meeting of the Anthropological Society of Washington, Washington, D.C.

1982   Archaeology of the Middle Atlantic. MS in preparation.

Gardner, W. M., and W. P. Boyer

1978   *A cultural resources reconnaissance of portions of the northern segment of Massanutten Mountain in the George Washington National Forest, Page, Warren, and Shenandoah Counties, Virginia.* National Forest Service, Washington, D.C.

Gardner, W. M., and J. F. Custer

1978   A preliminary cultural resources reconnaissance of the proposed Verona Lake Site No. 2 Department of Anthropology, Catholic University of America. MS on file.

Gardner, W. M., and G. Haynes

1978   A preliminary cultural resources reconnaissance of the proposed Hambrooks Boulevard extended, Cambridge, Dorchester County, Maryland. Department of Anthropology, Catholic University of America. MS on file.

Gardner, W. M., and C. W. McNett

1971   Problems in Potomac River archaeology. Department of Anthropology, Catholic University of America. MS on file.

Gardner, W. M., and R. M. Stewart

1977   A cultural resources reconnaissance of proposed disposal areas for maintenance dredging of the Barren Island Gap, Dorchester County, Maryland. Department of Anthropology, Catholic University of America. MS on file.

1978   A cultural resources reconnaissance of portions of the Middletown-Odessa regional sewer system, New Castle County, Delaware. Island Field Museum, South Bowers, Delaware. MS on file.

Gardner, W. M., and R. Verrey

1979   Typology and chronology of fluted points from the Flint Run area. *Pennsylvania Archaeologist* 49(1-2):13–46.

Gehris, C. W.
1964   Pollen analysis of the Cranberry Bog preserve, Tannersville, Monroe County, Pennsylvania. Ph.D. diss., Pennsylvania State University.

Goddard, I.
1978a   Eastern Algonkian languages. In *Handbook of North American Indians, Vol. 15: The Northeast,* ed. B. Trigger, 70–77. Washington, D.C.: Smithsonian Institution.

1978b   The Delaware. In *Handbook of North American Indians, Vol. 15: The Northeast,* ed. B. Trigger, 213–39. Washington, D.C.: Smithsonian Institution.

Goodyear, A. C.
1979   *A hypothesis for the use of cryptocrystalline raw materials among Paleo-Indian groups of North America.* University of South Carolina Institute of Archaeology and Anthropology Research Manuscript Series no. 156. Columbia: University of South Carolina Institute of Archaeology and Anthropology.

Goudie, A.
1977   *Environmental change.* Oxford: Clarendon Press.

Gould, R. A.
1971   The archaeologist as ethnographer: A case study of the Western Desert of Australia. *World Archaeology* 3:143–77.

Graybill, J.
1973   Shenks Ferry settlement patterns in southern Lancaster County, Pennsylvania. *The Kithuwan, Journal of the Anthropology Club, Franklin and Marshall College* 5:7–24.

Griffin, J. B.
1961   Some correlations of climatic and cultural change in eastern North American prehistory. *Annals of the New York Academy of Sciences* 256:710–17.

1967   Eastern North American archaeology: A summary. *Science* 156:175–91.

1977   A commentary on Early Man studies in the Northeast. *Annals of the New York Academy of Sciences* 288:3–15.

1978   Eastern United States. In *Chronologies in New World Archaeology,* ed. R. E. Taylor and C. W. Meighan, 51–70. New York: Academic Press.

Griffith, D. R.
1974   Ecological studies of prehistory. *Transactions of the Delaware Academy of Sciences* 5:63–81.

1977   Townsend ceramics and the Late Woodland of southern Delaware. Master's thesis, Department of Anthropology, American University.

1981   Prehistoric ceramics in Delaware: An overview. Paper presented at the Saint Mary's City Conference on Prehistoric Ceramics, Saint Mary's City, Maryland.

n.d.a   Report on the Warrington site. Island Field Museum, South Bowers, Delaware. MS on file.

n.d.b   Report on the Poplar Thicket Site. Island Field Museum, South Bowers, Delaware. MS on file.

Griffith, D. R., and R. E. Artusy
1977   Middle Woodland ceramics from Wolfe Neck, Sussex County, Delaware. *The Archeolog* 28(1):1–29.

n.d.   Report on archaeological investigations of the proposed Dover By-Pass
          Corridor. Island Field Museum, South Bowers, Delaware. MS on file.

Guilday, J. E.
1962   The Pleistocene local fauna of the Natural Chimneys, Augusta County,
          Virginia. *Carnegie Institute of Pittsburg Museum Annals* 36:87–122.

Guilday, J. E., P. S. Martin, and A. D. McCrady
1964   New Paris No. 4: A Pleistocene cave deposit in Bedford County, Pennsyl-
          vania. *National Speleological Society Bulletin* 26:121–94.

Handsman, R. G., and C. W. McNett
1974   The Middle Woodland in the Middle Atlantic: Chronology, adaptation,
          and contact. Paper presented at the 1974 Middle Atlantic Archaeological
          Conference, Baltimore, Maryland.

Harding, T. G.
1970   Trading in northeast New Guinea. In *Cultures of the Pacific,* ed. T. G.
          Harding and B. J. Wallace, 94–111. New York: Free Press.

Harris, M.
1968   *The rise of anthropological theory.* New York: Thomas Y. Crowell.
1979   *Cultural materialism: The struggle for a science of culture.* New York: Random
          House.

Harrison, D.
1974   Beyond Paleo-Indian: Chronology and patterning in the Archaic. Paper
          presented at the 1974 meeting of the Society for American Archaeology,
          Washington, D.C.

Harrison, W. R., F. Malloy, G. A. Rusnak, J. Teresmae
1965   Possible late Pleistocene uplift, Chesapeake Bay entrance. *Journal of Geol-
          ogy* 73:201–29.

Haury, E. W., E. Antevs, and J. F. Lance
1953   Artifacts with mammoth remains, Naco, Arizona, I, II, III. *American
          Antiquity* 19:1–24.

Haury, E. W., E. B. Sayles, and W. W. Wasley
1959   The Lehner mammoth site, southeastern Arizona. *American Antiquity*
          25:2–30.

Hawkes, E. W., and R. Linton
1916   *A pre-Lenape site in New Jersey.* Anthropological Publications of the Uni-
          versity Museum, University of Pennsylvania vol. 6(2). Philadelphia: Uni-
          versity Museum.

Haynes, C. V.
1964   Fluted projectile points: Their age and dispersion. *Science* 145:1408–13.
1977   When and from where did man arrive in northeastern North America: A
          discussion. *Annals of the New York Academy of Sciences* 288:165–67.
1980   Paleo-Indian charcoal from Meadowcroft: Is contamination a problem?
          American Antiquity 80:582–87.

Hester, J. J.
1972   *Blackwater Locality No. 1: A stratified early man site in eastern New Mexico.*
          Fort Burgwin Research Center, Rancho de Taos, New Mexico.

Hoffman, M. A., and R. W. Foss

1980   Blue Ridge prehistory: A general perspective. *Quarterly Bulletin of the Archaeological Society of Virginia* 34:185–210.

Holland, C. G., S. E. Pennell, R. O. Allen

1981   Geographical distribution of soapstone artifacts from 21 aborginal quarries in the eastern United States, *Quarterly Bulletin of the Archaeological Society of Virginia* 35:200–208.

Howard, P. A.

1969   Cache blades from the Miles River. *The Archeolog* 21(2):22.

Huff, D.

1969   Mastodon at Marshalls Creek. *Pennsylvania Game News* 40(2):2–7.

Humphrey, R. L., and D. Stanford

1979   *Pre-Llano cultures of the Americas: Paradoxes and possibilities.* The Anthropological Society of Washington, Washington, D.C.

Hunt, G. T.

1940   *The wars of the Iroquois: A study in inter-tribal relations.* Madison: University of Wisconsin Press.

Hunter, W. A.

1959   The historic role of the Susquehannocks. In *Susquehannock Miscellany*, ed. J. Witthoft and W. F. Kinsey, 8–18. Pennsylvania Historical and Museum Commission, Harrisburg.

Hutchinson, H. H.

1955a   Report on the work done to date at the Mispillion River site. *The Archeolog* 7(2):6–9.

1955b   Progress report on Mispillion site. *The Archeolog* 7(3):2–3.

1961   Indian reservations of the Maryland provincial assembly on the middle Delmarva Peninsula. *The Archeolog* 13(2):1–4.

1966   Shell Bridge site (7S-H-8). *The Archeolog* 18(2):15–16.

1967   A tentative closing report on the Willin site (18DO1). *The Archeolog* 19(2).

Hutchinson, H., W. H. Callaway, and C. Bryant

1964   Report on the Chicone site #1 (18DO11) and Chicone site #2 (18DO10). *The Archeolog* 16(1):14–18.

Hutchinson, H., W. H. Callaway, and D. Marine

1957   Report on the Mispillion site (7S-A-1). *The Archeolog* 9(2).

Ireland, W., and E. D. Matthews

1974   *Soil Survey of Sussex County, Delaware.* U.S. Department of Agriculture, Soil Conservation Service, Washington, D.C.

Jackson, R. W.

1954   The Sandy Hill Mound site. *The Archeolog* 6(3).

Jennings, F.

1966   The Indian trade of the Susquehanna Valley. *Proceedings of the American Philosophical Society* 110:406–24.

1968   Glory, death, and transfiguration: The Susquehannock Indians in the seventeenth century. *Proceedings of the American Philosophical Society* 112:15–53.

1975   *The invasion of America: Indians, colonialism and the cant of conquest.* Chapel Hill: University of North Carolina Press.

204 *References*

1978   Susquehannocks. In *Handbook of North American Indians, Vol. 15: The Northeast*, ed. B. Trigger, 362–67. Washington, D.C.: Smithsonian Institution.

Jepson, G. L.
1964   *A New Jersey mastodon*. New Jersey State Museum Bulletin, no. 6. Trenton.

Johnson, F.
1942   *The Boylston Street fishweir*. Papers of the R. S. Peabody Foundation for Archaeology, vol. 2. Andover, Mass.: R. S. Peabody Foundation for Archaeology.

1949   *The Boylston Street fishweir, II*. Papers of the R. S. Peabody Foundation for Archaeology, vol. 4(1). Andover, Mass.: R. S. Peabody Foundation for Archaeology.

Jones, E.
1963   The Frederica site and the Delmarva Adena problem. *Journal of the Archaeological Society of Maryland* 1(1): 12–15.

Jordan, F.
1880   *Remains of an aboriginal encampment at Rehoboth, Delaware*. Numismatic and Antiquarian Society, Philadelphia.

1895   Aboriginal village sites of New Jersey, Delaware, and Maryland. *The Archaeologist* 3(4).

1906   *Aboriginal fishing stations on the coast of the Middle Atlantic states*. Lancaster, Penn.: New Era Publishing Company.

Jordan, R. R.
1964   *Columbia sediments of Delaware*. Delaware Geological Survey Bulletin no. 12. Newark: Delaware Geological Survey.

Judge, W. J.
1973   *Paleo-Indian occupation of the Central Rio Grande Valley in New Mexico*. Albuquerque: University of New Mexico Press.

Kauffman, B., and J. Dent
1978   Preliminary flora and fauna recovery and analysis at the Shawnee Minisink site (36MR43). Paper presented at the 1978 Middle Atlantic Archaeological Conference, Rehoboth Beach, Delaware.

Kavanagh, M.
1979   Archaeological reconnaissance of proposed channel improvements in the Upper Chester watershed, Kent and Queen Anne Counties, Maryland. Mimeo. Maryland Geological Survey, Division of Archaeology, File Report no. 147. Baltimore.

Kent, B. C.
1971   Conoy Town on the lower Susquehanna River, 1718–1743. *Eastern States Archaeological Federation Bulletin* 30: 1.

Kent, B. C., and V. P. Packard
1969   The Erb Rockshelter. *Pennsylvania Archaeologist* 39(1–4): 29–39.

Kier, C. F., and F. Calverly
1957   The Raccoon Point site, an early hunting and fishing station in the lower Delaware Valley. *Pennsylvania Archaeologist* 27(2).

King, T. C., P. P. Hickman, and G. Berg
  1977   *Anthropology in historic preservation.* New York: Academic Press.

Kinsey, W. F.
  1958   Survey of fluted points found in the Susquehanna Basin, Report No. 1. *Pennsylvania Archaeologist* 28(2–3).

  1959a Survey of fluted points found in the Susquehanna Basin, Report No. 2. *Pennsylvania Archaeologist* 29(2).

  1959b Recent excavations on Bare Island in Pennsylvania: The Kent-Hally site. *Pennsylvania Archaeologist* 29(3–4): 109–33.

  1971   The Middle Atlantic culture province: A point of view. *Pennsylvania Archaeologist* 41(1–2): 1–8.

  1972   *Archaeology of the Upper Delaware Valley.* Anthropological Series of the Pennsylvania Historical and Museum Commission no. 2. Harrisburg.

  1974   Early to Middle Woodland cultures on the Piedmont and Coastal plain. *Pennsylvania Archaeologist* 44(4): 9–19.

  1975   Faucett and Byram sites: Chronology and settlement in the Delaware Valley. *Pennsylvania Archaeologist* 45(1–2): 1–103.

  1977a *Lower Susquehanna Valley prehistoric Indians.* Ephrata, Penn.: Science Press.

  1977b Patterning in the Piedmont Archaic: A preliminary view. *Annals of the New York Academy of Sciences* 288: 375–91.

Kinsey, W. F., and J. F. Custer
  1979   A cultural resources reconnaissance of south central Pennsylvania. North Museum, Franklin and Marshall College. MS on file.

  1982   Excavations at the Lancaster County Park site (36LA96). *Pennsylvania Archaeologist* 52(3–4): 25–56.

Kinsey, W. F., and J. R. Graybill
  1971   Murry site and its role in Lancaster and Funk phases of Shenks Ferry culture. *Pennsylvania Archaeologist* 41(4): 7–43.

Kraft, H. C.
  1970   *The Miller Field site, Warren County, New Jersey, Part I: Archaic and Transitional Stages.* Seton Hall University Archaeology Laboratory, South Orange, New Jersey.

  1972   The Miller Field site. In *Archaeology of the Upper Delaware Valley,* Anthropological Series of the Pennsylvania Historical and Museum Commission No. 2, ed. W. F. Kinsey, 1–54.

  1973   The Plenge site: A Paleo-Indian occupation site in New Jersey. *Archaeology of Eastern North America* 1: 56–117.

  1974   Indian prehistory of New Jersey. In *A Delaware Indian symposium,* Anthropological Series of the Pennsylvania Historical and Museum Commission No. 4, ed. H. C. Kraft, 1–56.

  1975   *The archaeology of the Tocks Island area.* Seton Hall University Archaeology Laboratory, South Orange, New Jersey.

  1976   The Rosenkrans site, an Adena-related mortuary complex in the upper Delaware Valley, New Jersey. *Archaeology of Eastern North America* 4: 9–50.

  1977   Paleo-Indians in New Jersey. *Annals of the New York Academy of Sciences* 288: 264–81.

206   *References*

Kraft, J. C.
    1971   Sedimentary facies patterns and geological history of a Holocene marine
            transgression. *Bulletin of the Geological Society of America* 82:2131–58.
    1974   Geologic reconstructions of ancient coastal environments in the vicinity
            of the Island Field site, Kent County, Delaware. *Transactions of the Dela-
            ware Academy of Sciences* 5:83–118.
    1977   Late Quaternary paleogeographic changes in the coastal environments
            of Delaware, Middle Atlantic Bight, related to archaeological settings.
            Annals of the New York Academy of Sciences 288:35–69.
Kraft, J. C., E. A. Allen, D. F. Belknap, C. J. John, and E. M. Maurmeyer
    1976   *Delaware's changing shoreline.* Delaware Coastal Zone Management Pro-
            gram, Technical Report no. 1. Dover: Division of Natural Resources.
Kraft, J. C., and C. J. John
    1978   Paleogeographic analysis of coastal archaeological settings in Delaware.
            Archaeology of Eastern North America 6:41–59.
Kraft, J. C., and R. A. Thomas
    1976   Early man at Holly Oak, Delaware. *Science* 192:756–61.
Lee, R. B., and I. DeVore
    1968   *Man the hunter.* Chicago: Aldine.
Leggett, W. C.
    1973   The migrations of the shad. *Scientific American* 228(3):92–98.
Leidy, J.
    1865   Report of investigations. *Proceedings of the Philadelphia Academy of Natural
            Sciences,* June 1865.
Lopez, J.
    1961   Pottery from the Mispillion site, Sussex County, Delaware, and related
            types in surrounding areas. *Pennsylvania Archaeologist* 31(1):1–38.
MacDonald, G. F.
    1968   *Debert: A Paleo-Indian site in central Nova Scotia.* Anthropology Papers of
            the National Museum of Canada no. 16. Ottawa.
Mac Neish, R. S.
    1971   Speculation on how and why food production and village life developed
            in the Tehuacan Valley, Mexico. *Archaeology* 24:307–15.
Malinowski, B.
    1922 (1961)
            Agronauts of the Western Pacific. New York: Dutton.
Marine, D.
    1957   Report on the Russell site. *The Archeolog* 9(1):1–9.
    1966   Recovery of a rhyolite blade from the subsoil. *The Archeolog* 18(1):21.
Marine, D., S. Bryn, and R. R. Bell
    1966   Further work on a shell deposit in the Wolfe's Neck archaeological com-
            plex. *The Archeolog* 18(1).
Marine, D., H. H. Hutchinson, O. H. Peets, J. L.Parsons
    1965a   Preliminary report on a shell heap deposit in the Wolfe's Neck ar-
            chaeological complex. *The Archeolog* 17(1).
Marine, D., J. L. Parsons, K. Hall

1965b Report on an outlying shell midden of the Rehoboth City site. *The Ar-cheolog* 17(1):18–24.

Marine, D., M. Tull, F. Austin, J. Parsons, and H. Hutchinson

1964 Report on the Warrington site (7S-G-14). *The Archeolog* 16(1):1–13.

Martin, D. S.

1958 Taiga-tundra and the full glacial period in Chester County, Pennsylvania. *American Journal of Science* 256:470–502.

Marye, W. B.

1936a Indian paths of the Delmarva Peninsula. *Bulletin of the Archaeological Society of Delaware* 2(3):5–22.

1936b Indian paths of the Delmarva Peninsula, Part I. *Bulletin of the Archaeological Society of Delaware* 2(4):5–27.

1937 Indian paths of the Delmarva Peninsula, Part II. *Bulletin of the Archaeological Society of Delaware* 2(5):1–37.

1938 Indian paths of the Delmarva Peninsula, Part III. *Bulletin of the Archaeological Society of Delaware* 2(6):4–11.

1939 Indian towns of the southeastern part of Sussex County. *Bulletin of the Archaeological Society of Delaware* 3(2):18–25.

1940 Indian towns of the southeastern part of Sussex County. *Bulletin of the Archaeological Society of Delaware* 3(3):21–28.

Mason, R. J.

1959 Indications of Paleo-Indian occupation in the Delaware Valley. *Pennsylvania Archaeologist* 29:1–17.

Matthews, E. D., and W. Ireland

1971 *Soil Survey of Kent County, Delaware.* U.S. Department of Agriculture, Soil Conservation Service, Washington, D.C.

Matthews, E. D., and O. L. Lavoie

1970 *Soil survey of New Castle County, Delaware.* U.S. Department of Agriculture, Soil Conservation Service, Washington, D.C.

Maxwell, J., and M. B. Davis

1972 Pollen evidence of Pleistocene and Holocene vegetation of the Allegheny Plateau, Maryland. *Quaternary Research* 2:513–29.

McCann, C.

1950 The Ware site, Salem County, New Jersey. *American Antiquity* 15:315–31.

McNett, C. W.

1967 Brodhead-Heller: A preliminary report on a stratified Transitional period site on the Upper Delaware. *Pennsylvania Archaeologist* 37(1–2):22–32.

McNett, C. W., and B. MacMillan

1974 Preliminary report on the initial season of the Upper Delaware early man project. Department of Anthropology, American University. MS on file.

McNett, C. W., S. B. Marshall, and E. McDowell

1975 Second season of the Upper Delaware early man project. Department of Anthropology, American University. MS on file.

Mead, J. J.

1980   Is it really that old? A comment on the Meadowcroft Rockshelter "over-
        view." *American Antiquity* 45 : 579–81.

Michels, J. W.
1967   A culture history of the Sheep Rock Shelter site. In *Archaeological investi-
        gations of the Sheep Rock Shelter, Huntingdon County, Pennsylvania,* ed. J. W.
        Michels and I. F. Smith, 801–24. Occasional Papers in Anthropology of
        the Pennsylvania State University no. 3. University Park: Pennsylvania
        State University Department of Anthropology.
1973   *Dating methods in archaeology.* New York: Seminar Press.

Michels, J. W., and J. S. Dutt, eds.
1968   *A preliminary report of archaeological investigations of the Sheep Rock Shelter.*
        Occasional Papers in Anthropology of the Pennsylvania State University
        no. 5. University Park: Pennsylvania State University Department of
        Anthropology.

Michlovic, M.G.
1976   Social interaction and point types in the eastern United States. *Pennsylva-
        nia Archaeologist* 46(1–2) : 13–16.

Milanich, J. T., and C. H. Fairbanks
1980   *Florida archaeology.* New York: Academic Press.

Moeller, R. W.
1975   Late Woodland faunal and floral exploitative patterns in the Upper
        Delaware Valley. In *Proceedings of the 1975 Middle Atlantic Archaeological
        Conference,* ed. W. F. Kinsey, 51–57. North Museum, Franklin and Mar-
        shall College, Lancaster, Pennsylvania.

Mouer, L. D., R. L. Ryder, and E. G. Johnson
1981   Down to the river in boats: The Late Archaic/Transitional Period in the
        Middle James River Valley, Virginia. *Quarterly Bulletin of the Archaeological
        Society of Virginia* 36(1–2) : 29–48.

Mounier, R. A.
1975   The Indian Head site revisited. *Bulletin of the Archaeological Society of New
        Jersey* 32 : 1–14.

Muller, J. D.
1978   The Southeast. In *Ancient Native Americans,* ed. J. D. Jennings, 281–325.
        San Francisco: W. H. Freeman.

Murdock, G. P.
1949   *Social structure.* New York: Free Press.

Neumann, G., and T. Murad
1970   Preliminary report on the crania from the Island Field site, Kent County,
        Delaware. *Proceedings of the Indiana Academy of Science* 1969 : 69–74.

Niering, W. A.
1953   Past and present vegetation of High Point State Park, New Jersey. *Ecolog-
        ical Monographs* 23 : 2

Odum E.
1971   *Fundamentals of ecology.* Philadelphia: Saunders.

Ogden, J. G.
1977   The Late Quaternary paleoenvironmental record of northeastern North
        America. *Annals of the New York Academy of Sciences* 288 : 16–34.

O'Kelly, L.

1975   The basis of human evolution and adaptation. In *Human ecology,* ed. N. D. Levine, 88–111. Belmont, Calif.: Duxbury Press.

Omwake, G.

1954a   Notes about the Phillips-Robinson-Benson site near Milford, Delaware. *The Archeolog* 6(1): 1–2.

1954b   A report on the excavations at the Ritter site No. 2 near Lewes, Delaware. *The Archeolog* 6(3): 4–12.

1954c   A report on the Miller-Toms site (7S-D-4), Lewes, Delaware. *The Archeolog* 6(2): 3–10.

1954d   A report on the archaeological investigation of the Ritter site, Lewes, Delaware. *The Archeolog* 6(1): 24–39.

1955   Recent local finds: Cached argillite blanks found. *The Archeolog* 7(2): 5–7.

Omwake, G., and T. D. Stewart   Late 1500s Bear ! ✕

1963   The Townsend site near Lewes, Delaware. *The Archeolog* 15(1): 1–72. Bear .

Owens, J. P., K. Stefansson, and L. A. Sirkin

1974   Chemical, mineralogic, and palynologic character of the upper Wisconsinian-lower Holocene fill in parts of Hudson, Delaware, and Chesapeake estuaries. *Journal of Sedimentary Petrology* 44: 390–408.

Parsons, J. L., H. H. Hutchinson, D. Marine, and L. G. Maeyens

1962   Report on an isolated double refuse pit—Indian or white? (7S-G-13). *The Archeolog* 11(2): 1–5.

Peets, O. H.

1951   The Old House site and the burning of Lewes in 1673. *The Archeolog* 3(4): 1–6.

1952   Remarks on the DeVries site. *The Archeolog* 4(2): 1–7.

1961   Site 7S-D-10 should be restudied. *The Archeolog* 13(2).

1962   An excavation project and some trade spangles. *The Archeolog* 14(1): 15.

Porter, F. W.

1979   *Indians in Maryland and Delaware: A critical bibliography.* Bloomington: Indiana University Press.

Potzger, J. E.

1945   The Pine Barrens of New Jersey, refugium during Pleistocene times. *Butler University Botanical Studies* 7: 1–15.

1952   What can be inferred from the pollen profiles of bogs in New Jersey Pine Barrens? *Bartonia* 26: 20–27.

Price, B.

n.d.   Competititon, productive intensification, and ranked society: Speculations from evolutionary theory. Department of Anthropology, University of Delaware. MS on file.

Purnell, H.W.T.

1958   The Draper site. *The Archeolog* 10(2): 1–16.

Ralph. E. K., H. N. Michael, and M. C. Han

1974   Radiocarbon dates and reality. *Archaeology of Eastern North America* 2: 1–20.

Rappaport, R. A.

1968   *Pigs for the ancestors: Ritual in the exhange of a New Guinea people.* New Haven, Conn.: Yale University Press.

Rappleye, L., and W. M. Gardner

1979   A cultural resources reconnaissance and impact assessment of the Great Dismal Swamp National Wildlife Refuge, City of Suffolk, Chesapeake and Nansemond Counties, Virginia. Department of Anthropology, Catholic University of America. MS on file.

1980   A cultural resources and impact area assessment, Bombay Hook National Wildlife Refuge, Kent County, Delaware. Island Field Museum, South Bowers, Delaware. MS on file.

Rasmussen, W. C.

1958   Geology and hydrology of the "bays" and basins of Delaware. Ph.D. Department of Geology, Bryn Mawr University.

Ray, C. E., B. N. Cooper, and W. S. Benninghoff

1967   Fossil mammals and pollen in a late Pleistocene deposit at Saltville, Virginia. *Journal of Paleontology* 41:608–22.

Regensburg, R. A.

1970   The Savich Farm site: A preliminary report. *Bulletin of the Massachusetts Archaeological Society* 32(1–2): 20–23.

1978   Peoples' relationship to soil. Paper presented at the 1977 Meeting of the Eastern States Archaeological Federation, Hartford, Connecticut.

Reich, J. R.

1974   *Caves of southeastern Pennsylvania.* Pennsylvania Geologic Survey Report no. 65. Harrisburg: Pennsylvania Geologic Survey.

Reynolds, G., and M. Dilks

1965   A preliminary report on a survey of fluted points in Maryland. *Journal of the Archaeological Society of Maryland* 1(1):8–10.

Richards, H. G.

1939   Reconsideration of the dating of the Abbott Farm site at Trenton. *American Journal of Science* 237(5): 345–54.

Ritchie, W. A.

1932   The Lamoka Lake site. *Researches and Transactions of the New York State Archaeological Association* 7(4): 79–134.

1959   *The Stony Brook site and its relation to Archaic and Transitional cultures on Long Island.* New York State Museum and Science Service Bulletin no. 372. Albany.

1961   *A typology and nomenclature for New York State projectile points.* New York State Museum and Science Service Bulletin no. 384. Albany.

1965   *The archaeology of New York State.* New York: Natural History Press.

1969   *The archaeology of Martha's Vineyard: A framework for the prehistory of southern New England.* New York: Natural History Press.

Ritchie, W. A., and R. E. Funk

1971   Evidence for Early Archaic occupations on Staten Island. *Pennsylvania Archaeologist* 41(3): 45–59.

1973   *Aboriginal settlement patterns in the northeast.* New York State Museum and Science Service Memoir no. 20. Albany.

Ritchie, W. A., and R. S. MacNeish

1949   The pre-Iroquoian pottery of New York State. *American Antiquity* 15:97–124.

Science Applications, Incorporated
1979   A cultural resource survey of the Continental Shelf from Cape Hatteras to Key West. Department of Anthropology, Catholic University of America. MS on file.

Shelford, V. E.
1963   *The ecology of North America.* Urbana: University of Illinois Press.

Schrader, J.
1978   Artifact. *Pennsylvania Archaeologist* 48(4):49.

Simms, S. R.
1979   Changing patterns of information and material flow at the Archaic-Woodland transition in northeastern North America. *Pennsylvania Archaeologist* 49(4):30–44.

Sirkin, L.
1977   Late Pleistocene vegetation and environments in the Middle Atlantic region. *Annals of the New York Academy of Sciences* 288:206–17.

Sirkin, L. A., and J. P. Minard
1972   Late Pleistocene glaciation and pollen stratigraphy in northwestern New Jersey. *Geological Survey Professional Paper* 800D:51–56.

Sirkin, L., J. P. Owens, J. P. Minard, and M. Rubin
1970   Palynology of some upper Quaternary peat samples from the New Jersey Coastal Plain. *U.S. Geological Survey Professional Paper* 700D:77–87.

Smith, J.
1907   *John Smith's Travels.* Glasgow: John Grant.

Smith, P. W.
1957   An analysis of post-Wisconsin biogeography of the Prairie Peninsula based on distributional phenomenon among terrestrial vertebrate populations. *Ecology* 38:205–18.

Smith, I. F.
1978   *A description and analysis of early pottery types in the lower Susquehanna Valley of Pennsylvania.* Pennsylvania Historical and Museum Commission, Harrisburg.

Snow, D. R.
1980   *The archaeology of New England.* New York: Academic Press.

Spaulding, A. C.
1960   The dimensions of archaeology. In *Essays in the science of culture,* ed. G. E. Dole and R. Carniero, 437–56. New York: Thomas Y. Crowell.

Spoljaric, N.
1967   *Pleistocene channels of New Castle County.* Delaware Geological Survey Report of Investigations no. 10. Newark: Delaware Geological Survey.

Spoljaric, N., and K. D. Woodruff
1970   *Geology, hydrology, and geophysics of Columbia sediments in the Middletown-Odessa area, Delaware.* Delaware Geological Survey Bulletin no. 13. Newark: Delaware Geological Survey.

Stanner, W. E. H.

1933   Ceremonial economies of the Mulluk Mulluk and Madngella tribes of the Daly River, North Australia: A preliminary paper. *Oceania* 4(2):156–75.

Starbuck, D. R., and C. E. Bolian

1980   *Early and Middle Archaic cultures in the Northeast.* Occasional Publications in Northeastern Anthropology no. 7. Rindge, N.H. Franklin Pierce College.

Stephenson, R. L.

1963   *The Accokeek Creek site: A Middle Atlantic Seaboard culture sequence.* Anthropological papers of the University of Michigan Museum of Anthropology no. 20. Ann Arbor: University of Michigan Museum of Anthropology.

Stevenson, C. M.

1978   Archaeological site survey and settlement-subsistence pattern recognition along the Allegheny Front, Centre County, Pennsylvania. Master's thesis, Department of Anthropology, Pennsylvania State University.

Steward, J. H.

1942   The direct historical approach to archaeology. *American Antiquity* 7:337–43.

1955   *Theory of culture change.* Urbana: University of Illinois Press.

Stewart, R. M.

1979   Review of "Paleo-Indian settlement pattern in the Hudson and Delaware River drainages," by L. Eisenberg. *Pennsylvania Archaeologist* 49(4):45–46.

1980a   Environment settlement pattern, and the prehistoric use of rhyolite in the Great Valley of Maryland and Pennsylvania. Paper presented at the 1980 Middle Atlantic Archaeological Conference, Dover, Delaware.

1980b   *Prehistoric settlement/subsistence patterns and the testing of predictive site location models in the Great Valley of Maryland.* Ann Arbor, Mich.: University Microfilms.

Stewart, R. M., and W. M. Gardner

1978   Phase II archaeological investigations near Sam Rice Manor, Montgomery County, Maryland, and at 18PR166 and 18PR172 near Acokeek, Prince George County, Maryland. Department of Anthropology, Catholic University of America. MS on file.

Stewart, T. D.

1945   Skeletal remains from the Rehoboth Bay ossuary. *Bulletin of the Archaeological Society of Delaware* 4(2):24–25.

1970   *Report on the skeletal remains from the St. Jones Adena Site near Lebanon, Delaware.* Delaware State Museum Series Bulletin no. 2. Dover.

Strong, W. D.

1935   *An introduction to Nebraska archaeology.* Smithsonian Miscellaneous Collections vol. 93(10). Washington, D.C.: Smithsonian Institution.

1940   From history to prehistory in the northern Great Plains. In *Essays in historical anthropology of North America,* 100:353–94. Smithsonian Miscellaneous Collections, Washington, D.C.: Smithsonian Institution.

Struever, S.

1962   Implications of vegetal remains from an Illinois Hopewell site. *American Antiquity* 27:584–87.

1965   Middle Woodland culture history in the Great Lakes-Riverine area. *American Antiquity* 31:211–23.

Stuckenrath, R.
1977   Radiocarbon: Some notes from Merlin's diary. *Annals of the New York Academy of Sciences* 288:181–88.

Swientochowski, J., and C. A. Weslager
1942   Excavations at the Crane Hook site, Wilmington, Delaware. *Bulletin of the Archaeological Society of Delaware* 3(5):2–17.

Thomas, R. A.
1966a   The Delaware Archaeological Board site survey: A progress report. *Delaware Archaeology* 2(1):2–15.

1966b   Paleo-Indian in Delaware. *Delaware Archaeology* 2(3):1–11.

1966c   7NC-F-7, the Hell Island site. *Delaware Archaeology* 2(2):1–18.

1966d   Archaeological investigations on Milford Neck. *Delaware Archaeology* 2(4). ✓ *p. 21+*

1970   Adena influence in the Middle Atlantic coast. In *Adena: The seeking of an identity*, ed. B. K. Swartz, 56–87. Muncie, Ind.: Ball State University.

1973a   Prehistoric mortuary complexes of the Delmarva Peninsula. Paper presented at 1973 Middle Atlantic Archaeological Conference, Penns Grove, N.J.

1973b   Cached blades from a Millsboro site. *The Archeolog* 25:1–4.

1974a   A brief survey of prehistoric man on the Delmarva Peninsula. *Transactions of the Delaware Academy of Science* 5:119–40.

1974b   Webb Phase mortuary customs at the Island Field site. *Transactions of the Delaware Academy of Science* 5:49–61.

1976   A re-evaluation of the St. Jones River site. *Archaeology of Eastern North America* 4:89–110.

1977   Radiocarbon dates of the Woodland Period from the Delmarva Peninsula. *Bulletin of the Archaeological Society of Delaware* 11:49–57.

1980   Routes 4, 7, 273: An archaeological survey. Department of Transportation, Dover, Delaware. MS on file.

1981   Excavations at the Delaware Park site (7NC-E-41). Department of Transporation, Dover, Delaware. MS on file.

1982   Excavations at the Hollingsworth Farm site (18CE129). *Maryland Archaeology* 18(1):9–28.

Thomas, R. A., D. R. Griffith, C. L. Wise, and R. E. Artusy
1974   A discussion of the lithics, ceramics, and cultural ecology of the Fox Creek-Cony-Selby Bay paradigm as it applies to the Delmarva Peninsula. Paper presented at the 1974 Middle Atlantic Archaeological Conference, Baltimore, Maryland.

Thomas, R. A., D. R. Griffith, C. L. Wise, and R. E. Wise
1975   Environmental adaptation on Delaware's Coastal Plain. *Archaeology of Eastern North America* 3:35–90. *Late Woodland — raccoon & possible fox* B) /NA

Thomas, R. A., and N. Warren
1970a   A Middle Woodland cemetery in central Delaware: Excavations at the *lots of bone* mid woodland Island Field site. *Bulletin of the Archaeological Society of Delaware* 8. → Fox 700–1000 AD

1970b   Salvage excavation of the Mispillion site. *The Archeolog* 22(2):1–23.

Thompson, T.A., and W. M. Gardner   *raccoon, fox, possible skunk*

1978   A cultural resources reconnaissance and impact area assessment of the Eastern Neck Wildlife Refuge, Kent County, Maryland. Department of Anthropology, Catholic University of America. MS on file.

Thornbury, W. D.
1965   *Regional geomorphology of the United States.* New York: Wiley.

Thurman, M. D.
1974   Delaware social organization. In *A Delaware Indian symposium,* ed. H. C. Kraft, 111–34. Anthropological Series of the Pennsylvania Historical and Museum Commission no. 4. Harrisburg.
1978   The "Hopewellian" occupation at Abbott Farm: A demurrer. *Archaeology of Eastern North America* 6:72–78.

Thurman, M. D., and W. P. Barse
1974   Mockley and Mockley-like pottery in the Middle Atlantic region. Paper presented at the 1974 Middle Atlantic Archaeological Conference, Baltimore, Maryland.

Tirpak, R. A.
1978   Activity analysis: A technique for the possible determination of seasonal occupation at the Mispillion site. *Bulletin of the Archaeological Society of Delaware* 11:22–68.

Trigger, B.
1978   Iroquois matriliny. *Pennsylvania Archaeologist* 48:55–65.

Tuck, J.A.
1978   Regional cultural development, 3000 B.C.–300 B.C. in *Handbook of North American Indians, Vol. 15: Northeast,* ed. B. Trigger, 28–43. Washington, D.C.: Smithsonian Institution.

Turnbaugh, W. A.
1970   A study of argillite points in eastern Pennsylvania. *Pennsylvania Archaeologist* 40 (1–2): 35–42.
1975   Toward an explanation of the broadpoint dispersal in eastern North American prehistory. *Journal of Anthropological Research* 31:51–68.
1977   *Man, land, and time.* Evansville, Ind.: Unigraphic Press.

Turner, E. R.
1978   Population distribution in the Virginia Coastal Plain, 8000 B.C. to A.D. 1600. *Archaeology of Eastern North America* 8:60–72.

Ubelaker, D. H.
1974   *Reconstruction of demographic profiles from ossuary skeletal samples: A case study from the tidewater Potomac.* Smithsonian Contributions to Anthropology no. 18. Washington, D.C.: Smithsonian Institution.

Vayda, A. D., and B. J. McCay
1975   New directions in ecology and ecological anthropology. *Annual Review of Anthropology* 4 293–306.

Walker, P. C., and R. T. Hartman
1960   The forest sequence of the Hartstown bog area in western Pennsylvania. *Ecology* 41:461–74.

Wedel, W.
1939   *The direct historical approach in Pawnee archaeology.* Smithsonian Miscel-

laneous Collections Vol. 97(7). Washington, D.C.: Smithsonian Institution.

Wells, I.
1981   A spatial analysis methodology for predicting archaeological sites in Delaware and its potential application in remote sensing. Master's thesis, College of Marine Studies, University of Delaware.

Wells, I., J. F. Custer, and V. Klemas
1981   Locating prehistoric archaeological sites using LANDSAT. *Proceedings of the 15th International Symposium on Remote Sensing of the Environment.* Ann Arbor, Michigan.

Wendland, W., and R. A. Bryson
1974   Dating climatic episodes of the Holocene. *Quaternary Research* 4 : 9–24.

Wendorf, F., and J. J. Hester
1975   *Late Pleistocene environments of the southern High Plains.* Fort Burgwin Research Center, Rancho de Taos, New Mexico.

Weslager, C. A.
1939a   Progress of archaeology in Delaware. *Bulletin of the Archaeological Society of Delaware* 3(1) 3–7.

1939b   An aboriginal shell heap near Lewes, Delaware. *Bulletin of the Archaeological Society of Delaware* 3(2).

1941   Indian artifacts from Delaware on display at Peabody Museum, Cambridge, Massachusetts, and at the American Museum of Natural History, New York City. *Papers of the Archaeological Society of Delaware* 4 : 3–15.

1942   Ossuaries on the Delmarva Peninsula and exotic influences in the coastal aspect of the Woodland period. *American Antiquity* 8 : 141–51.

1953   *Red men on the Brandywine.* Wilmington, Del.: Hamilton Company.

1961   *Dutch explorers, traders, and settlers in the Delaware Valley, 1609–1664.* Philadelphia: University of Pennsylvania Press.

1968   *Delaware's Buried Past.* 2d ed. New Brunswick, N.J.: Rutgers University Press.

1972   *The Delaware Indians: A history.* New Brunswick, N.J.: Rutgers University Press.

1976   A brief history of archaeology in Delaware. *Transactions of the Delaware Academy of Sciences* 5 : 11–24.

1978   *The Delaware: A critical bibliography.* Bloomington: Indiana University Press.

1983   *The Nanticoke Indians—Past and Present.* Newark, Del.: University of Delaware Press.

White, L.
1949   *The science of culture.* New York: Grove Press.

Whitehead, D. R.
1965   Palynology and Pleistocene phytogeography of unglaciated eastern North America. In *The Quaternary of the United States,* ed. H. E. Wright and D. G. Frey, 417–32. Princeton, N.J.: Princeton University Press.

1972   Developmental and environmental history of the Dismal Swamp. *Ecological Monographs* 42 : 301–15.

1973   Late Wisconsin vegetational history in unglaciated eastern North America. *Quaternary Research* 3 : 621–31.

Wigglesworth, J.
   1933   Excavations at Rehoboth. *Bulletin of the Archaeological Society of Delaware*
           3 : 2–6.
Wilke, S. and G. Thompson
   1977   *Prehistoric resources of portions of coastal Kent County, Maryland.* Maryland
           Geological Survey, Division of Archaeology File Report no. 139. Balti-
           more: Maryland Geological Survey.
Wilkins, E.
   1962   Preliminary report on the Harlan Mills Steatite quarry (18CE5). *Bulletin
           of the Archaeological Society of Delaware* N.S. 2 : 1–22.
   1978   A Selden Island vessel from the Minguannan site, 36CH3. *Bulletin of the
           Archaeological Society of Delaware* 11 : 17–22.
Willey, G. R.
   1953   *Prehistoric settlement patterns in the Viru Valley, Peru.* Bureau of American
           Ethnology Bulletin no. 155. Washington, D.C.: Smithsonian Institution.
   1966   *An introduction to American archaeology, Vol. 1: North and Middle America.*
           Englewood Cliffs, N.J.: Prentice-Hall.
Willey, G. R., and P. Phillips
   1958   *Method and theory in American archaeology.* Chicago: University of Chicago
           Press.
Willey, G. R., and J. A. Sabloff
   1980   *A history of American archaeology.* 2d ed. San Francisco: W. H. Freeman.
Winters, H. D.
   1968   Value systems and trade cycles of the Late Archaic in the Midwest. In
           New perspectives in archaeology, ed. S. R. Binford and L. R. Binford, 175–
           222. Chicago: Aldine.
Wise, C. L.
   1974   The Nassawango Adena site. *Eastern States Archaeological Federation Bulle-
           tin* 33 : 8.
   1975a   A proposed Early to Middle Woodland ceramic sequence for the Del-
           marva Peninsula. *Maryland Archaeology* 11(1).
   1975b   A proposed ceramic sequence for the development of pottery in the
           Middle Atlantic and Northeast. In *Proceedings of the 1975 Middle Atlantic
           Archaeological Conference,* ed. W. F. Kinsey, 1–5. North Museum, Franklin
           and Marshall College, Lancaster, Pennsylvania.
Witthoft, J.
   1953   Broad spearpoints and the Transitional period cultures. *Pennsylvania
           Archaeologist* 23(1) : 4–31.
   1959   Notes on the Archaic of the Appalachian region. *American Antiquity*
           25 : 79–85.
   1959a   Ancestry of the Susquehannocks. In *Susquehannock Miscellany,* ed. J. Wit-
           thoft and W. F. Kinsey, 19–50. Harrisburg: Pennsylvania Historical and
           Museum Commission.
   1963   General interpretations of the Townsend site. *The Archeolog* 15(1) : 59–69.
Witthoft, J., and W. F. Kinsey, eds.
   1959   *Susquehannock Miscellany.* Harrisburg: Pennsylvania Historical and
           Museum Commission.

Wright, H. E.
   1976   The dynamic nature of Holocene vegetation. A problem in paleo-climatology, biogeography, and stratigraphic nomenclature. *Quarternary Research* 6:581–96.

Wright, H. T.
   1960   The Hell Island report. Island Field Museum, South Bowers, Delaware. Ms on file.
   1962   The Hell Island report. Island Field Museum, South Bowers, Delaware. Ms on file.
   1973   *An archaeological sequence in the Middle Chesapeake region, Maryland.* Maryland Geological Survey, Archaeological Series no. 1. Baltimore: Maryland Geological Survey.

Yarnell, R. A.
   1976   Early plant husbandry in eastern North America. In *Culture change and continuity,* ed. C. E. Cleland, 265–73. New York: Academic Press.

Zukerman, K.
   1979a   Slaughter Creek comprehensive survey, phase I. Delaware Division of Historical and Cultural Affairs, Dover. Ms on file.
   1979b   Slaughter Creek comprehensive survey, phase II. Delaware Division of Historical and Cultural Affairs, Dover. Ms on file.

Index

DATE DUE

DEC 0 1 2010		
12/3/12		